Working for Children

Ethical Issues Beyond
Professional Guidelines

Judith S. Mearig
and Associates

Working
for Children

Jossey-Bass Publishers

San Francisco • Washington • London • 1978

WORKING FOR CHILDREN
Ethical Issues Beyond Professional Guidelines
by Judith S. Mearig and Associates

Copyright © 1978 by: Jossey-Bass, Inc., Publishers
433 California Street
San Francisco, California 94104
&
Jossey-Bass Limited
28 Banner Street
London EC1Y 8QE

Library of Congress Catalogue Card Number LC 78-1148

International Standard Book Number ISBN 0-87589-367-8

Manufactured in the United States of America

JACKET DESIGN BY WILLI BAUM

FIRST EDITION

Code 7808

The Jossey-Bass
Social and Behavioral Science Series

Preface

Professionals who work with or for children face difficult ethical and moral issues. One objective of this book is to better understand the complexities of these issues. An even more important objective is to understand that the most significant variable in the actual outcome for children is how individual professionals use the knowledge and perspectives they acquire. Professionals deal with similar problems in very different ways, and it is valuable to explore major factors influencing individual decisions in dilemma-producing situations. Numerous books have dealt with the more straightforward aspects of professional ethics, children's rights, and child advocacy; the present volume focuses on the dynamics of professional functioning itself.

Impetus for *Working for Children* comes from three sources. The first is from my own child advocacy experiences; over the years an impression has grown that professionals often miss unique oppor-

ix

tunities to significantly affect the direction of children's lives. Frequently we seem to view such opportunities as options rather than responsibilities, and we hesitate to take professional or personal risks. It is true that some situations in children's lives are so complex, or even desperate, that a moral resolution of problems appears impossible. But many times well-established and apparently inflexible institutional or bureaucratic procedures cause a professional to develop a safe, almost habitual reaction to issues involving values. Moreover, the professional's behavior may be acceptable according to traditional ethical guidelines even though the morality of such behavior is questionable when the child's best interests are not receiving priority. Professionals are granted more prerogatives by society than most people. Those with strength can demonstrate marked independence if they believe that the children they are working for have no other advocates and would be seriously hurt if they did not act. The ultimate question thus becomes, What is the responsibility of the individual professional?

The second impetus for the book is the genuine concern of students and recent graduates of professional programs. They become aware only too quickly of the many dilemmas they will face. Although they often realize that there are no simple solutions and that compromises may be necessary, they do not want to abandon an idealism that may have been a major influence in their choice of career. They do want discussion of, and practice in dealing with, the more difficult ethical and moral questions before having to take responsibility for important decisions. I hope this volume will meet at least part of that need and will also stimulate continual reassessment of ethical issues by helping professionals at all levels. Although this book is directed primarily toward graduate students and newly practicing professionals, most of the topics are equally important to more experienced individuals.

The third impetus for the book comes from my admiration of how some outstanding professionals working for children handle difficult ethical and moral concerns. Many of the contributing authors have previously written or spoken about such concerns but with a focus unlike the one in this book. The authors not only represent various professions but also have worked in interdisciplinary settings rather than within the confines of their own specialties.

Each of their topics has significance for all professionals. Moreover, children will be better served when those helping them more fully understand their problems.

I deeply appreciate the careful thought and concerted effort devoted to this book. The contributors demonstrated a commitment similar to the one they have to the issues discussed here and to the children they serve. In my own professional experience, Deborah Kaplan and Charles Turcotte over long careers have clearly demonstrated how to go beyond the guidelines to help children. I am grateful to Deborah Claflin for her assistance in organizing the materials for the manuscript and to Doris Strathdee for her patience in typing. There are three people to whom I am particularly indebted in this project: William C. Morse, whose influence in my own professional development has been inestimable, and Jane W. Kessler and Nicholas Hobbs, without whose early enthusiasm and continuing support this book would not have become a reality.

Potsdam, New York   JUDITH S. MEARIG
January 1978

Contents

The Authors

JUDITH S. MEARIG is professor of educational psychology at St. Lawrence University and coordinator of the graduate program in school psychology, which she began developing in 1964. Since 1967 she has also maintained a private practice in psychology.

She earned her bachelor's degree (1957) in psychology and kindergarten-primary education at Oberlin College and both her master's degree (1960) in educational psychology and her doctor's degree (1964) in the Combined Program in Education and Psychology at the University of Michigan.

Currently the president of the School Psychology Educators' Council of New York State, Mearig also is a monitor of the Executive Council of the School Psychology Division of the American Psychological Association. She is a member of additional professional groups as well as being a diplomate in school psychology of the American Board of Professional Psychology.

Mearig, an editorial consultant for the *Journal of School Psychology,* is the author of articles on child advocacy, creativity, school psychology, and the dynamics of muscular dystrophy, which is one of her continuing research concerns. Her awareness of the complexity of ethics has been heightened as a result of being a maverick professional in a rural area.

Mearig lives in Potsdam, New York; her nonprofessional interests include music and photography.

DOUGLAS BIKLEN, director, Center on Human Policy, Syracuse University, Syracuse, New York

MAUREEN F. CARDIFF, senior medical social worker, Pediatric Pavilion, Los Angeles County-University of Southern California Medical Center, Los Angeles, California

THEODORE J. DIBUONO, chief of Seguin Community Services, Syracuse Developmental Center, Syracuse, New York

CONSTANCE T. FISCHER, associate professor of psychology, Duquesne University, Pittsburgh, Pennsylvania

ALMA S. FRIEDMAN, pupil services counselor, Los Angeles City Unified School District, Los Angeles, California

DAVID B. FRIEDMAN, professor of pediatrics and director, Family and Child Development Division, Pediatric Pavilion, Los Angeles County-University of Southern California Medical Center; and co-director, Department of Health, Education and Welfare Region IX Resource Demonstration Project of the National Center on Child Abuse and Neglect, Los Angeles, California

NICHOLAS HOBBS, professor of psychology and preventive medicine and director, Center for the Study of Families and Children, Vanderbilt University, Nashville, Tennessee

JANE W. KESSLER, Lucy Leffingwell Professor of Psychology and director, Mental Development Center, Case Western Reserve University, Cleveland, Ohio

JANE KNITZER, staff associate, Children's Defense Fund of the Washington Research Project, Inc., Washington, D.C.

EDWARD R. LISBE, director of student relations and educational consultant, Ridge Consultants for Maximizing Human Resources, Cazenovia, New York

BRENDA G. McGOWAN, assistant professor, School of Social Work, Columbia University, New York, New York

ROBERT S. MENDELSOHN, chairman, Department of Family Practice, Forest Hospital, Des Plaines; and associate professor, Department of Medicine and Community Health, Abraham Lincoln School of Medicine, University of Illinois, Chicago, Illinois

WILLIAM C. MORSE, professor of educational psychology and psychology and chairman, Combined Programs in Education and Psychology, University of Michigan, Ann Arbor, Michigan

WILLIAM C. RHODES, professor of psychology and program director for psychology, Institute for the Study of Mental Retardation and Related Disabilities, University of Michigan, Ann Arbor, Michigan

ALAN P. SANDLER, director of ambulatory diagnostic services and instructor in pediatrics, Pediatric Pavilion, Los Angeles County-University of Southern California Medical Center, Los Angeles, California

EDITH SMITH, director of social work, Mental Development Center, Case Western Reserve University, and child therapist, Cleveland Center for Research in Child Development, Cleveland, Ohio

RICHARD M. SWITZER, superintendent, Human Resources School, Human Resources Center, Albertson, Long Island, New York

Working
for Children

Ethical Issues Beyond
Professional Guidelines

Introduction:
Working for Children

Judith S. Mearig

The focus of this book is upon the individual professional's dilemmas in meeting ethical responsibilities to children, with particular attention to the dynamics of professional functioning. Each of the authors brings to his* task some unique experiences in services for children. All have "been there" and "done it," so to speak, and have gone "beyond the guidelines" in their work. Many have made important scholarly contributions to their fields and all have been teachers or supervisors of young professionals and have coped with their dilemmas. It is hoped that these firsthand experiences have added to the authenticity of their messages. The authors communicate their ideas with much individuality in professional orientation

---

*The authors of this book will use either the masculine *or* the feminine pronoun and avoid awkward constructions that include both.

and style of expression, although there is consensus in the depth of their concern about the role of the helping professions in meeting the many needs of children.

Some chapters present rather straightforward, practical suggestions concerning issues and dilemmas, whereas others leave an impression that something is awry but offer no workable solutions. The authors have tried neither to avoid suggesting concrete guidelines for action where resolution—or at least progress toward it—is possible nor to imply that knowledgeable and experienced professionals have matters well in hand when they are actually far from that state. It is hoped that the case material frequently presented will illustrate these realities.

A major purpose of the book will be achieved if young professionals from different disciplines discuss together the dilemmas of being a helping professional in today's society. The general aspects of these dilemmas are presented in Chapters One through Four. The case presentations for problem-solving practice at the conclusion of Chapters Five through Fourteen provide the reader with an opportunity to weigh the options. All factors involved in a dilemma may be analyzed, and alternative approaches to its resolution considered. In some instances the reader may have difficulty in arriving at any reasonable solution. But many important issues can be brought to light in the attempt, and the necessity of having to deal with such problems on an everyday basis in one's professional life may become more apparent.

William C. Morse (Chapter One) introduces a number of the value dilemmas, frustrations, and challenges that face helping professionals. Many of these are explored in greater detail by subsequent authors. The reader may sense Morse's agonizing over many value issues. His orientation reflects the uncertainty and consternation felt by many individual professionals. It also is a forty-year perspective of one who sees issues in all their complexities and nuances and who has particular insight into the frustrations and ideals of student and neophyte professionals. Morse stresses the permeating of values in every dimension of the professional's functioning. Aspects creating dilemmas that he discusses include: professional power and the danger of arrogance, distinguishing between failure due to the system and that due to the individual, the expectation of instant change in our society, accepting and remaining in a job when there are value conflicts, institutional restraints and ethical responsibility, the stress on student and neophyte professionals in trying to meet their own as well as program expectations, and responsibilities and procedures of professional programs in transmitting values and other ethical judgments.

Nicholas Hobbs (Chapter Two) places the helping professional enterprise into the broader context of behavior control. This perspective is important for the individual's awareness of his potential power in other people's lives and should be incorporated into the ethical stance he develops for his everyday functioning. Hobbs discusses the nature and ramifications of the "invincible surmise," which is beyond prescriptions of ethical standards and customs of professions and which is necessary to exercise when another person's welfare is in jeopardy. In making difficult ethical and moral choices, a primary requirement is familiarity with all the issues involved. Hobbs cites major pragmatic and theoretical developments contributing to such awareness, concluding with a review of possible positions in determinism. The latter invariably enter into a professional person's choices and decisions. Noting the evolution of changes in ethical standards as knowledge and understanding grow, Hobbs notes that "the true professional must accept private responsibility for the constant reconstruction of what is right."

William C. Rhodes (Chapter Three) examines the helping professional's use of the concepts of normality and abnormality, stressing that one must first understand the former. He points out that new paradigms for interpreting behavior have challenged objective empirical science. Individual professionals have to make personal moral choices concerning these issues from the vantage point of very different theoretical positions, and Rhodes addresses implications of these choices in clinical work. He then discusses the concept of healing and psychological grace and argues that "normality" needs healing as much as abnormality.

Robert S. Mendelsohn (Chapter Four) presents a critical perspective on ethical and moral difficulties likely to be produced by the phenomenon of professionalism itself, particularly in medicine. He expresses great concern about the transformation in values many students seem to undergo during professional education and training and notes that present day professional ethics sometimes seem antithetical to traditional ethics. Mendelsohn's positions on various issues may be controversial, but they need to be considered by every professional who is formulating or examining his own ethical positions. After providing examples of practices that disturb him, Mendelsohn makes some recommendations to medical students who want to preserve earlier learned values.

Jane Knitzer (Chapter Five) examines the ecological forces impinging upon both families and professionals as they attempt to provide needed assistance to children. Case examples illustrate the futility parents sometimes feel because of the power and arbitrariness of some of these forces. Knitzer notes, however, that there are still a number of options professionals can exercise within the system to help children, but they must have adequate information, look at the total gestalt of a child's situation, and evaluate long-term consequences of their actions and decisions. Professionals also can help families to learn to cope more effectively with ecological forces. Knitzer goes on to describe the professional's relationship to the child advocacy movement, citing different ways in which individual professionals can respond to it. She stresses that the professional has an ethical obligation to see that an individual child actually receives needed services, using whatever means are necessary to achieve this goal.

Douglas Biklen's presentation (Chapter Six) begins with a rather graphic longitudinal record of a child in an institution. It is the kind of situation that professionals hope today no longer exists, but this expectation may be an unrealistic one. In any event, the children whom such records represent are still living, and the gravity of what professionals themselves consented to, or performed with client consent, cannot be overestimated. The record also illustrates the misuse by professionals of testing and treatment, which is discussed further in later chapters. Biklen extensively analyzes the components of consent, which he considers to be the cornerstone concept in the relationship between a professional and those he serves. He notes that consent has been poorly understood in the past and that many people do not even recognize the three necessary elements—capacity, information, and voluntariness. Also important is the distinction between client and professional protection under the rubric of consent.

Constance T. Fischer (Chapter Seven) analyzes nine dilemmas in the standardized testing process, grouped under headings of objectivity, professionalism, and efficiency. She cites initial conflicts of graduate students and newly practicing professionals that have been communicated to her and then explains what her own resolution of each dilemma would be. She notes that some dilemmas in assessment situations are self-imposed because of literal rather than logical interpretation of testing guidelines and directions. However, where there is an actual conflict, Fischer stresses that the child's welfare is the primary criterion in effecting resolution of the dilemma. The distinction between testing and assessment also is sharpened, and the blurring of assessment into treatment is emphasized.

Jane W. Kessler (Chapter Eight) discusses dilemmas in clinical practice with children, noting that professionals are under much scrutiny today, perhaps because of their own misuse of power. Accountability to third parties is increasingly required, with a professional having to demonstrate the competence represented by her degree and training. At the same time, the traditional image of a professional as someone with special expertise continues among the general public, and the individual professional is challenged to live up to this image. Kessler cites the importance of recognizing one's fallibility and illustrates seven categories of mistakes professionals frequently have made in children's lives: (1) collective ignorance, (2) individual ignorance, (3) the need for certainty, (4) denial, (5) projection, (6) displacement, and (7) frustration. She then discusses two difficult cases in which the professional has an opportunity and an obligation to exercise his best professional and personal judgment in order to help a child.

Brenda G. McGowan (Chapter Nine) presents a clear exposition of the major obstacles that confront individuals who work within a bureaucracy; she analyzes the dynamics, inner workings, and inevitable frustrations. However, she points out that bureaucracies are necessary to provide many services vital to children and stresses that professionals must learn to shape organizational structure and bureaucratic policies and procedures to use as tools to meet children's needs rather than be dictated by them. McGowan reviews similarities and differences between bureaucratic and professional functioning, noting how the latter generate ethical dilemmas.

The first step is for professionals to fully understand the general workings of bureaucracies as well as the specific setting in which they work. McGowan systematically outlines the steps by which an individual professional should proceed if he wishes to initiate change successfully and describes the appropriate use of different strategies.

Edith Smith (Chapter Ten) traces the history of care of children outside their families. She indicates the complications that professionals, particularly social workers, face in serving a child's best interests, such as individualizing arrangements for families who cannot cope at the moment with their children and protecting children from rigid or arbitrary rules and regulations of the "system," especially when their psychological identity is at stake. Smith describes the conflict professionals feel when they are thwarted in using their best judgment. Nevertheless, she states that workers have a responsibility to the children to try to change the system and that they cannot escape their role as decision makers. Examples of major dilemmas with which professionals in the child care field have had to deal recently are: (1) the knowledge of natural parents that should be given to adopted children and (2) the decision-making process of single mothers concerning custody of their infants.

Theodore J. DiBuono (Chapter Eleven) grapples with one of the most agonizing dilemmas confronting physicians: their part in the life or death decision-making process for severely impaired newborns. In addition to presenting the dilemma, he states a position and develops a clear rationale for it. A professional, often the pediatrician, can have tremendous influence in this determination; on the other hand, he also can allow himself to become the executor of a parental decision. DiBuono asks the reader to examine the value structure of individual professionals and society that contribute to a physician's judgment (or agreement) not to provide life-supporting measures for these infants and the implications for severely impaired children at later ages. DiBuono also cites the present inadequacies of medical education in communicating knowledge about, and providing positive experiences with, severely handicapped children. Another important lack is experience in working in concert with other professionals and community services to provide ongoing support for these children.

Richard M. Switzer (Chapter Twelve) provides a perspective of parents of disabled children. He opens his presentation with an account of parents' feelings when they first discover that their infant is severely disabled and that they are dependent upon professionals for direction. He stresses the significant amount of mutual learning that can occur when professionals step out of authoritarian roles and notes that questions about some children's potential must go unanswered because there is no knowledge base from which to make firm predictions. However, opportunities for maximum development should be provided. Switzer also emphasizes how necessary it is for parents to deal with a child's disability in its total dimensions as they live with him from day to day, whereas the professional can often limit his involvement to a few aspects. The problem is that the latter may not realize why parents cannot perform up to professional expectations in his particular area of concern, because he lacks the gestalt of the total family situation. Furthermore, parents' frustration and depression are often a result of not finding services and support they are told are available to them. Another important aspect of the disabled child's life that Switzer discusses is education, perhaps the most visible and open to criticism of all the helping professions. There are many dilemmas faced by both professionals and parents in this realm, some ameliorated and some increased by the recent federal legislation requiring as "regular" schooling as possible for disabled children.

Edward R. Lisbe (Chapter Thirteen) supplies the perspective of a perceptive neophyte psychologist who is thrust into a public school system with a host of dilemmas. Quick response is often expected on his part, but changes he would like to initiate must proceed slowly. His chapter is a sensitive exposition of soul searching and value examination as he is frustrated by a system that does not seem to share his goals for children. But it also is a testimony to the potential for achieving substantial progress if the individual professional will persevere, establish a coherent guiding philosophy, and analyze carefully all interacting variables in his own behavior as well as in the system itself. Then other supportive personnel can be identified, and a workable plan of action developed. The reader should be reminded of McGowan's guidelines for initiating change in Chapter Nine.

Alma S. Friedman, Maureen J. Cardiff, Alan P. Sandler,

and David B. Friedman (Chapter Fourteen) present an extensive analysis of eight sources of major dilemmas professionals confront in coping with child abuse and neglect: (1) gray areas in the identification process, (2) confidentiality in the relationship between professional and client, (3) the professional tradition "to do no harm," (4) the professional's training, (5) the fine line between punishment and abuse, (6) rights of parents and children, (7) the definition of neglect, and (8) the trauma of working in child abuse and neglect. They suggest a holistic model for problem solving as the only effective approach to child abuse and discuss guidelines to cope with the dilemmas. The necessity of interdisciplinary understanding and cooperation is stressed, although present professional programs are providing little preparation in such an approach to child abuse or even to child abuse itself. Much attention is devoted to parent sensitivities and to techniques in working with them. The need for flexibility in regulations and procedures in all types of child abuse and neglect is emphasized.

The final chapter of the book is an editorial discussion of the conclusions, recommendations, and other significant points arising from the issues explored by the authors. Implications for professional education are frequently cited, and the ultimate responsibility of the individual professional for ethical and moral decisions is stressed.

Chapter 1

Professionals in a Changing Society

William C. Morse

Until recently many child "upbringers" went about their activities with little question. Parents and those professionals who served as parent surrogates had the responsibility of directing the young in the ways they should go. Professionals knew what was good for those they were helping because they were professionals; that was their role. Should they disagree, institutions had a hierarchy of decision makers. Like the Animal Farm, all professionals were equal except that some were more equal than others. Outside the home, parents had little power, since they were less equal than professionals; children were least equal and hence given the least power. Of course, there were many professionals who felt the gravity of making decisions about the lives of others, but, overall, the system lumbered on. "Clients" or "patients" were worked on, worked over, and seldom worked with. Being a certified expert bestowed the right to make better qualified judgments.

No one has put the peculiar role of professionals better than Shore (1977, p. 359) as he reviews Koocher's book, *Children's Rights and the Mental Health Professions:* "Through an unwritten social contract, society gives special privileges to the professions. Professionals are believed to be people with special expertise. They foster implicit trust because of their dedication to high-quality services and their commitment to people's welfare." Would that it were so simple and self-evident. Shore goes on to indicate that these assumptions give the professions their permit to design their own training without outside interference, and he concludes that the major occupational hazard is arrogance, which must be countered by consciousness raising and vigilance. Whatever one's professional persuasion, complacency about one's role is no longer acceptable. The bottom has fallen out of the certainty market, and the repercussions of the crash are all around us. The social revolution we are experiencing has brought tremendous changes in concepts of helping. At its crest this revolution was a discrediting process for all professionalism. To be trained as a career professional helper came to have a negative stigma rather than a privileged status. Training was considered dehumanizing. Anyone who represented the establishment was suspect. Lay knowledge was always better. The counterculture developed its own mores with indigenous workers.

When it comes to helping children, a special difficulty is added to these other professional uncertainties. How does one enhance the potential children and youth have for self-responsibility and at the same time use the wisdom gained from experience, especially if the child to be helped is disturbed? Deciding how much and in what ways children can participate in important decisions affecting their lives can be difficult. Child development literature does not deal directly with this issue to any extent. It is true that we sometimes vastly underestimate children's ability to assume responsibility for their own lives; but, on the other hand, when they have emotional conflicts, they may not be able to function very well at all. This, of course, is true for adults as well, but children are especially vulnerable since they have little accumulated personality stability to fall back on. They may not know of alternatives or really appreciate alternatives if such were explained to them. For example, being asked to decide by themselves whether they want to go with their mother or father in a divorce situation may be unfair. The child's age may be a general guideline, but there are often more significant factors that determine variation among individuals. Presumably the professional knows what the child does not yet know. How can we teach what is useful of what we know with the proper balance, so that neither domination nor unfair expectations of independence result? If failure is the outcome, the child may be even less inclined to accept responsibility the next time around.

Moreover, many persons may have rightful interests in a conflict situation. This changes the objective of achieving what is best for the child to one of attaining a positive outcome for all concerned, although the child's interests can still have priority. However, when caring extends to all people involved, complications can become acute. There are the rights of the child, the rights of parents, the rights of siblings, as well as the rights of society. These are seldom reconciled easily. The professional often stands in the middle of these forces, experienced or naive, with wisdom or with ignorance, hoping—and expected—to help resolve the dilemma morally. Furthermore, many decisions that might have been within the purview of professional judgment in the past have now been transferred to the courts. The professional still has an important role but not a decisive one.

It is well to remember that the social revolution has not been a fabrication of a few radicals but a response, at least in part, to inhumane processes in the mental health enterprise. There may be excesses, but behind the excesses is a struggle for a new ethic in human relationships and a new awareness of a person's psychological as well as legal rights. The effects are felt by both seasoned practitioners and neophytes.

First, we may look at those who make their living by certified intervening. A school psychologist recently exclaimed that he gave the same good tests he always had, but nobody paid any attention anymore. He found that the valuable knowledge emanating from his work equaled low power or no power. Professionals have always had rituals by which they have been spared personal responsibility for the lives of others. We develop codes. We categorize in ways that predetermine results. We have batteries of tests that we let decide for us regardless of the test validity and reliability. We fractionate, each doing a part of the action, and then put it all together in a case conference where a coordinator may make the decisions. The group dynamics of the professionals' decision-making process is fascinating in itself.

The dilemma was analyzed lucidly by Hersch (1968) in his classic presentation of the devastating disintegration of certainty in the mental health field. We used to feel assured about who was the patient; now even the question of who is sane depends on definition and perspective. Earlier we thought we knew the methodology to be taught to would-be helpers. Now almost every method has advocates, and at times, it seems that anything goes. We had illusions about who could be selected as helpers, and this, too, has gone the way of other certainties. Young aspirants come to be "certified" but really believe "it takes one to help one." We used to think we knew when a person was helped enough to be called cured; however, the concept of cure as well as the judgment is now in doubt.

It is most important to have the insights that leaders in the helping professions can give, so that what we only ominously sense or blindly react to in our own day-to-day work may be illuminated and clarified. But it is easier to analyze than to prescribe. It remains to put all this in an historical context so that the evolution of an ethically based helping process for our time is delineated. The day of carrying Binet kits or stethoscopes as proud signs of status, without uneasiness, is past.

As Hersch (1968) remarked, in actual helping practice almost anything goes, and the devotees of the iconoclastic treatments match the staid establishment in dogmatism and universal application. It also has been suggested that for each ill perpetrated by the uninitiated and atypical helpers, one can point to equally poor treatment from the traditional experts. New cults develop at every conference. The lack of old certainties does not reduce the search for new ones, pronounced by the gurus of the moment. New therapies are proposed for the couch. Control of charlatanism and exploitation by professionals themselves is almost nonexistent, and the courts are given the problem. Licensing is a struggle. The pseudosolution to responsibility currently gaining ground is to insure against lawsuits for professional malpractice.

As the need for change began to be acknowledged and the painful difficulties of it became apparent (Sarason, 1972), there was considerable frustration and depression among professionals. Both those who practiced and those who were training new professionals were challenged. Even the economic security of the established professional was not always a palliative for cultural status demotions. It is not easy to be told that your important work is, in fact, a charade. Because of the continued, if not increasing, anxieties of modern living, the demand for services has not diminished, but new therapies now share the clientele.

One cure for this professional depression is achieving an analytical–historical perspective. Particularly in America, where we expect instant everything and our material environment changes before our eyes, unreal expectations of change are common. We are given to waves of preoccupation, which become spent before the goal is reached. Knowing this, those interested in change become anxious, as well they might. In the midst of a revolutionary time, given the common pragmatic or existentialist outlook, we forget how changes in a social order take place. We expect a straight line of progress without regression. We expect new legislation, which in essence represents codified societal hopes, to substitute for the hard work of social change. As an example, the latest special education law (Public Law 94–142) requires a totally new approach in programming and evaluation, but the same professional people do the work. It assigns new responsibilities and roles to some unsuspecting persons. It substitutes philosophical hopes for psychological reality. It tries to do more for less cost. Yet, is this chain of events not the way we have made improvements in the past?

The dissonance between what is and what should be generates various reactions in professionals. Some continue professional work as zombies and search for satisfactions elsewhere. What one does away from work becomes the only reason for working, the means by which one acquires the necessary resources. Some blame themselves and grab onto any new approach, hoping to get by osmosis what only difficult and continual effort toward growth and self-renewal will produce. The escape into primary levels of feeling and mysticism is the newest frontier for some. Rather than work to develop more appropriate methods of research and evaluation, others move to a nihilistic escape from seeking knowledge.

At least one can grapple directly with the dissonance between aspiration and accomplishment. The established professional learns to forgo the illusion of any final resolution. There is no promise of a rose garden in the matter of professional values. The struggles to maintain hope can be shared, though the exact resolutions are idiosyncratic. Resolutions must be worked out individually; they cannot be borrowed from colleagues.

Becoming a psychologist of social change has been useful to some professionals in their effort to keep perspective. Sarason (1972), among others, has given the beginner and the experienced professional considerable help in converting the hope for change into reality. Naive expectations are the most demoralizing. The seasoned professional's role is to know the odds and yet keep at the task, working with the young professional who supplies both the drive for change and time myopia. Restricted vision can be an asset when it frees one to act with hope and imagination in spite of a poor prognosis generated by past failures. Different tactics are effective at different times and in different institutions.

As a student of social change, one must confront the etiological dilemma. How much of the failure for change lies within the individual professional and how much lies within the system? In seminars designed to develop more effective helping approaches by professionals, one finds vacillation in designating primary responsibility to internal or external factors. One polarization is the "catch-22" explanation. The system holds us back—"those guys downtown, the establishment, the director." Then some very effective individual indicates how that problem can be solved, that the incompetent individual is really at fault. The blame for no change returns to each individual professional. Consultants who do not have to face the reality of situations often exacerbate the latter state of affairs with *ex cathedra* advice, implying how easily some change can be brought about.

The personal side of the etiological dilemma must also be dealt with, lest it surface in indirect symptomatic ways. What is the orbit or social system in which I can feel positive about my efforts? How big a world can I influence? Should I take a given job? Should I stay in the job? How does it violate my professional and personal ethics? As one astute observer said, we should find out who is getting rich on the poverty program: certainly not the poor. Pollak (1976) discusses the moral dilemmas posed by institutional restraint. One earns a livelihood in an institution that, according to the professional's views, is deleterious for the youngster. Of course, this goes beyond one's employing agency: the entire society has ills that have to be rectified. Is it ethical to live on or be any part of a corrupt operation? How corrupt? What can one do, especially in a decision-making role with little authority? What if one's colleagues go along with the corruption? Or other disciplines than one's own perpetrate what appears to be an error? The extensive recommendation of drugs for some children in school is an example.

Profound exploration of what the social revolution means for professional practice cannot be avoided. All practice has moral implications, from recommending a drug to interpreting a test. How can I behave to be in tune with my beliefs? It becomes necessary to be a philosopher! What do I believe? Do I have any *essential* role in helping to solve the *underlying* problem with my professional skills? There are some other questions that have to do with my personal maturity, my openness and whether or not I deserve trust. How many of my own vulnerabilities are being activated? How much empathy and respect have I for the client? Has the "client" or "patient" disappeared and become a person even as I am a person? What rights of that person's self-determination do I foster? A decision from an interpretation of a test or behavior observation may have as much influence on a life as an incision on an operating table.

The burden of being an ethical agent in what is at best a quasi-ethical society (or agency) is not an easy one to bear. Those who work with children or adolescents have even a greater press, since children's rights are receiving more emphasis. What protection do children need? What social contract implies a limit to the child's freedom? Currently we see this struggle for a new and more humane synthesis being argued by various advisory caretakers—lawyers, parents, and mental health professionals. All professionals have to reassess their concepts in such matters and relate those concepts to the goals they hold. It is surprising how seldom the busy, seasoned professional gives time to "first causes" that underlie the application of values to contemporary moment-by-moment decisions. First causes have to do with basic human rights, with our concepts of human nature, and with our trust and mistrust of the human capacity for change and the impact of a given method. The first-cause study is the examination of our own beliefs about human nature and change.

When the odds against sane, humane behavior and the opportunity to influence the system in some professional positions are weighed, the chances appear to be zero. In fact, what we often see is a migration of the caring professionals from the least promising but most needing systems. Although one can admire the lone crusader, each individual has to assess his ego strength. Those who cannot cope and find themselves disintegrating must reassess where they can function and how much stress they can handle. Thus, ego strength and professional humility are in constant interplay. The skill required of an effective advocate, who shows how others are wrong and causes them to move in desired directions, is minimally understood. The too aggressive advocate will, with righteousness, announce the self-selected correct decision regardless of what happens. However, since many decisions about children are now required to be made by a group, one can hide behind one's own role and contribute to a disastrous decision without feeling any guilt. One has only one's job to do, and if it is done well, let the results go as they will. "I did my part correctly."

In a way, there has been tacit collaboration of the various professions to break the youngster into many pieces, each of which is the responsibility of a particular professional. The mosaic is put together in conferences, although we may not recognize the picture when it is assembled. The image of the child we all started out to understand has been lost. A study in process of school psychology assessment and intervention (Beebe, in process) suggests that there is really little linkage among diagnostic processes, decision-making meetings, specific planning, responsibility for action, actual interventions, and ultimate change.

One rather common opinion today is that professionals should take risks, as if they, not the people they are trying to help, are risking something. The professional only takes a genuine risk when she puts her position in jeopardy. That may well be the real test of ethics. The risk is usually that the client may have to pay a price if an action fails. The person to be helped is obviously risking more if there is a debate over the best action to take. The risk for the professional is usually not of a career but of compatibility with, or regard of, peers. Charity is rare in vigorous professional disagreements. But something else also can happen: hierarchy becomes significant in disagreement. The person in charge usually takes over and the decision is taken "out of our hands." Of course, if we are in a multidisciplinary situation, we often use the power-holding profession as a scapegoat.

The dynamics of group decision are interesting and perplexing. A worker once said, "It was a foregone conclusion the meeting would give the principal the right to place the child in spite of differing viewpoints presented. He had lost his last four attempts and he was set for a real fight." Regardless of the official roles, meetings revolve around the assertiveness, persuasiveness, and nature of interpersonal feelings. Each person has a professional self and a personal self that must be considered at a meeting; decision making is never restricted to a professional process.

Certainly, these are times that try professionals' souls, the trials becoming proportionately more acute as more individuals with differing perspectives are involved. For example, what should school professionals do if the principal believes in character development via the wooden paddle, if the parents support him, and if the value differences are not resolved by the mutual commitment to the education enterprise? School professionals might consider offering some alternatives to punitive retaliation other than talking to the student. What might the youngster do to restore his status besides receiving a spanking? In the recent resurgence of school corporal punishment (denied to prisons!), one can refrain from participating in or recommending the practice, but it will take solid organization to effectively combat it. Moreover, corporal punishment too often provides an illustration of mental health professionals philosophizing rather than giving specific guides to action. We have suggested few alternatives to corporal punishment except talking, which is not considered a viable disciplinary method by many schools or parents. We must develop skills in alternative planning; we must be creative

when our sense of what is right is being violated. There is more to
ethics than debate. There is the strategy of ethical alternatives. Even
then, it may be a compromise because the most desirable alternative
is not available.

If it is confusing for experienced professionals to face the
current myriad of values, what must it mean for young persons
preparing to enter the helping professions? Never having assumed a
placid certainty, some students may actually be better prepared to
respond. Or, some may not sense any conflict until they are out in a
job because they are trained in programs where some fairly arbitrary practice is taught as the *modus operandi*. Yet, as stressful as the
social revolution may be on the established professionals, they do
operate from a base of experience and usually have financial security. For the trainee or the neophyte seeking a position and becoming established, the impact is greater, and conditions change so
fast that it is difficult to gauge what survival tactics will be necessary in the years ahead.

What are the responsibilities of training programs in the
establishment of professional values? Do they have the right to inculcate a particular set? Regardless of claims of neutrality, there is
no question but that all professional education and training involves
direct or indirect efforts to influence values of students. The question
is one of the kind of these efforts and the nature of the values. Understanding official statements of ethics of the various professions is
a valuable first step for students. Although such guidelines do not
suggest actual solutions to dilemmas, they do provide some guidance
and form the basis for discussion of policy. We would all prefer concrete answers to general principles, but that is saying we would
prefer being in a trade to being in a profession. The illusion is that
there may be a clear-cut solution. Applicants to professional programs should be made aware of the relevant codes and react to them
as part of the initial application process.

Do training programs provide ample opportunity for definition and clarification of ethical professional behavior? Or is most
attention focused on "how to" rather than "when to" or "what if"?
For example, if a physician knows how to save a neonate's life,
whatever the prognosis, what about the ethical consequences of intervention on an obviously high risk, extremely poor prognosis, case?

There are numerous other examples. Unneeded operations are sometimes performed on request or even suggested by professionals. One can give an intelligence test in the approved manner knowing the distorted use intended. Or, the results of a published but poorly designed experiment can be considered scientific by unsophisticated readers and also become part of the folklore of treatment methods.

Individual trainers will use different modes of exposure to ethical matters. Since we are dealing with attitudes, the affective–cognitive blend involved in each case will differ. But there seem to be several program components, curricular and otherwise, that could enhance ethical sensitivity. One is provision for direct, systematic attention to values and other ethical matters in seminars on professional behavior. The second is to incorporate ethical and moral considerations on an ongoing basis at all levels and in all kinds of experiences in the professional program.

More profound ethical instruction perhaps takes place via modeling and identification with the instructor or practitioner who is a member of the training team. So great is the need for guidance and solutions to ethical questions that visible or vocal carriers of resolution behavior have a great deal of influence on students. The end result may be very positive, but the experienced professional should always ask whether conformity is expected or demanded for student survival. Some programs permit the model to be rejected, and the student is allowed to create his own ethical stance as a counterposition. However, the teaching of one approach to solving all helping problems has a seductive quality for the student who has so many practical problems that ethical concerns can become obscured.

Because the application of a given methodology always has ethical implications, the training program must not indoctrinate one point of view. Worse is blind indoctrination that ignores even the presence of alternative solutions. Programs must often deal first with undergraduate students' arrival for training in a graduate helping profession with a single understanding. They may be so neobehavioristic or Freudian that they know nothing else. There are two fundamental issues. The first is one's position on the nature of human beings. As Matson (1976) notes, in the "nurture of nature" a professional has no right to his position without knowing well what has been rejected. This issue should be related to the second one of choice of interventions, in which stereotypes are equally suspect. The professional should know exactly what the end product of intervention will be; intervention is not justified merely because it is how he has been taught to deal with certain presenting problems. We must also never lose sight of the fact that, in therapeutic settings, those adults with money and wisdom can make selections of the type of service they wish. The uninformed, the poor, and children usually have no choice. How do professionals reconcile all this inequity in terms of their theories of human nature and of intervention—must they have different ones for different people?

Since we now know the power of roles in dictating behavior and something about the socialization of a profession, we cease to think of ethical behavior dissociated from the circumstance. A corollary is that "doing your professional thing" is no longer sufficient: the life of the person to be helped must be improved. Awareness of this accountability puts a tremendous strain on the professional in training.

Culture shock often hits the young professional first when practica are introduced. Moving from theory and laboratory to supervised practice is a huge step. The teaching faculty and the field supervisors may have differences; the latter are likely to have more influence since they are with students in "real" situations. How individually "good" professionals can sometimes add up to corrupt institutional practice is a mystery to the neophyte. Certainly, professionals in training who are undergoing initiation rites are in a vulnerable position, even more so than when they are certified, although they are still lowest on the totem pole in a first position. Not yet being eroded by practical reality, the young worker often displays more sensitivity about personal ethical behavior than more experienced professionals in charge.

There appear to be two levels of reality-shock malaise. The first is the level of obvious corrupt practice. The other is professional fragility, which is human being fragility. No professional is perfect, and the worship that some young workers have for able seniors may result in intolerance for the errors that even the best occasionally make. This may stem, in part, from the hopes we all have for ourselves as well as from fears of failure. To see the masters not measure up to rigid standards is the first forced recognition that the young professional may also not measure up in the future. There is an awakening realization about pressures of institutional forces that may well shape our ends in spite of our best efforts. Punitive and demeaning supervision certainly makes the working through of this personal process most difficult.

Students and neophytes should become aware of possible support for their ethical beliefs and desire to make changes through affiliation with groups and formal organizations working toward these goals. The social advocate function keeps alive the hopes, and professionals and consumers can often work effectively together. Student associations might initiate this involvement.

There are some first jobs in which the choice for the ethical professional is to become a martyr or move. Even the most skilled can be consumed in trying to change some situations. This raises the dilemma, suggested earlier, that young workers often articulate: In unethical programs, ethical professionals are more needed than anyplace else. The challenge becomes one to withstand the torment and strife without sacrificing integrity. This usually requires a great deal of supportive consultation and a step-by-step effort. The power of retribution against a young professional by a defensive agency is terrible to behold.

For the most part, we have neglected to include the study of agency and organizational dynamics in training. A professional needs self-diagnosis, and client diagnosis we study systematically. But it may be equally important to be able to diagnose a work system to see what can be changed, and how. Sarason (1972) has been one of the leaders in providing understanding in this area, which is critical for sustaining ethical effort. In Chapter Nine McGowan analyzes the dynamics of a bureaucracy and suggests some sequential steps for the individual professional who wants to bring about change.

The "socializing" of young professionals—which often amounts to trading ethical sensitivity for survival—has been the subject of research and observation (Cherniss, in press). But the path of many professionals who resist and learn to function with their values intact has been less studied. We should know how they manage, for they may provide guidelines for new workers as well.

Professional values emerge from many sources, undergo a series of transformations or alterations, and pose many dilemmas. Some crucial factors are under the individual professional's control and are conscious, but a few are not. Whatever their origins and means of sustenance, application of these values has profound ramifications for the well-being of the children and adults professionals serve. Students and neophyte professionals have a responsibility to become aware of, and evaluate, all perspectives and possibilities. Educators and other experienced professionals have a responsibility to assess continuously their own value systems and the manner in which these are communicated to both younger colleagues and their clients.

Chapter 2

Ethics of Behavior Control

Nicholas Hobbs

There is a line in one of Santayana's poems that goes like this: "To trust the soul's invincible surmise was all his science and his only art" (1923, p. 5). The poet suggests that there are issues in the affairs of man that are of such profound consequence that both art and science are insufficient guides to choice. A higher intuition, an invincible surmise, is required when the well-being of another person is seriously at stake. The conscientious professional person must be able to draw upon sources of wisdom that transcend the prescriptions of ethical standards and the customs of professions. Therefore, this chapter will examine the question: How does the professional helper achieve an "invincible surmise" sufficient to the high moral requirements of his calling?

Involved is the professional person's private responsibility for the control of the well-being of others. There are prerogatives and sanctions assumed by professions and granted by society that can result in significant control over people's lives. Physicians' control of the well-being of others is perhaps the most overt, autonomous, and fully sanctioned. Pratt (1976) cites many examples of physicians' prerogatives, including deciding who is ill, who is admitted to hospitals, who receives surgery, who gets what kinds of treatment, and even who shall survive. The responsibility is enormous, and physicians are appropriately surrounded by many protections, including restricted external monitoring and limitations of access to records. But there is a real question as to whether or not physicians gain in moral competence and authority from the privacy they enjoy. The social worker may often be in a position of carrying out orders from a court or an agency where responsibility for control of the life of a child, for example, seems displaced to a higher authority, but ultimately the choice must rest with the professional person. The psychologist deals directly with human behavior and therefore must confront squarely the ethical and moral problems involved in controlling, in some measure, the conduct of others.

Psychologists of different theoretical persuasions vary in the explicitness of their control and in their awareness of their control. The behavior modifiers make no bones about it; they agree (sometimes with the client) on the behavior to be modified and set about arranging contingencies to achieve results specified in advance. The humanistic psychologists, on the other hand, shy away from admitting such manipulation; they prefer to see their role as helping other persons increase their self-awareness, to realize themselves, to achieve their full potentials, with minimum intrusion of the psychologist in directing the outcome. But both the behavior modifiers and the humanistic psychologists are engaged in the control of behavior. The teacher of psychology, or any subject for that matter, also has the modification of behavior as a goal. As long as teaching is as inefficient as it is, ethical and moral issues remain in the background; however, should teaching ever become highly effective, ethical and moral issues would surge to the fore. All of the professional relationships here cited—those of the physician, the social worker, the psychologist, the teacher, and others as well—intrinsically involve ethical and moral issues, a point to be elaborated upon later. Professional codes of ethics often provide sufficient guidance for making decisions affecting the well-being of others. Not infrequently, however, the professional person will be confronted with choices that require wisdom far beyond what can be prescribed.

The choices the professional person must make in the exercise of his competence may be thought of in three categories: (1) the level of professional courtesy and custom, which simply eases professional intercourse, (2) the level of good professional practice, which implies competence and responsibility, and (3) the level of moral choice, in which decisions must be made that embrace considerations beyond the scope of ethical standards. Indeed, it is helpful to realize that all statements of ethical standards are inherently inadequate and, in some measure at least, in error. The final authority for ethical and moral choice must be the individual professional person. As knowledge and understanding grow, the most astute, sensitive, and responsible professional people must begin making choices in advance of, and at odds with, established ethical standards. New circumstances will require new kinds of ethical and moral decisions. The true professional must accept private responsibility for the constant reconstruction of what is right.

To discharge this profound responsibility (a requirement that differentiates the professional person from the technician or tradesperson), the helping professional must invest steadily in expanding his own awareness of the issues involved. There are two sources to draw upon to enhance understanding: (1) pragmatic developments, or accounts of ways in which ethical and moral issues have actually been addressed and (2) theoretical developments, or analyses of the underlying, timeless issues that must inform ethical and moral choice.

First, let us consider pragmatic developments. Thirty years ago the literature on professional ethics was meager, and concern for the problem of ethics largely was confined to philosophers. In an early symposium, Landis (1955) presented a collection of essays concerning the effectiveness of existing codes of professional ethics. The essays indicated that codes of ethics had little influence on the conduct of the professional people covered, unless the profession had some means of imposing sanctions on violators. Since that day, there have been many developments of a pragmatic character that provide sources for understanding the ethical and moral issues facing members of the helping professions.

The American Psychological Association pioneered in an approach to the definition of ethical standards that had several unique characteristics. First, the ethical principles were derived from critical incidents supplied by thousands of psychologists, each incident involving some ethical issue, in the psychologist's judgment. The standards derived were only partly concerned with gross violations that might incur sanctions; rather, their primary emphasis was on improving the choices of psychologists who were assumed to be committed already in principle to the highest ethical conduct. Finally, the committee responsible for developing the first statement of *Ethical Standards of Psychologists* (American Psychological Association, 1953) recognized that the process of developing the statement was perhaps more important than the product, that a continuing examination of ethical issues by psychologists would be the source of enlightened decisions, and that a constant restructuring of the *Standards* should be expected. A major revision has recently been completed (1977). This commitment to continuing inquiry and reformulation of the *Standards* is also evident in the work of the Committee on Ethical Standards and Psychological Research, whose report was issued in 1973 by the American Psychological Association. Following earlier procedures, Chairman Stuart Cook and his associates collected a large number of incidents judged by psychologists to involve ethical choices in the pursuit of psychological research, a topic not touched on in earlier statements of the *Standards*. Drawing on the critical incidents, the committee formulated a number of principles covering such issues as the use of deception in research, the right of a person to withdraw from an experiment, the confidentiality of research protocols, the use of stress and means for removing it after an experiment, the requirements of disclosure, the locus of responsibility for adherence to high standards, and the imperative of professional consultation in doubtful situations. Adhering to the concept of the importance of participation, the draft document was widely circulated among psychologists. There were intense debates, some critics asserting that the *Standards* imposed undue restraints on investigators. The debate resulted in some revisions of the statement, but it succeeded mainly in raising the general level of psychologists' awareness of ethical issues involved in research.

Perhaps the most remarkable development of a pragmatic character over the past two decades is the involvement of government in issues once left to professional discretion. The conscience of the community has expressed itself through legislation, administrative guidelines, and court orders. Issues covered range widely from diagnosis and treatment to research. In 1954 Judge David L. Bazelon ruled that in order to hold a mental patient involuntarily, hospital officials would have to make public what they were doing for him (*Durham* v. *United States,* 1954). The ruling was denounced as an unwarranted intrusion on the responsibility of the professional person. Nonetheless, it set the stage for a number of subsequent court rulings assuring right to treatment (*Donaldson* v. *O'Connor,* 1972), right to education (*Pennsylvania Association for Retarded Children* v. *Commonwealth of Pennsylvania,* 1972), freedom from institutional peonage (*Dale* v. *New York,* 1973), and a number of other similar issues, previously considered the private domain of professional people. In each, the ruling asserted the right of the state to concern itself with the welfare of people receiving professional assistance and to demand a higher level of performance than had been achieved under professional standards only.

Research has long been the most private of pursuits, presumably governed sufficiently by the canons of science and the traditions of universities. That these were insufficient safeguards became apparent in two widely publicized episodes involving the injection of live cancer cells in aging patients and the withholding of treatment from patients with syphilis. These actions now seem morally reprehensible, but it is clear that scientists (in these and other experiments) had let the pursuit of truth, an intrinsically worthy endeavor, blind them to their obligations to the well-being of others. To prevent such abuses, government grants involving experimentation on human subjects must now go through a rigorous review by a special committee at the sponsoring institution, by the staff of the granting agency, and by a national council. Subsequently, requirements have been set forth to ensure due process, confidentiality of records, and informed consent for research subjects and patients, prisoners, and school children. Courts have prohibited the use of intelligence tests in ways that perpetuate discrimination in schools (*Larry P. v. Riles,* 1972). The Law Enforcement Assistance Administration has limited the use of behavior modification procedures in federal prisons, holding them to be an undue infringement on a person's rights. Government action is responsive to public concerns, of course, but in these instances, especially, it has been remarkably successful in raising the general level of awareness of individual rights in settings in which professional people have held responsibility for many years, in research laboratories, in hospitals, schools, prisons, and other settings where ethical and moral issues are ever-present.

Some professional people have argued that government intrusion into the ethical practices of professions is unwarranted and counterproductive. Just the opposite would appear true. The scientist or professional person who insulates himself from public criticism runs a great risk and deprives himself of a valuable source of ethical and moral insight. The professional person must ultimately be responsible for his own conduct. Professional traditions of privacy and secrecy often deprive him of a valuable source of instruction. Candor, openness, and full disclosure within the limits of confidentiality are important sources of moral rectitude and authority. It goes against the grain of most professional training, but an informed public with open avenues for criticism can be the professional person's best friend.

The flowering of behavior modification—the translation of B. F. Skinner's laboratory observations to practical matters of training, education, and therapy—has been one of the truly remarkable developments of the past several decades. Regarding behavior modification, I have written elsewhere (Hobbs, in press):

> This development is important to discuss in ethics and morality precisely because it requires serious address to the idea of *man as machine*. The metaphor, advanced by Descartes and made explicit by LaMetrie, has been around for a long time, but behavior modification has stripped the concept of its metaphorical character and made it an operational reality (under certain conditions). Control of behavior by other means, by surgery or drugs, for example, does

not seem to join the issue of man as machine as explicitly as does behavior modification, which replaces individual "will" by individual "reinforcement history." Behavior modification is based on the assumption that the behavior of both mice and men is controlled by environmental contingencies, and, further, that these contingencies can often be externally controlled with precision (Skinner, 1969). Literally thousands of experiments support this mechanistic view in principle. Knowledge of the experiments had already created anxiety in philosophical and theological camps when B. F. Skinner's book, *Beyond Freedom and Dignity* (1971) appeared. Since then the debate has raged furiously, with moral and ethical considerations foremost. The arguments have to do with the assumptions about the nature of man, with various assessments of the efficacy of behavior controlled technology, with free will and determinism, and with the responsibilities of controllers.

The Skinnerian proposition that positive contingencies work better than negative sanctions is persuasive. But what positive reinforcers modify behavior? Pellets and lab chow seem sufficient for rats and pigeons. M-and-M's serve well with children, for a while. For hungry and destitute adults, food, clothing, and shelter are powerfully reinforcing. But when these basic needs are satisfied, what contingencies shape human behavior? In the history of humanity with its many ups and downs, what seem most powerfully to shape the behavior of men and women are the exercise of competence; the commitment of oneself to others; the intimacy and comfort of reciprocated private affections; the delights of discovery in nature, art, and music; the intimations of immortality through gods or good works; the benison of needed aloneness; the belief in the possibilities of the future; and the valuing of freedom and dignity. When such complex contingencies as these are to be contrived, by what name shall we call the contriver?

Members of the helping professions—whether medicine, psychology, social work, counseling, nursing, or the ministry—have joined with laypeople in recent years to address the complex issues of the sanctity of life, expressed in controversies over abortion, experimentation on the fetus, the prolongation of life by heroic measures, and euthanasia. These issues involve the most profound moral choices, and they present the professional person with a challenge to extend his own knowledge and understanding, his sensitivity to the perceptions and values of others, and his patience and resourcefulness in achieving an invincible surmise when he himself is called upon to help make such a decision. With practice in such complex matters, lesser issues should be handled with greater ease. It is important to note that the debate on the termination of life has moved out of the academy and into public forums. It is conducted in newspaper columns, on television programs, in magazine articles, in churches, and even in political campaigns. This widespread involvement of the public is extraordinarily valuable in raising the general level of moral perceptions, including those of members of the helping professions.

The professional person who wishes to maintain and enhance his sensitivity to ethical and moral issues involved in helping other people can now find much assistance in doing so. Indeed, the increase in the number of journals, institutes, and professorships devoted to issues of ethics and morality is remarkable, even astonishing, considering the scant attention paid to the problem less than two decades ago. Scholarly journals established during this period include *Soundings, Philosophy and Public Affairs, Journal of Medicine and Philosophy, Bioethics Digest,* and the *Hastings Center Report.* The Hastings Center in New York City also publishes the *Bibliography of Society, Ethics, and the Life Sciences.* New institutes include the Institute of Society, Ethics, and Life Sciences and the Joseph P. Kennedy Institute of Bioethics at Georgetown University.

It is easy for a professional person to accept without examination the philosophical foundations of his discipline. After years of training and long association with teachers and colleagues who share a common set of values, it is extraordinarily difficult to step aside and question one's value postulates or even to be aware that some questioning of assumptions would be productive. Members of helping professions can thus wisely welcome the work of thinkers who question the very foundations of what they are doing. One need not agree with their iconoclastic stance, but their work derives its value from requiring a sorting out of the good and the bad in one's accustomed modes of thought. One might cite, as examples, the work of Ivan Illich in education (1971), of Thomas Szasz in psychiatry (1970), of Alvin Gouldner in sociology (1970), and of Samuel Bowles and Herbert Gintis in economics and education (1976).

Now, let us turn our attention to theoretical developments. In the Harvard *Lampoon* a few years ago there appeared a cartoon showing a couple of rats in a Skinner box. One rat says to the other: "Boy, do I have that guy conditioned! Every time I press this bar, he gives me a pellet of food." This epistemological joke invites speculation on several theoretical issues involved in the ethics and morality of the control of human behavior, including the nature of choice, the meaning of responsibility, the problem of who is in the system and who is not, and the necessary assumptions of the scientific and clinical helping professional enterprises. Beliefs about human beings' freedom to choose inevitably enter into choices and decisions made by professional people in their effort to help others. One's initial choice of approach to a problem, preventive or therapeutic, reflects a position on the issue. Furthermore, the very nature of the relationship established between the helper and the person helped, usually controlled by the professional person, says something about beliefs concerning human freedom. The Harvard-educated, epistemological rat probably did not intend all these inferences, so let the author simply assume responsibility for them and thank him for making the point that truth depends on how one looks at things. He (the author, not the rat!) will now consider some common ways of looking at a set of issues roughly related to the central problem of determinism and then describe his preference for resolving the many paradoxes involved.

Benton Underwood (1957, p. 4) asserts simply: "Determinism is a necessary assumption for the scientific enterprise." B. F. Skinner (1953, p. 6) is equally explicit: "If we are to use the methods of science in the field of human affairs, we must assume that behavior is lawful and determined." And Perry London (1969, pp. 265–266) writes to the same effect but with more passion: "The message of behavioral technology, sent more forcefully by drugs and psychotherapy and conditioning and brain implants than it could ever be by proposition, is that will is ultimately not free, nor is ideology, nor man." (That London proposes a solution to this seemingly dead-end state does not diminish the significance of this forceful statement.) Finally, Anatol Rapoport states that, without freedom of choice, the very concept of ethics is meaningless. What are we to make of these contradictions?

As long ago as 1880, William James (1948, p. 37) wrote: "A common opinion prevails that the juice has ages ago been pressed out of the free-will controversy and that no new champion can do more than warm up stale arguments which everyone has heard." He then goes on to say: "But this is a radical mistake." Although frequently put to eternal rest by one author or another, the issue refuses to die; it is as alive today as it was almost a hundred years ago when James yearned plaintively that it would go away. As recently as 1976, at the annual meeting of the American Psychological Association, the issue was debated by such distinguished psychologists as Kenneth E. Clark, D. O. Hebb, David McClelland, Carl Rogers, B. F. Skinner, and others.

In 1959 I wrote a passage that I do not feel I can improve upon today:

> The psychologist is concerned with understanding and explaining behavior, mostly human behavior. One of the ways in which a psychologist tests the validity of his explanation is to make predictions derived from some explanatory system. If a particular prediction is confirmed, as through an experiment, his confidence in the system is increased. If the prediction is not confirmed and if he is confident of the adequacy of his experiment, he must go back and rework his explanations. Psychologists, like other scientists, work to advance understanding by testing specific "if–then" equations and working the results into more general formulations. The ground rules of science say that these equations cannot contain variables which are nonrandom in their operation but which at the same time are considered to be unavailable to any possible quantitative assessment. No scientific equation can contain an "X" variable which turns out to be the influence of any

demon, pixie, gremlin, fate, entelechy, god, or spontaneous individual will. Now there is nothing in science
that can disprove the existence and effective operation
of demons, pixies, gremlins, fates, entelechies, gods, or
undetermined individual choices. It is just that science
is not set up to deal with these kinds of problems. There
is no way for the scientist ever to write an equation incorporating such variables. The famous equation
$E = mc^2$ does not suggest that engineers should build
into an atom bomb a little man to decide whether or
not the bomb is to explode. The psychologist cannot
write such an elegant equation as this one of the physi-
cist, but he, too, must write his equations without benefit of little men. Insofar as psychological science is concerned, the notion of free choice is a homunculus.
Psychology cannot prove that the behavior of the individual is determined, but for purposes of inquiry he
must assume so and be content to live with whatever
limitation this assumption may (or may not) make on
his activities as a scientist (Hobbs, p. 222).

However, helping professionals and people in general often
have a difficult time with this kind of formulation, and many, even
ardent behavior modifiers, keep looking for a way out, for a solution
that will incorporate the canons of science without extinguishing
completely that spark of freedom so cherished by human beings over
the ages.

There are four familiar ways of handling the freedom-de-
terminism argument. First, one can take a deterministic position and
hold that it can encompass all natural phenomena, including human
beings and the artifacts that we call culture. This formulation is one
of great power and utility. When they do science, scientists live by
this idea. I object only when scientists try, through various kinds of
foot-in-the-door arguments, to stretch a deterministic system to embrace nondetermined and nonrandom events, such as "choice" or
"freedom." Second, one can maintain, not unreasonably, that human beings are simply different from other animals. We may be said
to have an immortal soul, or we may be said to be the only animal
that guides our own evolution by creating environments to our own

choosing. The implication is that our essence is unavailable to scientific inquiry and formulation. Third, one can argue that determinism is an obviously valid idea in reference to simple organisms with simple life histories and is applicable to human beings in some measure (a person in jail cannot choose to go for a walk), but that in important human matters the determinants of choice are so many, so complex, and so constantly in flux that it is useless, boring, or even silly to discuss the idea. This approach may seem the most attractive to many helping professionals. Nevertheless, the complexity-of-human-life aspect has important implications for diagnoses and therapeutic interventions that are sometimes overlooked. Fourth, one can argue that there are new discoveries in science that invalidate deterministic arguments, which are referred to as old hat, Newtonian, or Cartesian. The concepts come mainly from physics where probability, entropy, and indeterminacy in the Heisenberg sense are familiar notions. When some biologists and physicists speculate about the human nature, they find dispensation for choice and freedom in these technical matters.

There is yet another approach to the determinism issue that seems to have merit and to have implications for helping professionals. It starts with the postulate that science is a system that has been invented by people for the purpose of imposing order on events that often appear to be more or less randomly organized with reference to their existence. We have invented other construct systems to achieve the same grand purpose or to permit orderly transactions in some more limited sphere. Each of these construct systems may have its own unique validity. The criterion for the validity of each is not its consonance with another system but its utility in giving order and meaning to human experience. The dilemma for the helping professional is in achieving "goodness of fit" between the theoretical model followed, the diagnosis or assessment of the problem, and the intervention to be initiated. If forcing seems required, another system or model should be considered. But even if a goodness of fit is achieved without much difficulty, professionals should never lose sight of the fact that their theoretical constructs, language, classification systems, and therapeutic procedures are their own invention; they do not "reside" in the person helped and in that sense have no reality of their own. Different systems for ordering exist within as well as among different professions.

Within a scientific construct system, the assumption of determinism (plus randomness, perhaps) is required. There are also construct systems in which assumptions other than determinism rule. For example, the individual scientist getting up in the morning construes the world with the assumption of substantial freedom of choice. The legal system for interpreting the world assumes a middle position on determinism and individual freedom; the criminal behavior of the young person or of the psychotic is considered to be determined by circumstance, whereas the sane adult is construed as being responsible for his behavior. A religious system for understanding the world obviously has to assume the effective functioning of some supraindividual influence. And a poetic system might make even other assumptions. It is when we attempt to shift from one construct system to another, without explicit recognition of what we are doing, that we get into trouble.

Assessment of needs by various helping professionals may be another case in point. Those who deal in more overt or direct forms are often suspicious of projective or indirect methods of eliciting needs. On the other hand, those whose specialty is the latter may claim that surface responses are masking the "real reality." An additional possibility, of course, is that the professional's own needs will be projected and enter into the needs assessment of the other person. In his work in community psychology at George Peabody College in Nashville, J. R. Newbrough asks another question regarding help provided to people supposedly in need. Is giving help to someone who does not ask for it legitimate (or ethical) just because the professional sees a need for it? Also, if people are satisfied with help that the professional knows is not of high quality, or even adequate by professional standards, should ethical concern be expressed? If so, how?

It is our tendency to impose order on experience. Although nature may indeed be orderly, the very concept of an orderly universe is a human cognitive achievement, still vastly reassuring, but considerably less so today than before all the rules were revised by Einstein not too long ago. We may confidently expect the rules to be revised again. This is not meant to imply that nature is intractably obscure or our purpose whimsical, but that experience has constantly to be reconstrued to make it ring true, to make it serve particular human purposes at particular times.

The point is that we constantly engage in erecting cognitive structures to make sense of our being, to reduce absurdity, to constrain anxiety, and to bring coherence to disparate experience. This process is ultimately personal, in science no less than in art, as the physical chemist Michael Polanyi argues convincingly in his remarkable book, *Personal Knowledge* (1958). The product is ultimately metaphorical, whether in science, history, poetry, or theology. In these ventures we define anew both ourselves and our world, so there can be no end to the endeavor. Every achieved simplicity, every elegant equation, every brilliant truth achieved opens new domains of obscurity and perplexity, and this it will ever be, world without end.

The criterion of success in these most human of efforts is not the discovery of truth, though we may call it thus. Nor, as noted earlier, is it consonance among explanatory systems, for accord depends much on purpose, not alone on fact. The short-run criterion for the worth of a construct system is its utility in furthering particular human enterprises; the long-run criterion is neither truth nor utility but esthetic appeal, a sense of rightness between us and our world.

In 1965 I wrote that "to assert that a clinical psychologist is a scientist who has a hard time shaking off the weight of scientific tradition (the hand of Descartes is on one shoulder and the hand of Comte on the other) and then to add that the clinical engagement is a moral and ethical enterprise at its center is to lay bare the clinical psychologist's most exquisite dilemma. He has got to make up his mind about the issue of determinism. He will not solve the problem because it probably is not solvable, but if he is conscientious he will live with it examined and unresolved as one of the existential impossibilities of his chosen profession. Sisyphuslike, he will advance the stone uphill one day, only to have it roll back the next" (p. 1509).

The professional person who commits himself to helping other people make sense of their lives comes in time to recognize that his relationship with the person he aspires to help must be ethical to be effective. In some professions, perhaps, the primary function of ethical standards is to protect the client from harm at the hands of the professional person. This is not a sufficient standard for the kind of professional functioning with which this book is concerned. The practice of helping children to grow up trusting the world and all people to live meaningful and satisfying lives requires adherence to exemplary conduct. This is not solely to protect the person when he is in a vulnerable position but, more importantly, to provide him with an immediate and enduring experience of an intrinsically moral relationship with another human being. The relationship must be a living, immediate act of ethical discovery. Its product, for the helper and the helped, is an invincible surmise as to which is the greater and which the lesser good.

The professional person is asked to consider his functioning within the context of behavior control, since the very nature of his work often involves the exertion of much power over other people's lives. Attention then must focus upon the manner in which he deals with the ethical and moral issues inherent in this potential for control, especially when existing knowledge and formulated professional standards are insufficient guides to choice. At these times, the professional person may have to exercise an "invincible surmise," believing that this is the only ethical approach that will serve the best interests of another person whose well-being is seriously at stake. It is important that the person helped experience an intrinsically moral relationship with the individual who aspires to assist him.

In order to assume private—and a profound—responsibility for the reconstruction of what is right, the individual professional person must be thoroughly familiar with pragmatic and theoretical developments related to ethical and moral issues. Pragmatic developments include the evolution of ethical standards as experience provides new insights; involvement of government and an informed public in issues of research, diagnosis, and treatment; the flowering of behavior modification; the debate concerning sanctity of life issues; and the proliferation of journals, institutes, and professorships devoted to ethics and morality.

Theoretical issues important in the ethics and morality of

the control of human behavior include the nature of choice, the meaning of responsibility, the problem of who is in the system, and the necessary assumptions of the scientific and clinical helping professional enterprise. One's position on determinism is reflected in most of the choices he makes as a professional person.

The professional person should never lose sight of the fact that science is only one of many construct systems invented to impose order on, and to give meaning to, experience. Each has its own unique validity. The dilemma for the helping professional person is in achieving "goodness of fit" between the theoretical model followed, assessment or diagnosis of the problem, and the intervention approach to be initiated. Also, he should not shift from one construct system to another without recognition of what he is doing. The clinical engagement is a moral and ethical enterprise, and the clinician must live with the issue of determinism as one of the existential possibilities of his profession.

Chapter 3

Normality and Abnormality in Perspective

William C. Rhodes

Today, as professionals, we find ourselves in a world of upheaval and ferment in human care. Yet, most of us somehow go on with our usual activities, acting as though we are oblivious to the tremors and threatened eruption of the ground beneath our feet—the ground of theories, service systems, intervention techniques, and bodies of knowledge. These upheavals are everywhere. What was solid, firm ground just a few years ago is now like a river of lava in which certainty and solidity have liquefied beneath us.

Even the bedrock of research and theory is dissolving in the process—normal and abnormal have become questionable mental

structures. Our accustomed world has suddenly become peopled
with myths—myths like mental illness (Szasz, 1961; Schatzman,
1973) or madness (Foucault, 1973). Abnormality becomes conditions of cultural or social relativity (Benedict, 1961; Paul and Des
Jarlais, 1978).

In this mixture of dissolved structures there is a certain sense
of freedom. At the very least, we have been made aware of some of
the psychosocial dimensions that lead us to construct the services of
human care in the way we do. For example, in arriving at conclusions about who is normal and abnormal, labeling theorists have
turned our attention to our own mind processes as these processes
have been shaped by culture (Becker, 1963; Ryan, 1971). This is
extended to all major nosological constructs in the human care
arena—retardation (Mercer, 1973), homosexuality (Reiss, 1964),
alcoholism (Jackson, 1965), and mental illness (Scheff, 1966).
These theorists have talked about professionals as agents of social
control. The agents include police, courts, psychologists, psychiatrists, teachers, social workers, and others. They are the invokers of
the labeling process. As construed in this perspective, they are responsible for selecting out of a whole society of rule breakers or
image breakers the particular social members who will play deviant
roles.

In the current fluid, shifting perspective we are experiencing,
behavioral disorders, learning disabilities, developmental disabilities,
neurosis, and psychoses become relative states. They take their
meaning from the idiosyncrasies of the particular culture in which
they are embedded, reflecting cultural agreements or fictions that
can assume one guise in one culture and a totally opposite guise in
another (Benedict, 1961).

Such countervailing views may have opened windows, but at
the same time they have raised moral dilemmas for the professional.
By what right, moral or scientific, do we diagnose people and proceed to intervene in their lives? If, as held in labeling theory, we are
agents of culture, enforcing cultural proscriptions regarding character traits, behaviors, physical conditions, and states of being, how
did we come to this position of power, and how will we find our
way out of this cul-de-sac? By what route did our minds convince
us of the scientific rigor and accuracy of our belief systems about

normal and abnormal, behavioral order and disorder? Are these constructs merely mirrors of collective minds shaped by the same culture, the same social forces?

But wait, we say, we cannot accept this extreme subjective view. There are objective realities, objective states and conditions that depart from health, soundness, order, and other identifiable dimensions. Even as we contemplate the counterperspective to our former convictions of scientific objectivity, our minds, with their great capacity for perceptual alteration, frequently shift our thinking to the opposite side of this inquiry. But, yes, we insist, there really are such conditions as insanity or mental retardation in people. We have all kinds of evidence that they exist. They are undeniable facts. Then we marshal the arguments of the deviance theorists, who criticize labeling theory's lack of emphasis on the contributions of the "rule breaker" in the process of becoming deviant (Matza, 1969; Gove, 1970). Thus, the professional mind today holds within itself two irreconcilable conclusions concerning deviance: "It is a phantom," and "It really exists."

If there are two realities side by side in our own heads, what is our stance toward "our" patients, "our" clients? If we can both prove and disprove the existence of abnormal states as scientists, what direction does that give us for our professional behavior? These questions seem particularly relevant for our work with children, whose ongoing development is so open to being influenced by the orientation we take.

We are thrown back upon ourselves. We are forced into individual choice. We cannot refer to a "body of accumulated data," "the most solid research findings," "the consensus of the field." None of these gives us our authority. Of course, we have the authority of our legal position; our legislated role as interveners; our official system, title, and power as licensed clinical psychologist, certified school psychologist, or board-certified psychiatrist. But we are suddenly bereft of the authority of a body of knowledge. We are individual "helpers" who have to ask ourselves by what right do we help and whom do we help. Our professional associations or affiliative organizations can give us a sense of comradeship, a human support system, in arriving at the answer to this question, but they cannot supply us with answers because they do not have them. Each one of us must grapple with the question ourselves and come to our own conclusions to guide our actions.

Even if we reject the various observations and framework of thinkers like Laing (1964), Szasz (1970), Kitsuse (1964), and Schatzman (1973) and hold to their opposite—that is, to a rigorous acceptance of absolute standards of normative states or conditions— we are now confronted with a perspective that forces social scientists and helping professionals to examine the actions of all the actors involved in the process through which certain human states and persons come to be perceived as deviating from physical and psychosocial norms. We now find ourselves included among these actors. Because the framework within which we define people leads us to decide how we shall treat them in our schools, our hospitals, our prisons—in all of society's institutions—we are forced into choosing perspectives to guide our actions.

The perspective of objectivity and the particular scientific method by which we have accumulated the idiosyncratic "data" that have guided us over the last half-century have been seriously questioned by such investigators as Quine (1969), Berger and Luckmann (1967), and Feyerabend (1975). Objectivity, too, dissolves into social conditioning, into the end product of the way in which we learn to perceive the world. Therefore, even when we chose objectivity and empiricism, it can be argued that such choice is one of faith. In the past we had no questions about empirical data. Now, we have to go through a mental process simply to reject the reasoning that raises questions about objectivity and empiricism.

The very essence of normality—that is, "reality"—the solid universe in which we dwell, is under examination (Berger and Luckmann, 1967). Berger (1969), following Schutz (1962), has pointed out that reality is a socialized symbolic universe and that socialization is never completely successful. Some individuals inhabit the transmitted universe more definitely than others. He says that even among the more or less accredited inhabitants of a culture's symbolic universe there will always be idiosyncratic variations in the way the universe is conceived. Berger says that precisely because the symbolic universe cannot be experienced as such in everyday life, because it transcends the latter by its very nature, it is not possible to teach its meaning in the straightforward manner in which one can teach the meaning of everyday life. He says that the questions raised by children about the symbolic universe have to be answered in a more complicated way than their questions about institutional realities of everyday life. The questions of idiosyncratic adults require further elaboration.

According to Berger, this intrinsic problem becomes accentuated if deviant versions of the symbolic universe come to be shared by groups of inhabitants of a particular culture's symbolic universe. In such a case, he says, the deviant version, for reasons evident in the nature of "objectivation," congeals into a reality in its own right, which, by its existence in the society, challenges the reality status of the symbolic universe as originally constituted.

In this connection, some of the newer specifically labeled groups, such as the Delancey Street Foundation (Hamden-Turner, 1977), have become self-help activists who challenge both the official symbolic universe of the greater society and the specific subset of this version held by the professional community. They also become a threat to our concept of reality. This type of collectivization of the alternative universes of labeled people may be the most serious challenge to the psychological reality we purport to explain. If groups like Narcotics Anonymous, Psychotics Anonymous, Recidivists Anonymous, Sexual Child Abusers Anonymous, Schizophrenics Anonymous (Jones, 1977), and Synanon and Delancey Street should coalesce into a single body, they would posit not only a theoretical threat to our professional version of reality but a practical one to all the institutional forms of care giving within the ambience of that particular symbolic universe. This would include the schools, the legal correctional system, the mental health system, and vocational rehabilitation. As pointed out in a recent meeting of professionals and mutual help system members, fiscal cutbacks and personnel shortages in the official service organizations have created an environment in which the rise of self-help efforts among the labeled groups is especially propitious.

In their analysis of the social construction of reality, Berger and Luckmann (1967) state that "The appearance of an alternative symbolic universe poses a threat because its very existence demonstrates empirically that one's own universe is less than inevitable" (p. 108). These investigators view therapy as an application of universe-maintaining conceptual machinery. In this connection, the term *therapy* applies not only to our own version but also to the many forms it assumes in various societies. Berger and Luckmann go on to say, "Therapy entails the application of conceptual machinery to ensure that actual or potential deviants stay within the institutionalized definitions of reality, or in other words, to prevent the inhabitants of a given universe from emigrating" (p. 108). They maintain that, since therapy must concern itself with deviations from the "official" definitions of reality, it must develop a conceptual machinery to account for such deviations and to maintain the realities so challenged. "This requires a body of knowledge that includes a theory of deviance, a diagnostic apparatus, and a conceptual system for the 'cure of souls' " (p. 113).

Drawing upon the model in Plato's *Republic*, they invert the psychoanalytic version of homosexuality as practiced in therapy until recently. Their paradigm concerns a collectivity that has institutionalized military homosexuality in which the stubbornly heterosexual individual is a sure candidate for therapy, both because he constitutes a threat to the combat efficiency of his unit of warrior lovers and because his deviance is psychologically subversive to the others' spontaneous virility. Some of them might be subconsciously tempted to follow his example. More fundamentally, such a deviant would be a challenge to the societal reality by questioning its cognitive ("virile men by nature love one another") and normative ("virile men should love one another") operating procedures. Furthermore, their deviance is a challenge to their gods who love one another in the heavens as their devotees do on earth. Berger and Luckmann then say that such a challenge to a socially constructed reality would provoke a theory of deviance, a body of diagnostic concepts, the prompt development of preventive and treatment measures and a group of specialists who master the theory and methods.

Berger and Luckmann's inversion of psychiatry's treatment of homosexuality as psychopathology could have been taken directly from Ruth Benedict's (1961) comparison of homosexuality in our culture and the opposite treatment of warrior love in Plato's *Republic*, as well as from other examples of cultures that treated homosexuality as a normal condition. Benedict's examples of the cultural nature of normality and abnormality, sickness and health, may seem remote to us because the cultures examined are both remote and esoteric compared with our own. However, one way to appreciate this relativity is to look at a culture closer to our own geographically and sociologically to fully grasp the cultural *construction* processes and images that condition normalcy and abnormalcy. In doing this we can use the cultural–historical framework employed by Foucault (1973). An example, which seems eminently suitable to this framework, is the startling inversion of sickness and health and life and death that occurred in Germany in the twelve years of its Nazi period. From this reference point, cultural constructions of normalcy and abnormalcy are very embedded in the cultural matrix. It is difficult to separate the reciprocal conditions of normalcy and abnormalcy out of that matrix and specify which is the property of groups, which is the property of individuals, and which is the property of the sustaining environment. Furthermore, cultural artifacts and institutions associated with normalcy and abnormalcy are such a part of the natural history of the culture's belief systems that they not only exemplify the belief system but also become the social–action expressions of that system.

One way in which to try to understand the German inversion of sickness and health and life and death is to go back to the writings of Alfred Rosenberg, the major conceptualizer of the Nazi framework, and the writings and speeches of his pupil, Adolf Hitler.

Responding to the mood of the nation after its disastrous defeat in World War I, Rosenberg and Hitler interpreted its feeling of sickness and pinpointed the cause. As in all cultures, both the cause and the cure lay in certain human qualities and characteristics. Also, as in all cultures, atonement was possible through isolation and curing of the cause. The sickness of the nation was due primarily to the sickness of certain groups of imperfect or contaminating individuals. Based upon the diagnosis supplied by Rosenberg and Hitler, the architects of the Reich made use of the current technology, along with the nation's central planning and organizational skills, to map out a radical social treatment that transformed Germany into a treatment society. Hitler (1939) talked about the rights of personal freedom receding before the duty to *preserve the race:* "Only after these measures are carried out can the medical struggle against the plague be carried through with any prospect of success. It is a half-measure to let incurably sick people steadily contaminate the remaining healthy ones—the demand that defective people be prevented from propagating equally defective offspring is a demand of the clearest reason and if systematically executed represents the most humane act of mankind. For if necessary, the incurably sick will be pitilessly segregated—a barbaric measure for the unfortunate who is struck by it, but a blessing for his fellow men and posterity" (p. 255).

The metaphors of sickness, health, and treatment were used in a very literal sense. They were an active and central part of the language of the Nazi leaders and the Third Reich. They were the foundation of the belief system that they and the German nation translated into social reality. Nor was it just the Nazi party that acted out this belief system in a search for cultural identity. It was the total nation, including business and industry, science and education, the judicial system, the care-giving systems, the army, and the police. All of these social institutions were geared to the curative cause. All of these directly participated in the elimination of the identified sources of sickness. "The proof is implicit in scores of documents introduced at Nuremberg. The prosecution did not introduce these documents as evidence against the German people, for the German people were not on trial at Nuremberg. But the evidence is there, nonetheless—evidence the more convincing for the very reason that it was not part of the prosecution's case, but grew almost accidentally, as it were, out of the facts themselves" (Bernstein, 1947, p. 246).

The Reich's "work-to-death" decree was carried out under private enterprise. Industries competed for inmates of labor camps under this decree. Medical journals of that time gave reports indicating the use of endocrines and other body parts of individuals who "died a sudden death" and who "had been living under absolutely identical conditions, even so far as nourishment was concerned" (Bernstein, 1947, p. 127). Bernstein also reports the case of the Kaiser Wilhelm Institute, "Germany's equivalent of the Rockefeller Foundation" (p. 177). For five years the laboratory technicians at the institute microscopically studied brain smears from children who had died in the asylum at Harr-Eglfing. The death certificates reported pneumonia or circulatory disorders. "Actually these children had been murdered systematically with injections of luminal, iodine, or evipan under the Nazi nationwide plan for destruction of 'useless eaters' " (Bernstein, 1947, p. 177).

The survivors of Bergen-Belsen claimed: "Large segments of the German people were drawn into the implementation of this plan of extermination—persons of all walks of life and all classes of society—scientists, diplomats and workers, soldiers and civilians. It would be a falsification of history to maintain that the German people were ignorant of the massacres and robberies. The auto-da-fe, the Nuremberg trials, the Crystal Night, the press and so called literature had pointed without any doubt to the direction in which they were going" (Black, 1965, p. lxv).

These quotes from other books are not offered as further condemnation of the German people of that period. Rather, they are intended to demonstrate how a total society can be caught up, or at least participate, in carrying out the culture's imagery of health and sickness. The imagery of Rosenberg and Hitler helped turn Germany into a treatment-by-death culture. This particular society is chosen as a case example of the cultural embedment and social construction of normal and abnormal because it is close in time to current history; and because, like our nation, it is also part of modern European civilization. Although it took an exaggerated form in Germany, the meaning of "sick" is no different in cognitive–emotional structure from what occurs in any culture. Although the cure of the disease turned out to be the most drastic in the history of collectives, the Nazis chose familiar victims with whom to begin. They began the purge of the imperfection and unhealthiness of the social body with the same populations that occupy our attention in our schools, disability programs, and institutions—the retarded, the mentally ill, the delinquent and criminal, and the "incurably" ill. To show the counterparts of thinking even in our own society in that period, H. H. Goddard, the renowned psychologist who was one of the introducers of intelligence testing in this country and who made social Darwinism a force in this nation's views of human imperfection, had singled out the same population just a few years before. (The Nazi architects used the same frame of reference and the same language of social and individual imperfection.) In his argument for segregation and sterilization of the feebleminded, delinquent, and mentally ill, Goddard (1921, p. iv) said, "There are two million people in the United States who, because of their weak minds or diseased minds, are making this country a dangerous place to live in. The two million is increasing both by heredity and training. We are breeding defectives. We are making criminals."

Rosenberg and Hitler also saw these feeble, sick, and criminal minds as sources of infection for the German society, and individuals so designated were slated as the first to be eliminated from the social body. It was in the extermination of the crippled, the retarded, the mentally ill, the criminal, and other so-called "incurables" that techniques such as segregation camps and gassings in the social planning blueprint were developed and perfected. This technically perfected arsenal of destruction was later used against Jews, Gypsies, Freemasons, Bolsheviks, ministers, and priests. In Hitler's disease ideology, to be declared healthy and Aryan was to be declared normal, and this had to be attested to by a listing on a central registry and a card carried to verify that fact. This is unlike our own situation in which only the condition of occupying a state of abnormality is labeled.

Peter Berger (1969, p. 92) has said that "There is a dichotomy in the human situation between a middle ground, which is the realm of the ordinary, everyday life in society, and various marginal realms in which the taken-for-granted assumptions of the former realms are threatened. As Alfred Schutz has shown, the middle ground which we take for granted as normality or sanity can be maintained (that is, inhabited) only if we suspend all doubt about its validity."

It would seem that in a few short years Hitler and his followers effectively made disease and cure a part of the realm of ordinary, everyday life in society. One was able to occupy the middle ground by taking for granted Hitler's assumptions about the plague that contaminated the German nation, the existence of a folk society, an Aryan race, and the assumption that one could identify the defective people contaminating the springs of racial purity. These assumptions were reinforced by social institutions and the respectability of institutions such as courts and schools. This strange middle ground was taken for granted as normality or sanity. By inhabiting it, one maintained one's sanity only by suspending all doubt about its existence no matter how it was seen from a more distant perspective. If one had questioned these assumptions, one would have threatened the realm one was occupying and (1) moved psychologically into the shadowy, marginal realms of abnormality occupied by hordes of other citizens banished to these "no-places" (beleaguered ghettoes and collecting and exterminating camps, outside the social stream of Germany), (2) challenged the reality status of the symbol universe occupied by the Third Reich.

The psychological threat of moving into marginal realms outside the shared reality is probably as great as the threat of institutional retaliation for having challenged the validity of the ensconced symbolic universe. One looses one's moorings; one ruptures the major relationships that make psychological existence possible. There is a loss of self anchored in a real world. The psychological cost is great in the loss of symbol foundations. There is a dissolution of not only internal but also external coherence. There is a loss of trust in oneself. There is a loss of connectedness to others. Institutional retaliation is experienced as perhaps legitimate since one has wandered into the desert of the abnormal outside the range of the middle ground.

The unbearable penalty is to create one's own alternative reality with no tie to institutions or to the enduring symbols and artifacts of the culture one inhabits. Furthermore, even if one chose to do so, it would be difficult to identify with the hordes of abnormals also wandering in the forbidden marginal realms. There is no coherent substitute reality that unites them in an alternative symbol universe. One experiences "not being" at the same time that one is aware of life. Therefore, the marginal realms are very difficult to dwell in. So, one does not lightly question a given reality. To have that reality taken away, when not prepared to voluntarily emigrate, is to experience psychosis.

Societies have always banished those they labeled abnormal into places of "not being." In his book *The Heresy of Self-Love,* Paul Zweig (1968) pointed out that abnormalized members of early towns (fools, lepers, outcasts, among others) were banished into the unstructured social spaces outside the society's institutional bounds, the resident reality of the life of the town. Foucault (1973), who says that madness suddenly burst upon the symbolic landscape of European civilization in the fifteenth century, reviews the literature, art, and iconography that depicts madness as being transported to nowhere. He cites the frequent artistic theme of the *Ship of Fools* (Bosch, 1973) and Sebastian Brant's *Narrenschiff* (1974) and says that in the fifteenth to seventeenth centuries in Europe, "fools" were actually put onto ships where the sailors or masters were paid to transport them away from the city. Thus, they were made wanderers or "floaters" from town to town. According to ethnographic data collected by Frazer (1950), the gesture of the community casting into limbo its "poisonous bacilli," its carriers of the sickness of the society, its bearers of pestilence in order to purify the culture is a pancultural and panhistorical human process. The towns transferred ills and threatened calamities upon these scapegoats and cast them out of the gates into the "wilderness"—the place of loss of social being. In this act the collective was purified. Like the German example, such bearers of the evils and calamities of the culture were also frequently put to death or had their bones broken so they could not return to the purified soil.

It is psychologically excruciating to voluntarily take upon oneself the calumny of the collective, to sacrifice oneself psychologically or physically. One experiences being "lost" both to society and to oneself. One experiences the awful psychological dread of sacrificial "shunning," of being bereft of psychosocial existence, of having moved out of reality, of being nowhere in an inchoate space.

From such a perspective, one begins to comprehend why people cling so desperately to the cultural ethos of "normality," no matter what crooks or turns it takes in the society one inhabits. Just as psychological theory has applied its efforts to the roots and meaning of abnormality, it must begin to apply itself to the psychological construction of normality. In fact, normality has been the missing equation in all psychological discussions of abnormality. It has been a taken-for-granted construction, a reality that psychology, in its own tie to the symbol universe of its culture, generally accepted as given. Although the rejected states of abnormality have been thoroughly investigated, the middle ground symbol universe has rarely been open to examination.

Otto Rank (1945) did attempt a phenomenological investigation of normality in his studies of that specific abnormality called neurosis. According to Rank, Nietzsche questioned alienists as to whether there are also neuroses of health. If one confronts the situation of the masses in Germany during the Nazi period, one is tempted to reply, "Of course." This answer comes from our own cultural judgments. In order to have certainty, one must go deeper into oneself, make choices, and then answer the question, independent of the conditioned reality of one's own culture or professional subculture.

In Rank's conception of the construction of reality, he offers a psychological counterpart to Berger's and Luckmann's (1967) notion of the social construction of reality, except that he moves us into the marginal realms outside the middle ground and offers a beginning roadmap of the uncharted areas. He presents the development and potentially autonomous nature of the "onlooker," the individual ego. "This involves not only the duality of actor and self observer, but has yet another meaning, in that, for civilized man, the milieu is no longer the natural reality, the opposing force of an external world, but an artistic reality, created by himself which we, in its outer as in its inner aspects, designate as civilization" (p. 211). For Rank the neurotic is one who has taken a look at socially constructed reality as it exists in its inner psychological aspects and in its outer cultural aspects and has made an abortive, creative move into the realms surrounding the middle ground of socialized sanity— for example, the sanity of Nazi Germany.

Kierkegaard (1971) describes the sickness of normality as permitting oneself to be defrauded by "the others," as seeing the multitude of others, as engaging in all sorts of worldly affairs, and as knowing as much as possible about "how things work" in the world. Such a person forgets himself, does not dare believe in himself. Rather than thinking for himself, rather than venturing into the marginal realms outside the conditioned symbol universe, he finds it easier and safer to be like the others, to imitate, to become a number, a cipher in the crowd.

Rank (1945) and Becker (1973) both see normality as having, at its roots, the same qualities as abnormality. It flourishes in "sickness." This sickness can be viewed as the normality of the German masses in the twelve-year span of the Nazi period. It can also be applied to normality in any culture, at any time. This is Benedict's (1961) culturally normal person. Rather than venture into oneself and get lost in those marginal realms, it is better to become embedded in a safe framework of the symbolic universe that constitutes the reality of one's own culture, the application of oneself to the safety of social and cultural obligations and duties.

According to Becker (1973) most of us dwell together in the middle ground of Kierkegaard's "philistinism." Most people figure out how to live within the probabilities of a given set of rules. The philistine trusts that by keeping herself at a low level of personal intensity she can avoid being pulled off balance by experience. All the forces of culture surrounding her help hold her in that orbit.

In the atrocities of the Nazi situation we observe some of the social consequences of "philistinism"; and, yet, for those vast numbers of individuals who occupied the symbol universe of sickness, health, and cure supplied by Rosenberg and Hitler, there were no devastating psychological consequences.

Becker (1973, p. 81) notes: "philistinism works, as Kierkegaard said, by 'tranqualizing itself with the trivial.'" He calls such philistinism "normal neurosis." This is very much like Freud's (1949) "social neuroses," the "pathology of whole cultural communities." According to Rank and Becker, when it does not work for the individual, when he awakens from the tranquilized sleep of life in the middle ground, he may either make the leap to creativity, or be suspended in the purgatory of neurosis. Rank sees the neurotic type as a miscarriage of the heroic creation of one's own reality, the creation of one's own sanity, independent of the cultural images of sickness and health, normal and abnormal: "The creative man of every type has a much stronger ego than the average man, as we see not only in genius but also in the neurotic, whose convulsed hypertrophied ego is just what creates the neurosis, psychologically a creative achievement just as much as any other" (p. 212). He characterizes the creative type as one who evolves his ego ideal for himself, not only on the grounds of the given but also for self-chosen factors that he strives after consciously. As a result, Rank says, instead of being caught between the two powerful forces of fate, the inner (id) and the externally derived (superego), the ego develops and expresses itself creatively. This creative alternative to the inevitability of adaptation to the cultural ideal of normality allows one to construct one's own ego ideal, one's own symbol universe. Rank locates this capacity in a spiritual rather than a biological principle. In *The Trauma of Birth* (1929) he compares the creative drive of the individual physically and psychically to the "rebirth experience." In *Will Therapy and Truth and Reality* (1945) he says that the rebirth experience is psychologically the actual creative act of the human being. For in this act the psychic ego and the human being become at once creator and creature, or actually move from creature to creator. In the ideal case, the person is creator of herself, her personality.

Thus, for Rank, unlike Freud, the ego is not only a wrestling ground of (id) impulses and (superego) repressions but is also a conscious bearer of a striving force. It is the autonomous representation of an individual will and individually chosen ethical obligation in terms of a self-constituted ego ideal. Berger and Luckmann have presented the social construction of reality, the middle ground symbol universe that is taken to be synonymous with normality and sanity. In her cross-comparison studies of normality Benedict (1961) has clearly shown that the ego-ideal is radically different and frequently the opposite from culture to culture. The Nazi example has shown us the ephemeral nature of the psychological construction of normal and abnormal and sickness and health, and it provides a vivid illustration of the sickness of normality described by Kierkegaard, Rank, and Becker.

As professionals we are a group rethinking ourselves and our relationship to our charges and to society. Although we go about our business as usual, we are unsettled and dissatisfied with our relationship to the symbol universe of normal and abnormal. Some of us have taken a giant step, have jumped the wall that separates the normal from abnormal, and have taken up residence in that "nether realm." Although we do not idealize those who are socially alien, we have become all too aware of our own creatureliness in them and the need to search out our own ego ideal among them. It is easier to do this when not dwelling in the middle ground where one has to constantly figure out how to live within the probabilities of a given set of rules. It is precisely because the vast masses of abnormals have not developed a unified, coherent alternative symbolic universe that it is possible to begin fashioning one's own reality among them.

Even for those professionals who have no need to dissociate

themselves from the culture, new guidelines are being fashioned. Perhaps the paradigm constructed by Terrance Des Pres (1976) in looking at the survivor of the death camps of Russia and Nazi Germany can offer a modified professional framework. We might think of our clients in the existential reality of their social situation, as survivors, and our task as that of helping them to survive the pressures of their human condition. Des Pres stated this thesis in the following way: "My subject is survival, the capacity of men and women to live beneath the pressure of protracted crisis, to sustain terrible damages in mind and body and yet be there, sane, alive, still human. I am not directly concerned with concentration camps, but with the people who suffered those places, who endured that evil and returned to bear witness. . . . I could not take a stance of detachment, could not be "clinical" or "objective" in the way now thought proper [for] to write about terrible things in a neutral tone or with descriptions barren of subjective response tends to generate an irony so virulent as to end in either cynicism or despair. On the other hand, to allow feeling much play when speaking of atrocity is to border on hysteria and reduce the agony of millions to a moment of self-indulgence" (pp. v–vi).

In our own reappraisal, we must take a look at our preventive and therapeutic apparatus, at our scientific ideology, and examine the extent to which they are marshalled to reinforce the society's version of reality. We must analyze the extent to which human services, as now constituted, set out to maintain creatureliness and abort evolvement into creativity. We must look at our schools particularly, because the educational systems of cultures tend simply to be transmitters of their own ethnocentric version of normalcy. As Foucault (1976) has pointed out, a society uses its educational system to create a symbol world that distorts its culture by smoothing conflicts and contradictions within it and by reflecting these distortions indirectly through myths that excuse it.

The myths of the Nazi regime disguised its tyranny and psychopathology by idealizing its *herrenmenschen* (master human beings) and demonizing its *utermenschen* (inferior human beings). The myth was further compounded by eulogizing the "duty to preserve the race," by not letting "incurably sick people contaminate the remaining healthy ones. . . . By preventing defective people [from] propagating equally defective offspring [is] a demand of the clearest

reason [which] if systematically executed represents the most humane act of mankind. . . ." (Hitler, 1939, p. 255).

As professionals we have believed until recently that we could
defend ourselves against the creatureliness inside ourselves and the
idealization of the culture outside ourselves through the magic circle
of objective science. Perhaps we have deceived ourselves. In his
essay, *Speaking of Objects,* Quine (1969, pp. 5–6) has said: "Even
we who grew up together and learned English at the same knee, or
adjacent ones, talk alike for no other reason than that the society
coached us alike in a pattern of verbal responses to externally observed cues. We have been beaten into outward conformity to an
outward standard. . . . When we compare theories, doctrines,
points of view, and cultures, on the score of what sorts of objects
there are said to be, we are comparing them in a respect which makes
sense provincially."

If Quine's thesis prevails, our choices cannot derive directly
from the evidence of our science when we apply psychological knowledge. The apparent solidity of the language of our theories and doctrines could be nothing more than an "outward" conformity to an
"outward" standard. We may have been coached alike in a pattern of
outward verbal responses to externally observed cues. Therefore,
each of us must individually go into ourselves and make our own
decisions about how we serve and whom we serve. The labeling
theorists have made us conscious of all the actors in the paradox of
abnormality.

In recent years we have been made all too aware by writers
like Szasz (1961) and researchers like Rosenhan (1973) of our own
role in the metaphorical drama of disability and disease. The necessity for attending to our own role as actors in the drama is pressed
upon us as never before.

Each of us may have to go through the psychological rebirth
trauma described by Otto Rank (1945) in *Will Therapy and Truth
and Reality* in order to make these awesome personal choices. The
first necessity is to begin to separate ourselves from our culture, both
the larger culture of the general society and the microculture of our
profession. This means stepping away from the middle ground and
exposing ourselves to the psychological and physical dangers of the
marginal realms.

There are no charts for this journey. Each person must map it for herself. However, there is a direction we can take beyond our professional guidelines. It is the direction we can take beyond normality, beyond neurosis suggested by Rank. It is a move beyond philistine creatureliness to creation of ourselves and our own ego ideal rather than borrowing the ego ideal presented by culture as the healthy human. In the process we need a guiding star by which to navigate. If we are to heal ourselves of cultural normality in order to heal others, this guiding star can be the state of human grace, in the human arena a psychological counterpart to that striven for throughout history in the spiritual arena. In the journey toward psychological rebirth and self-creativity we can refer back to the negative guidelines of the Nazi experience. We can use these shoal-markers to help us avoid the dangers of our own creatureliness.

To develop healing strength in ourselves and in others we must try to awaken from our dream of normality and stop trying to figure out how we and others can live within the probabilities of a given set of rules. We have to guard against being defrauded by "the others," whether the others are our colleagues or the larger society. We must practice thinking for ourselves rather than relying on our "body of knowledge" to think for us. We must turn our eyes away from the multitude of other professionals about us into the experiential creativity within ourselves. In moving toward such personal, psychological grace, we must develop ego strength as "onlookers" of the psychological scene in which we are both actor and self-observer. The familiar milieu, the so-called "environment," must be transformed in the process from the "natural reality"—that is, the opposing force of an external world—to an artistic reality created by ourselves.

As we look at the task at hand in moving toward personal grace, we can borrow the model that Des Pres (1976, p. 121) summarizes from Camus' novel *The Plague:*

> There are two kinds of people in *The Plague,* the "townspeople" and the "volunteers." Both react to the plague, the former on its terms, the latter on terms partially their own. The "townspeople" remain subject to necessity, at one with the situation destroying them.

The "volunteers" respond to the same necessity, but by opposing it. They turn reaction into action self-directed, and in this way move far enough beyond death's rule to keep themselves intact as human beings. Rieux, Tarrow, and their coworkers pit themselves against the plague, with no conviction of success, but only determined not to stand idle while others suffer. Together, therefore, they organize hygienic programs, they tend the stricken, they dispose of the dead. They work twenty hours a day amid the stench and agony of the dying, spending themselves in that endless, empty time of day upon day, without the encouragement of visible progress, without the hope of an end in sight, and always with a knowledge that death may win. They carry on all the same, because "they knew it was the only thing to do."

This chapter asks professionals to consider the origins of their concepts of normality and abnormality and the implications for the people they serve. It reviews the recent challenging of traditional concepts and notes that professionals today are faced with two irreconcilable conclusions about deviance. The individual professional must grapple with the question of how these two existential realities affect his orientation and actions toward those he is trying to help. The Nazi version of sickness and health is used to illustrate the relative nature of concepts and how cultural construction processes and images condition ideas of normality and abnormality. The psychological advantages of inhabiting a middle ground—by taking for granted assumptions underlying a particular concept of normality—are then discussed, followed by an overview of the ways in which a society treats people who dare to venture into the marginal realms of socially constructed reality. Rank's creative individual does make this leap, and constructs his own ego ideal and symbol universe. It is important for professionals to take a direction beyond normality and to realize that choices they make in applying psychological knowledge cannot derive directly from the evidence of science. Rather, such choices must come from within themselves. The state of human grace can guide professionals in developing healing strengths in themselves and others and in awakening from a dream of objective normality.

Chapter 4

Rights and Rites of Professionalism

Robert S. Mendelsohn

Professional had a good meaning during my childhood years and for some time thereafter. To say of someone, "He is a professional" meant he was a doctor, a dentist, or a lawyer. He had a certain level of education, a certain dignity and, of course, the highest standards of ethical behavior. His performance was consistently and predictably excellent, and a high compliment was "done like a pro."

The professional could be trusted to keep a confidence, to treat people fairly and conscientiously, and to regard the exchange of money as a matter secondary to the quality of service. Besides, one did not usually discuss money with the professional, especially the physician. The service was given, a bill was submitted, and prompt payment was expected except in the most unusual circumstances. Even then, a certain ethical code prevailed in that one might discuss a financial adjustment, but one never bargained. Such discussions were often held with an intermediary, such as a secretary or bookkeeper, rather than with the professional himself. Interest charges were for businessmen, not professionals.

Somewhere in my early adult life, after I finished my medical training, I recognized that the word *professional* applied not only to doctors, golfers, tennis stars, plumbers, actors, journalists, photographers, administrators, and other perfectly honorable occupations; it also was used in some less savory connections, such as a "professional witness," "professional blood donor," and "professional liberal." In these instances, the word denoted something less than excellence, honesty, integrity, and ethics.

The professional witness's testimony was bought; the professional donor's blood was likely to be contaminated with viruses dangerous to the recipient; the professional liberal's stances were more likely based on considerations of personal gain than on deep moral conviction. All these professionals had a certain expertise in their fields and even a certain code of ethics (for example, honor among professional thieves). Nevertheless, they did not exactly conform to my earlier concepts of the "professional person." It was no longer possible to use the word with the same confidence that there was consensus about its definition and the image it conveyed.

Indeed, pejorative images, particularly among "helping" professionals, began to sprout up all around me. A "professional" social worker, a doctor who behaved "professionally," a "professional" nurse all denoted, at least in part, a certain detachment, emotional coolness, lack of involvement, concern for the person helped only up to a point, distanced objectivity, narrowness and—not intentionally, but also not infrequently—cruelty. In addition, I began to notice more sinister implications of professional ethics. Thus, the taboo on advertising carried more than a hint of an economic conspiracy, even among professionals. The restriction on criticizing one's colleagues carried some of the connotations of the criminals' code prohibiting "ratting on your buddies." And all the professions, learned and otherwise, began to look more like ordinary trade guilds, labor unions, and business associations.

My early University of Chicago education, which included reading and listening to Milton Friedman, Frederick Hayek, and others who claimed that any licensed profession is a conspiracy against the public, suddenly became relevant. Nevertheless, professionals in the fields of health, welfare, and education retained their image of goodness in my mind longer than any of the others. For decades, I regarded them as positively and exclusively favorable and beneficial to their clients, patients, and students.

I then became aware of Greenwood's (1957) often-quoted criteria for defining a profession: (1) a systematic body of theory, (2) authority, (3) community sanction, (4) ethical codes, and (5) a culture of values, norms, and symbols. I certainly agreed with the necessity of a systematic body of theory, community sanction, and ethical codes, although much in this present chapter expresses my skepticism about how we as a medical profession have dealt with them. However, I was always bothered by the concept that authority (derived from specialized education) affords the professional a monopoly on judgment in his specialty, leading to a monopoly on the services offered. I was especially uncomfortable with Greenwood's observation that, when there is resistance toward the profession's claim to authority, the professional associations try "to persuade the community that it will benefit greatly by granting the monopoly" (p. 49). Apparently the monopoly itself was not to be questioned. It would seem that in recent years, however, some monopolies are breaking up. Because of lawsuits, the medical profession has had to at least consider following its legal colleagues in lifting the ban on advertising. The emergence of career ladders in most professions is another example, perhaps reflecting Moore's (1970) concept that professionalism is more a scale than a cluster of attributes. To a certain extent, the professions themselves have supported and even developed the idea of a continuum of services; but in some degree it was forced upon them by the scarcity, or at least very unequal distribution, of these services. It is also true that many of what have been everyday professional functions can be performed quite competently by individuals with less than the traditional training. Unfortunately, in medicine the increased use of so-called paraprofessionals has resulted in a strengthening rather than a weakening of the monopoly, since physicians tightly control the functioning (and salaries) of these helpers.

Another aspect of the authority criterion that may be weakening slightly is peer control over standards for performance, as increasing numbers of community and citizens' boards become involved in organization and delivery of services. I think peer *responsibility* is essential, but I have always been uncomfortable with a concept of peer control that in practice has allowed only professionals to judge their own work. Perhaps Greenwood's (1957) criterion of community sanction has functioned in the sense that it was meant to censure or limit authority of a profession if misuse of its monopoly occurs. Rhodes (1972) noted the inevitability of a revolt against traditional care givers if care receivers feel shortchanged and resent the power exercised over them. Some, such as the poor and minority groups who have worked to develop services indigenous to their own communities, have also felt exploited. However, major change initiated by care receivers is ordinarily a slow process. A profession has long traditions of performing in a certain way, and the authority, special privileges, and autonomy of functioning it has been granted have led to a significant power base. This is particularly true in my own profession.

A colleague has reminded me that over the course of history society has chosen to invest more power in the medical profession than in any other because of its unique association with the very beginning and end of life, intrinsic with feelings of loneliness and fear. A close interweaving of healing and spiritual powers has been evident in many very different cultures since ancient times. There remains almost a "witch doctor" mystique in many people's minds, and they do not want to acknowledge fallibility in these individuals. However, because of the very fact that a society is willing to grant physicians extra power and independence of judgment, they have a special responsibility not to misuse it. I do not believe that as a profession we have lived up to this trust, although certainly there are many individuals who have. The challenge for neophyte physicians is not to be swayed by "traditions" that are in conflict with their more basic values.

Early changes in my own positive attitudes also had a

clinical basis, as I analyzed some negative effects of helping professionals on family life. Modern medicine, together with social work, psychology, and education, has had an inherent and strong antifamily bias. I use the word *inherent* because it is the nature of nurses to try to take the role of mothers, social workers that of concerned brothers or sisters, physicians that of wise grandmothers, and teachers that of fathers. The antifamily campaign starts right at the outset of life. Physicians separate mothers from their husbands during labor and delivery (although this shows some sign of changing as the exploding home delivery movement threatens traditional hospital practice); they separate the laboring mother from her infant by analgesia and anesthesia, and they separate the baby in a newborn nursery. Older siblings, grandparents, and other relatives are almost always excluded from visiting. Pediatricians recommend a separate room at home for the baby, or at least a crib since taking a child into the parents' bed is considered a minor form of sexual deviation (breast feeding being a major form), and the "family bed" is practically unknown to professionals.

Breast feeding, advocated by more nurses than physicians, is frequently discouraged by modern hospital practices even though there is considerable talk about it. Dry-up shots, four hour schedules, supplementary bottles, and ridiculous reasons for discontinuing breast feeding continue to be promulgated. This opposition to breast feeding occurs despite the scientifically and historically established facts that mortality and morbidity rates are lower in breast-fed babies. Since certain life-threatening diseases practically never occur in breast-fed babies (tetany of the newborn, *E. coli* meningitis, necrotizing enterocolitis, sudden infant death, hypothyroidism), how can the ethical professional condone hospital practices that favor bottle feeding?

Hospitals separate families at other critical times by not permitting children to visit hospitalized parents and by not allowing parents to stay overnight with hospitalized children. Of course, many people must die isolated and alienated in intensive care units, where visiting periods are limited to five minutes every hour. The doctor (often hiding behind the hospital administrator) orders the visiting restrictions; the nurse implements the order; the social worker helps any rebellious family members to understand, "accept" and "adjust to" the situation; the psychologist is always available to diagnose a difficult parent as "uncooperative, hostile, overprotective, or denying." What an ethical team!

After the baby reaches a few months or a few years of age, the daycare center or nursery school is prescribed. A new field emerges, now euphemistically called "early childhood education," and, at this point, educators take over from pediatricians the family-division effort. In school children are always taught something new whether it is true or not, as long as it ensures that children know something their parents do not. Take, for example, the three-generation switch from old math to new math and back to old math. Other examples include the change from traditional to liberal sex education, which is now moving back to traditional; and the teaching of controversial concepts like Darwinian evolution versus special creationism, arbitrarily choosing one as definitely superior to the other. The effect is to create a gap between one generation and the next, with insufficient justification. In the schools, the family-division situation is reversed professionally. The educator/teacher prescribes; the social worker helps with "adjustment"; and, if some students rebel, the friendly doctor stands in the background with his prescription pad, ready to pass out tranquilizers, sedatives, and behavior modifiers. Another ethical team! Education also makes a major contribution to family breakup at the time of entry to college, separating adolescents from their homes and cultures in the midst of crucial physical, endocrinological, and emotional changes and encouraging them to go to college at least 500 miles away from their homes.

Thus, my image of even the helping professional changed from one of naive trust to one of considerable suspicion. This suspicion, based originally on general observations and theoretical deductions, became further supported by the real cases that appeared month after month during my tenure on a state medical licensure committee, first as a member and later as chairman. There were an amazing number of physicians brought before us for disciplinary action (licensure suspension or revocation) for a variety of causes, ranging from conviction of felonies and other criminal behavior, narcotic addiction, insurance fraud, income tax evasion, and counterfeiting to incompetence and unprofessional conduct. It appeared that the special status afforded physicians had been misused, or perhaps my early idolizing of professionals led me to believe that physicians would not become involved in such activities. Disillusioned, I was all ready for Ivan Illich (1971) and other recent thinkers who claim that teachers produce stupidity, doctors produce illness, and police produce crime; that the criminal has a better chance of rehabilitation if he is not apprehended, the student a better chance of learning if he is not schooled, and the patient a better chance of recovery if he is not diagnosed.

If there is some question about the physician's professional ethics, how should the student physician or nurse respond in some day-to-day situations? What is his responsibility when the surgeon discovers a sponge in the belly, left there from the previous operation? Does he ensure that the patient and his family receive this information with full candor and honesty, or does he leave the decision to the surgeon, who may or may not decide on a course of deception? What decision-making process does the surgeon go through? What are all the factors that enter in the decision?

What does the physician do when passing the scene of an automobile accident? Does he follow the dictates of religious or personal ethics or morality, which demand that he stop and assist his fellow human being? Or does he waver, contemplate the presence or absence of good Samaritan laws in this particular locality and, unless he feels completely protected against litigation, pass by?

The physician is well aware—or should be—of the risks, including death, of many of the tools in his bag. Yet, how often does he trade health for convenience, esthetics, cosmetics, and other psychologic considerations? How often does he serve as the counter-attendant in a cafeteria, catering to patients' tastes regardless of the dangers that he, not they, fully knows? How should medical and personal ethics enter into a physician's decision to: (1) prescribe the pill or the intrauterine device, (2) perform abortions on demand, (3) tell a mother that formula feeding is as good as breast feeding, (4) prescribe tranquilizers, (5) prescribe the new antiarthritic drugs, (6) recommend plastic breast implants, or (7) perform vasectomies?

There certainly are analogous questions and concerns in each of the other helping professions. I am focusing on medicine not only because I know it best but also because its ethics are imitated or at least used as guidelines by other professions. This imitation is not necessarily good for the consumer or the professional.

Let us examine a few initially medical situations that quickly involve other helping professions. Can the ethical nurse ever stand by silently as the physician prescribes, performs, and recommends the above seven actions? Can he ethically assist the physician in carrying out these procedures? Can the ethical social worker or psychologist just disregard the physician's actions on the grounds that medical concerns are not his business? Can he condone the hospital rules that prohibit parents from visiting children and children from visiting parents? Can he ethically assist in helping patients to "adjust" or "accept" their doctor's advice, or should he recommend a second opinion? Can the ethical social worker ever tell parents of a victim of sudden infant death (SID) that they are not to blame, without introducing them to the considerable literature, particularly in foreign countries, documenting the linkage between bottle feeding and sudden infant death (Camps and Carpenter, 1972)?

The fields of SID, battered children, and hyperactivity have all become growth industries, and I usually advise ambitious fledgling professionals to go into these fields if they want a successful career. But they should consider what commitment to doing something about the causes of these conditions they are willing to make. They must ask themselves whether SID has anything to do with bottle feeding; battered children are more common when birth is by Caesarian section (now 25 to 33 percent of all hospital deliveries); or hyperactivity and learning disabilities are related to drugging and undernutrition of pregnant and laboring women. They must not accept the self-serving statement of the medical profession that "our failures are due to our successes," a claim that the ability to save infants who otherwise might die is responsible for the existence of many malformed, defective children and adults. After physicians decide their position, the social workers have an ethical choice to make. If they stay away from causation, if they tell parents that nothing is known about causes, then they can go the counseling route, removing guilt as fast and as completely as possible and probably gaining an ever-increasing caseload.

I am aware that all of us have been taught not to generalize, but I reject that teaching, along with many other poor lessons I learned in school. Ethics demands generalizations to cover the overwhelming majority of situations and the necessity of justifying each exception. Individualization without generalization means moral chaos rather than ethical standards.

A few physicians will escape the fate of the majority. They will reject modern professional ethics for traditional ethics. They will reject the death-oriented customs of the ancient Greeks and Romans, of Plato, Aristotle, and Seneca, who recommended exposure on the mountainside for the crippled and the aged, abortion for population control, and killing of the retarded. They will reject "situational ethics" and Joseph Fletcher's teaching that a baby need not be considered fully human until the third day of life. These are but modern versions of the ancient Greek philosophy. Instead, they will reach out for the traditional ethical systems that abhor zero population growth; that proscribe abortion, homosexuality, sodomy, transsexual surgery, elective sterilization and euthanasia; that carefully limit human as well as animal experimentation; that emphasize patterns of living as the best preventive and curative medicine. Traditional ethical standards of both Eastern and Western civilizations will be examined by these few physicians. Thus, Buddhism, Macrobiotics, The Book of Mormon, the Christian New Testament, and Jewish law will all be compared in double column fashion to the teaching of modern professional ethics.

However, the great majority of physicians will fail to take this approach. The selection process for medical students and their subsequent education guarantees a high degree of abandonment of the ethics they may have learned as children and youths, whatever their religious beliefs. After all, medical students, interns, and residents are usually physically separated from their families and home cultures by many miles, under the policy of "geographic mix."

Even those who stay in their home towns are effectively isolated from their families, old friends, and cultures by the long hours spent on education and the monastic environment of the teaching hospital. Students are separated from each other by frequent competitive examinations, particularly the system of "grading on a curve" where, regardless of everyone's excellence, someone must fail. Therefore, the incentive is toward secrecy, exclusion, suspicion, and hostility in relating to one's "fellow" students. This isolation from the outer world weakens students' loyalty to family and previous cultural ties and makes them vulnerable to a new ethical system as promulgated by their new masters, the medical faculty, who have major power over their present and future lives. Thus, the stage is set for the acquisition and acceptance of "professional ethics."

Actually, the acculturation process begins much earlier. The power of the medical school is great enough to seep into the life of every premedical undergraduate, so that much of "professional ethics" is already present before entry to medical school and, indeed, plays a major role in determining selection for admission. One example, the frequent questioning of applicants for admission regarding their views on abortion, should suffice to make this point. At the other end of the continuum, mandatory continuing medical education (CME) ensures "booster doses" throughout life, since the justification for CME stems from the realization that many physicians forget (reject?) their education (brainwashing?) after some years out of the teaching environment (monastery?). CME will ensure that the same faculty that controlled fledgling doctors will continue to control graduated doctors throughout life. Thus, for almost all physicians, professional ethics will continue its domination over more traditional standards.

Most practicing and student physicians will be perfectly satisfied with professional ethics as a way of life. Therefore, I address myself not to the satisfied, comfortable majority but to those who cling to a different ethical standard and who wish to escape the fate of the majority. How can they manage to survive? The answers are simple to state, yet difficult to implement.

These individuals can try to stay close to home, to family, to their community, to nonmedical friends, and to their culture. Some years ago, in an opening talk to the freshman class of a local medical school, I gave this exact prescription. My talk was followed by one from the Dean, who began by stating, "I agree completely with everything that Dr. Mendelsohn has said. Yet, you entering students must understand that you are starting a new life." Students who are not willing to give up their old life must begin by rejecting this radical recipe. If they decide to maintain continuity, a concrete place to start is in the area of study habits. They must not spend too much time studying; forty to sixty hours weekly is more than enough to invest in the schooling process. They must not confuse schooling with education. The primary purpose in attending medical school is to acquire a degree. Any relevant education they receive in school is peripheral and accidental to this main purpose. Their real education will have to take place outside of school hours or after they have graduated. Some medical schools claim to have innovative programs but, once graduates are in practice, many more similarities than differences are observed. After graduation, they must secure their license to practice medicine as soon as possible and "drop out" —rejecting the modern residency programs that guarantee further isolation, further feelings of inadequacy and inferiority, and further acculturation to professional ethics. Above all, they must rear their own families, and be always aware of the danger of confusing career with life.

Someday, perhaps, we will have medical schools that train a different kind of physician, that teach home care (delivery of babies, house calls, care of terminally ill) as superior to hospital institutionalization, that encourage and enable students to marry and properly rear families, and that give students a firm grounding in more time-honored ethical systems. There may not be a separate ethics course in this new medical school, and esoteric ethical questions will not be prominent on the agenda. Instead, the ethical issues to be considered will be drawn from the daily newspapers to ensure that students are always dealing with the problems that are relevant to the greater society around them. Physicians must be able to participate fully in discussions with people outside medicine, particularly with those in the news media.

Thus, the internal medicine course will discuss the ethical implications of the Saul Krugman–Willowbrook hepatitis experiment. The infectious disease course will discuss the ethical implications of the Tuskegee syphilis experiment. The oncology course will discuss the ethical implications of the Sloan–Kettering painted mice. The psychiatry course will discuss the ethics of the Ventura, California, mental institutions for the retarded. The immunology course will discuss the ethics of the swine flu vaccine program. The pediatric program will consider the ethics of the Johns Hopkins practice of rejecting corrective digestive tract surgery on Downs Syndrome babies. The obstetric program will address itself to the ethics of amniocentesis for sex determination. The nutrition course will address itself to the New Testament teaching that what comes out of the mouth is more important than what goes into it (*Matthew* 15: 11–20) and will consider the impact this religious teaching has had on the exclusion of nutritional information from Western medical education. Finally, all courses will consider the ethics of what to tell a dying patient, ranging from the modern practice of "honesty" and getting the patient to "accept" his impending death to the Jewish ethic of concealing the patient's fate and never removing hope.

Ethical behavior will radically affect the conventional curriculum. Thus, pediatrics will largely disappear as students are taught to tell patients the truth about the superiority of breast feeding and the dangers of bottle feeding. (The LaLeche League can provide extensive references.) This is the recipe for losing a pediatric practice, since the bottle-feeding mothers, feeling guilty, will switch to another pediatrician, leaving the honest ones with only breast-fed babies—who hardly ever get sick anyway!

Home delivery of babies will cause the disappearance of 95 percent of obstetrics and much of gynecology. If the hospital habit can be kicked at birth, it will not become an addiction for the rest of life. Psychiatry will be unmasked as Thomas Szasz (1970) and Jay Ziskin (1976) become standard works in the curriculum and as the "paralysis by analysis" syndrome becomes widely appreciated. Internal medicine will lose most of its highly lucrative products— routine annual exams, hypertension screening and treatment, and modern antiarthritis drugs—as they are fully disclosed as either irrelevant or risky. Finally, as the surgical treatment of cancer and its adjuvants—irradiation and chemotherapy—are revealed as basically irrational and scientifically unsupportable, the entire field of orthodox oncology will wither. Thus, the big five specialties—medicine, surgery, psychiatry, pediatrics, and obstetrics—will largely disappear as a result of the powerful effect of the ethical spotlight.

Present-day preventive medicine will also be exposed as a sham operation in many instances. I can still remember decades ago when the field of preventive medicine and public health was held in poor repute by organized medicine. That, of course, was the era in which public health physicians stressed environmental control—clean water, food, and air. All of these measures tended to diminish the number of patients in doctors' offices. Recently, however, preventive medicine has turned largely to screening for disease and identification and labeling of deviants, increasing the patients who fill up doctors' waiting rooms. Thus, the public health physician has increasingly assumed the role of procurer for the other doctors, and his popularity has proportionately grown. He is naive enough to believe that the reason for his acceptance as a full-fledged colleague stems from a new and enlightened attitude on the part of physicians about public health. This wishful thinking interferes with his vision, so that, basking in the warmth of colleague approval, he has almost completely lost his sense of mission as well as his ability to objectively view even the key items in his own doctor's bag, such as immunizations. Furthermore, preventive medicine, through its promotion of paramedical personnel and the expanded role of the nurse, has contributed to the medicalization of everyone in this country, thus increasing physician power by enlarging the professional–client relationship. Finally, by their support of national health insurance, public health physicians may be guaranteeing that the entire population will become patients and the whole country a hospital. Thus, the poor will have access to the same questionable medical care now available to the rich. However, as the truth about modern-day preventive medicine becomes known, it will also disappear along with the other medical specialties.

Television programs and movies such as "Let's Hear it for the Patient" and *Hospital* will be standard parts of the curriculum offerings of this new medical school, and iatrogenic disease will be discussed every day in every course. Indeed, it will rapidly become clear that it is impossible to teach any subject matter that is not laden with weighty ethical overtones. However, until this day arrives, the only option must be each student for himself. Survival techniques for minorities do not come easily, but, as long as candidates for admission are asked their views on abortion and as long as homosexuality is defined as an "alternative life style" on examinations, the individual student who carries a minority standard of ethics will have to master these survival techniques. As everyone who has closely watched minorities knows, the survival techniques include duplicity and deception. The medical student must rapidly learn what kind of behavior is desirable, what limits are permitted to his questions, what responses are acceptable. These lessons are not quite as important in the basic science courses, where mass lectures usually ensure a safe degree of anonymity, as they are in the clinical years where the contact with faculty is close and surveillance of student performance and attitudes is intense. It is in these years that duplicity becomes the order of the day.

Occasional students in this minority believe the system is what it claims to be—open, honest, tolerant, fair, and rational. These students sometimes challenge their teachers, and they sometimes are successful. They may even come to regard other minority-ethics fellow students as paranoid! Yet, their very success is fraught with danger, since, flushed with enthusiasm, they may be encouraged toward more openness, more trust, more challenging, and more confrontation of the majority group. Eventually, they confront the wrong person. The results of an unfortunate confrontation with a powerful faculty member determined to maintain the status quo in medicine can range from dangerous to catastrophic. I have seen students who challenge conventional psychiatric concepts receive final evaluation reports on their course performance that contain statements damaging their chances for selection of desirable internships. I have seen students who openly question accepted obstetric practices referred for psychiatric consultation. And I have witnessed students who question orthodox cancer therapy receive failing grades.

These students, now endangered, require strenuous rescue techniques if they are to receive their degrees and continue to successful licensure. Some drop out. But most can be convinced of the importance of sticking it out and of "going underground" for the rest of their education. They then become expert at the doublethink, at learning the acceptable answers, the acceptable behavior, the acceptable questions, the acceptable attitudes. Of course, the price paid in emotional terms for this technique can be considerable unless defenses are erected. The best defense consists of frequent—even nightly if necessary—meetings with others who share their views. Thus, the young students can receive—at night and on weekends—validation of their thinking, extension of their "real" education, and psychological support from the encouragement of their freely chosen role models.

Now, who is ready for this kind of courageous behavior in support of their ethical beliefs? Obviously, courage is doing what one must do, acting in a certain manner because there is no choice! Therefore, one must always be ready to give up the trappings and perquisites, the wealth, power, and status associated with being a usual physician. Unrealistic hopes for quick changes in the system must be abandoned. Neither socialized medicine, government health insurance, peer review, consumer participation, producing of more paraprofessionals, nor any of the other popularly advocated solutions represents any major threat to the tyranny of the modern medical establishment. Rather, the hope lies in the continual erosion of public faith in modern medical treatment. Dr. Quentin Young, founder of the national organization, The Medical Committee on Human Rights, has aptly termed "iatrogenicide" as the most serious public health problem today.

There can be no illusion that patients have inherent "rights." But a bill of rights for patients is meaningless unless there is a powerful mechanism available for enforcing these rights. In medicine, might makes right, and the medical establishment has plenty of might, plenty of muscle, plenty of power. The only right a patient has is to threaten his physician, overtly or covertly with effective counterforce, legal and otherwise, should the latter cause damage without proper justification.

Medicine is not the dispensing of drugs; it is not sociology or psychology; it is not politics. Medicine is basically ethics. Modern medicine is basically amoral and has in its present nonethical system the same standards that characterized the German physicians of several decades ago who prepared the way and later implemented the Nazi death camps, always "with the best of intentions."

But we will not be judged on our best intentions, with which as everyone knows, the road to hell is paved. It will be of no avail if every helping professional receives an "A" for effort. The real question is whether we do actual damage to the clients we attempt to "take care of." After all, the prime rule in medicine is not directed toward doing good, but *primum non nocere,* first, do no harm! Only deep and committed attention to ethics can give us an approach to achieving that goal.

It is far too late for pipe-smoking, armchair, casual deliberation. The reasoned papers on medical ethics already fill libraries. I offer this inadequate call to arms in the hope that it will encourage and stimulate others more capable than I to more lucid statements and stronger action. Ethics is not a question of motivation or deliberation. Ethics is judged by behavior.

Professionalism has come to have many negative connotations, which the individual professional, especially the student, must assess. Some beliefs and practices are harmful to the people served; some damage the individual professional's integrity and personal values. Of all the professions, medicine has the greatest concentration of power. There are too many practices it perpetuates that are self-serving rather than in the best interests of the patients. Some of these involve basic ethical dilemmas, which must be confronted by the individual professional. Analogies, of course, can be found in other professions, but medicine is the most difficult to change because of its significant power. It also deserves special examination because it is often imitated by other professions.

Medical students who want to retain basic values inculcated in their early life must resist the pressure during their education and training to convert to "professional" ethics. Perhaps, they can best accomplish this by learning responses needed to pass through the medical school favorably while, at the same time, maintaining their original values through an "underground" support system of like-thinking students and established professionals.

Chapter 5

Responsibility for Delivery of Services

Jane Knitzer

One of the fundamental realities of today's society is that the family is no longer a self-contained unit. Whether, in fact, it ever was is the subject of considerable academic debate. But regardless of the historical facts, the current situation is clear. Families and the children in them are affected by available support systems and are influenced, sometimes controlled, by externally generated stresses. A family's capacity to cope may be significantly altered by whether or not day care is available in a given community and whether or not it earns too much or too little to be able to use it. This, in turn, is determined by the politics of child care, both locally and nationally.

The services received by a handicapped child depend upon the concern and resources within a local community and on the efforts of the professionals within that community to help a particular family. But the concern and the resources have been inadequate. It is estimated that of the seven million handicapped children, only a little over three million are adequately served (Weintraub and Abelson, 1972). In partial response to this grim picture of undeveloped services, federal legislation (Public Law 94-142) has been passed requiring that all handicapped children receive an appropriate education. Significantly, the law gives a child's parents a legislatively protected right to participate in the development of a service plan for the child and to challenge any part of the plan with which they are dissatisfied.

To put it another way, it is becoming increasingly clear that the processes of child development are significantly affected not only by the action and inaction of those in the child's immediate world. They are also shaped by local, state, and national fiscal policies and practices; legislative realities; professional ideology and skills; and administrative and regulatory procedures that shape the institutions—the schools, the mental health clinics, the developmental centers, the welfare departments, the courts, the hospitals—with which families daily interact. These social and political forces do not affect all families equally. The poor, for example, have much more exposure to them than the nonpoor. And families with handicapped children have more exposure to them than families whose children have no such problems. No family, however, with a child to rear can possibly avoid the impact of these ecological forces.

As a result, families and their children must develop skills in understanding and coping with such forces. But so, too, must the professional. The realities and the power of legislative, administrative, budgetary, and professional processes challenge or should challenge each individual professional invested in "helping children" to reconsider what, in fact, it means to "help" a child. What new strategies are appropriate, what new ethical responsibilities are posed, and, above all, what dilemmas must be faced and sorted out?

The answers are not clear. Indeed, even the questions are not always clear. But by drawing on the ecological perspective, it is possible to identify at least two crucial questions that professionals must take into account in defining ethical responsibilities: Given the complex service delivery network, what is and should be the professional's responsibility to children and their families? And what is and should be the professional's response to the emerging child advocacy movement? The issues involved are often ignored in professional training, so students receive little supervision and help in dealing with them. This chapter will explore some of the critical dimensions implicit in these questions.

It is increasingly rare that only one professional be involved in the delivery of services to children. More typically, several professionals representing different agencies—some private, some public —are involved. Theoretically, this should enrich the quality and increase the quantity of services. In fact, the result for the family and the child is often fragmentation and frustration. Problems begin even at the point of referral. Consider, for example, Jimmy's plight.

When Jimmy was two years old, his parents, concerned about his behavior and failure to develop as his sister had, took him to a well child clinic. The pediatrician on duty told the parents that Jimmy was autistic and referred him to a psychologist at a developmental center. There, the parents were told that there was an eight-month waiting list for a diagnostic test, as the center served a six-county area. The parents waited the eight months, and Jimmy's diagnosis was confirmed. At that point, the psychologist informed them that the developmental center no longer worked with autistic children. There had been a change in state policy some six months earlier. The state no longer considered autism a developmental disability, but a mental illness. Therefore, the parents were told to go to the mental health clinic.

The parents, with Jimmy now almost one year older, made an appointment at the mental health clinic. There, once again, after a second and even more thorough diagnostic workup, this time by a team of four people, the diagnosis was confirmed. But the psychiatrist leading the team told the parents that the program of the clinic was in transition and that although there had been plans for a special program to help the parents of autistic children, now the staff had decided that it could only concentrate on setting up a consulting program within the schools. Unfortunately, Jimmy could get no help at the clinic until he was of school age.

Jimmy's parents, desperate and discouraged, did not know where to turn. At that point, a neighbor said she had heard of a special preschool program in a town about an hour and a half away. The parents made inquiries. Such a program did in fact exist. But its funds had just been cut by the state department of mental health, and the director explained to Jimmy's parents that the program was not taking any new children.

After a search lasting more than one year, Jimmy's parents gave up. They stopped seeking help for Jimmy, and they tried to live through the remaining time until Jimmy could get help in the school.

Consider the roles of the professionals involved in this futile quest. Jimmy and his parents were seen by a pediatrician, several psychologists, a psychiatric social worker, a psychiatrist, and a specialist in special education. Not one of these people took the responsibility for seeing that Jimmy and his parents got help. Each responded to the parent's needs from the perspective of his own agency. That was what they protected, not Jimmy. Indeed, the message to the parents was clear and consistent. "Your needs do not fit what we have to sell. You are on your own." In fact, the professionals were both misinformed and uninformed about how to help Jimmy. The pediatrician wrongly referred the parents to the developmental center. The developmental staff did not know what the mental health center could and could not do; the psychiatrist at the clinic refused to help the parents and offered them no alternatives. He did not even mention the relatively nearby therapeutic nursery. (When questioned later, he said he had never heard of it, although it had been cited as a model program in the state.) Ironically, the most helpful referral came from a neighbor, who could hardly be expected to know that the program was no longer admitting children.

But the failure of the professionals goes beyond their lack of constructive strategies to cope with limited resources and beyond restrictive agency policies. It goes beyond their grossly inadequate information about the service network. The fact is that no professional with whom the family had contact was required to accept, or voluntarily accepted, the responsibility to see that Jimmy got help. As a result, Jimmy got nothing, at a time when intervention was developmentally crucial to both him and his family. The question we professionals must grapple with is who, indeed, should have responsibility for mobilizing services to a particular child? What are the limits of the professional's responsibility in the absence of a clearly structured mandate?

The issue is a very difficult one, for it challenges the boundaries of professional functioning. Should professionals identify among themselves a type of "service ombudsman"; should they form a committee in each community to ensure that the Jimmys are served? One thing is clear. It hardly seems ethical for professionals simply to ignore what happens to children and to continue to do business as usual.

Jimmy's problems began at the point of referral. But the impact of professional control over the distribution of services is not limited to the referral stage. The experiences of two siblings growing up in a large suburban area rich in human service agencies and repeatedly cited for its community planning efforts typifies another dimension of the ethical issues we professionals must raise in thinking about our relationship to the service network.

The two children, Jill and Samantha, were twelve and fourteen, respectively. Their father had disappeared years ago. Their mother was unable to find employment. They lived in a public housing project. The family had been on welfare for at least five years. The social worker assigned to the case became increasingly troubled because she suspected that the mother was abusing the younger girl. On two separate occasions the girl had severe bruises on her face. She said that she had been in a fight on the way home from school with a gang of rough boys. But the social worker suspected the mother because the mother had told her that sometimes she gets so angry at the children she could kill them. The social worker discussed the case with her supervisor, who said that such evidence would not be acceptable in court. However, if the social worker was that concerned and the mother that angry, perhaps the mother should file a petition to have the girls declared incorrigible by the court. That way they could be separated without the evidence of abuse.

When the social worker proposed that the mother petition the court, she agreed. In the petition she said that the girls did not always go to school and that sometimes they stayed out late. She said she felt she needed some help with them. At the court proceeding, the judge, relying solely on the caseworker's testimony that the girls should be removed from the home, ordered them immediately sent to the chil-

dren's shelter. No one from the schools was ever asked about the girls, nor was there ever any discussion with the mother about how she might deal with the problem without removing the girls. After the court session, the mother and her daughters were visibly shocked. The mother said she had no idea this could happen, and repeated she had just wanted some help.

The girls, who had committed no delinquent offense, were placed temporarily in one of the three shelters in the community. Those shelters, according to a recently released report from a group of community advocates, lacked any educational program at all, provided nonnutritious meals to the children, lacked any recreational facilities except television and were suffering from severe staff shortages, so that many of the teenage inhabitants were simply running wild. The report recommended that the shelters be used only as a last resort, that all other options be considered first.

The sisters remained in the shelter for two months, until a foster home could be found for them. They had been in that home for just three months when the foster mother complained that she had wanted to have only children under ten. The girls then returned to the shelter for another two months, until there was space in a group home. By this time the girls, average students, had fallen badly behind in their school work. Throughout this period, the mother visited the girls regularly, and often, when she left, both she and the younger child were crying.

The two sisters did have a caseworker assigned to them. She visited once a month. There is nothing in the record to indicate that she ever talked with the mother's caseworker or that she ever talked with the girls about their "incorrigibility." The mother's questions about when she could have her daughters back went unanswered. A year later, however, the social worker who originally encouraged the mother to petition the court said that at that time she was new to the community. She was no longer sure she did the correct thing in separating the girls from their mother.

In this instance, the problem was not so much the failure of the professional to take responsibility to help a child and to be appropriately informed about possible services. It was the assumption by the professional of too much responsibility without any forethought as to the long-term consequences to the children and their mother. But the social worker was not alone in her failure. The judge's decision to remove the girls without any real analysis of either their needs and circumstances or the alternatives available reflects the very great amount of control the professional can exert over other people's lives.

These two cases have several implications for professionals trying to sort out new responsibilities. The first is that professionals must know what community resources are available. It is simply not sufficient to be a good speech therapist or a good clinician. Responsible professionals must also keep themselves informed about the resources in the community and the policies and practices that govern who has access to these resources. This is sometimes a frustrating task as eligibility guidelines and even programs undergo arbitrary changes that seem to be in no one's best interest. But the effort should be made. Furthermore, professionals ought to know firsthand as much as possible about the programs to which they refer families. The last thing a family seeking help needs is an inappropriate referral.

Most importantly, the professional must see that the family does, in fact, get help—if not with the professional's own agency, then with another. Professional responsibility does not stop at the agency doors. It stops only when a family is connected with the appropriate service. This is not an easy responsibility to accept, and it poses many dilemmas for professionals. Realistically, there may be no service or no appropriate service within a reasonable geographical area. Professionals may be forced to refer children to agencies in which they have little faith, or the children and families may be forced to use services that are inappropriate. For example, a handicapped child may have to be placed in foster care because no day treatment or respite services exist, without which the child cannot remain with his family. But the realities of limited services only strengthen the professional's obligation to work for a better delivery system and a stronger statutory or policy framework to ensure that children's rights and needs are met.

Finally, however unpleasant it may be, the professional must learn to analyze the difference between help that is merely a form of social control and help that enables clients to assume more control over their own lives. This is especially crucial for those who work with the poor, for it is the poor who are most vulnerable to the whims, biases, and misplaced benevolent intentions of those who "serve" them.

In recognition of the significant role that social structures, regulations, legislation, fiscal policy, and professional ideologies play in determining the availability and the adequacy of help for children, a new set of strategies—broadly termed *advocacy*—has emerged over the past decade.

Child advocacy is a helping strategy, but unlike traditional helping strategies, the target of change is not the child or her family but those forces beyond the family that act as barriers to the child's growth and development. Thus, child advocacy efforts center on identifying, exposing, and correcting policies and practices, both within the service network and beyond, which are seriously detrimental to either individual children or classes of children. Child advocates seek to fill the gap when professionals, politicians, and administrators fail to take responsibility for children, for the Jimmys and Jills and Samanthas in every community. In effect, child advocacy is a direct response to the awareness that children do indeed exist in an ecological context. It is an effort to apply that knowledge for the benefit of children.

Sometimes the advocates are citizens with a special concern for children. The Junior Leagues, for example, are involved in a national advocacy effort. Sometimes the advocates are parents, joining together to ensure better responsiveness to their children from community institutions. Sometimes they are professionals. The strategies, goals, and targets for intervention used by advocates vary depending on the problem, the political context, and the resources of the advocates. There is no one set of approaches. Advocates engaging in case advocacy—that is, advocacy on behalf of individual children—rely on such strategies as persuasion, negotiation, coercion, and indirect pressure (McGowan, 1973). Class advocates working for groups of children also make use of these approaches. In addition, class advocacy often involves administrative advocacy (efforts to change restrictive regulations or to ensure that new regulations adequately serve the needs of children), legislative lobbying (efforts to ensure that the local, state, or national legislative framework serves the needs of children), and litigation (efforts through the courts to modify discriminatory or harmful practices that systematically affect large numbers of children). Whatever the chosen strategy or combination of strategies, advocates must learn all the facts of a situation and then generate workable, realistic solutions to problems identified in order to be effective (Knitzer, 1976).

Child advocacy poses new demands and new dilemmas for professionals. This example of case advocacy in operation can be used as a framework for considering these.

Sara is an eleven-year-old child. Like Jimmy, she had been diagnosed as autistic. She lived at home with her parents—who were devoted to her. Her father received disability insurance; her mother did not work. Both spent many hours trying to stimulate her with books, large toys, and "Sesame Street" on television.

After Sara's last year in special class, at age ten, the school informed her parents that she needed full-time psychiatric hospitalization and recommended that Sara's parents voluntarily commit her to the nearest state facility—three and one half hours from where the family lived.

The parents did so, but on each of the visits they made to Sara, they became increasingly disturbed at the treatment she was receiving. Sara cried when they left and complained that the attendants were hitting her. Sara's parents were always shaken by the locked doors and the barren atmosphere. Finally, unable to stand it anymore, they took Sara home after three months, against staff advice.

On the way home, they stopped at a special diagnostic clinic they had heard about, where they and Sara stayed for a two-week intensive evaluation. The team evaluating Sara supported the parents' decision to take her from the hospital and recommended that she be in a special school program in her own community. The clinic discussed this with the parents and sent a report to the school.

By the time the parents returned home, it was August. Mrs. B went to the school to talk with the school officials about Sara. They said they would see what they could do. Mrs. B heard nothing for a month; her calls were not returned. Finally, the week school started, Mrs. B received a brusque memorandum from the school saying they could not accept Sara and that they recommended Mr. and Mrs. B do one of two things—rehospitalize Sara or move to a different community. The memorandum also warned that if the parents did not do either of these, they would be charged with neglect. (The community the B's lived in was known nationally for its fine school system.)

*On receiving the memorandum, Mr. B panicked and said he
would hide Sara so he could not be charged with neglect. Mrs. B
remembered hearing about a new children's group forming in the
community. She called the local newspaper, tracked down an article
announcing a planning meeting, and called the contact person. The
group was beginning to plan for an advocacy coalition, and one of the
convenors agreed to try to help the B's. Thus, an advocate was identified who began to track down what had happened and to plan possible
solutions with the parents. The advocate discovered that:*

*1. The school officials held a meeting without telling Sara's parents or
inviting their participation. At that meeting they discussed only the
report of the state hospital, recommending Sara's continued hospitalization. They did not discuss the report from the clinic.*
*2. The clinic team leader, a psychiatrist, had specifically called to find
out what kind of program had been developed and was outraged to
find out that "nothing had been done." He called Sara's mother to
offer to help in any way he could.*
*3. The school official responsible for placing handicapped children had
made contact with a special four-county coordinator, paid for by the
department of mental health, to see if he had any suggestions about
Sara. The school official had been told by this professional that there
was a day program forty-five minutes from Sara's home but that it was
in the wrong catchment area and, therefore, Sara was not eligible.*
*4. The mental health professional employed by the state's department
of mental health was misinformed about the state's policies regarding
catchment boundaries.*
*5. A court settlement required the state to provide an education to all
children, and appropriate school officials were so notified by official
memoranda.*

*Armed with all these facts and with the decision by Sara's par-
ents to enroll Sara in the special day treatment program rather than
pressure the school to modify the special class, the advocate averted the
crisis. After many phone calls, clarifications, and, at one point, threat
of a lawsuit, Sara's exclusion from the educational process and her
parents' ordeal ended. Advocacy had made a difference.*

The response of professionals to child advocacy, as is clear
from this example, is ambivalent: Some of the professionals involved reached out to fight for Sara's well-being and rights; others

simply perceived all the activity in her behalf as an inconvenience. The school officials complained repeatedly to the advocate about how much of their time she was wasting. These are individual reactions. As a group, professionals have raised at least three specific types of objections to advocacy. First, some professionals are simply offended that other professionals raise questions about their judgment. They particularly resent the intrusion of the "nonprofessionals," such as parents and citizen advocates, who seek to learn how services actually work for children, how to challenge gaps and inadequate services and how to deal with the overt hostility sometimes encountered by families seeking help.

This protective, narrow response of professionals, however, ignores the fact that children exist in an ecological context and that services are rarely delivered in isolation but rather through a network of participants, with professionals facing many difficult constraints.

A second objection is the argument that advocacy siphons off time and resources needed for direct service. This line of reasoning ignores the fact that, in general, the outcome of advocacy is the provision of services to an individual child or group of children previously unserved or inadequately served. Still other professionals who see the merits of an advocacy approach take the position that advocacy is fine as long as others do it. They are glad that someone is willing to tackle the complex and sometimes frustrating process of working for change for children, particularly systemwide change, provided they are not in any way bothered, questioned, or asked to help.

These are some of the reasons for the less-than-enthusiastic embrace of the concept of advocacy by professionals. There is one other. Advocates increasingly seek not only to identify and correct problems but to create and apply mechanisms to monitor what actually happens to children served by different programs in an ongoing way. Advocates are becoming more sophisticated and expert in monitoring local, state, and federal programs for children. They are asking tough questions, demanding answers, and, if necessary, gathering the data themselves. Are the programs serving all eligible children? Is the quality of services adequate? Are changes in regulations or legislation necessary? How does performance in one community compare with performance in another? Are minority children given the same access to services? Are handicapped children given appropriate services?

Monitoring is part of the effort to increase fiscal and service accountability, to ensure that funds are used to do what they are supposed to do and that service providers do what they are supposed to do. Monitoring is a powerful means to see that handicapped children in a community *do* receive an appropriate education, that children served by the Early Periodic Screening Diagnosis and Treatment (EPSDT) program *do* receive treatment for health problems uncovered through screening, that children in foster care *do not* remain in the system, moving from place to place because no one will determine that they should be returned home or freed for adoption, and that institutions *do not* overdrug or seclude children.

As with some of the other objections to advocacy, the professionals' resistance to having someone review their effectiveness is rooted in two long-standing tenets of professionalism: the value placed on individual autonomy and the so-called expertise of the professional that sets her apart from nonprofessionals. But, in fact, neither a resistance to monitoring as an accountability tool nor any of the other objections to advocacy described above are realistic or professional. They deny the multiple factors involved in children's services. It is more appropriate for professionals to learn about advocacy, to come to some understanding of its strengths, and to examine in the light of their own patterns of functioning where advocacy can be helpful and what dilemmas it poses. The significant question is how professionals and advocates can work together to improve services to children and families in the face of limited resources, structural barriers, and limited professional knowledge about what *can* really help a child.

This task is a difficult one. There is no easy way to work out the relationships between professionals and case and class advocacy activities. Consider case advocacy first. What is the ethical obligation of a professional to be an advocate for an individual child, not in the sense of providing high-quality service, which is an obvious professional obligation, but in the sense of manipulating systems on behalf of that child? What is the obligation to challenge a decision made by another professional or by bureaucrats that will hinder a child's progress or actively harm the child? There are risks to parents in questioning well-worn bureaucratic and professional routines, and there may also be risks to professionals. How many are willing to take these risks? On the other hand, the risks are often not as great as we perceive them to be. It is also true that some professionals, who may be excellent at providing direct service, may simply not be good advocates. The balance of professional activities between traditional roles and advocacy is, in part, an individual decision. But if the professional chooses not to take an advocacy stance, there is nevertheless a clear ethical obligation to see that *someone* does fulfill that role on behalf of the child. It is simply irresponsible to ignore the impact of structural forces on the child while purporting to help. It is also unethical. In a provocative discussion of this issue, Justine Wise Polier (1975) has gone so far as to call such avoidance of responsibility the "professional abuse of children." Perhaps only with such a dramatic label will we attend more seriously to what happens to children as a result of this typical professional stand.

Second, consider class advocacy activities. Again, individual preference and style will shape individual decisions. But professionals can at least lend important support to advocates by sharing information—not only "professional expertise" but accumulated knowledge about how the system works, how decisions are made, what the consequences are for different groups of children, what the leverage for change is, and who and what are the obstacles to change. One of the most difficult and fundamental tasks the advocate faces is learning the facts—finding out what the problem really is—not in vague generalities but in specific detail. The professional can be a crucial resource for important information.

Other professionals, with different styles and concerns, may take a more active role, offering expertise and sometimes leadership to advocacy groups. For these professionals, the relationship between ecological forces and help to children is not an academic one but a vital part of professional effectiveness, consonant with the realities of service to children. In the early days of advocacy, it was fair to say that nonprofessional advocates were suspicious of the professionals who took an advocacy stance. Today it is clear that there is room for all who seek to change systems to better ensure that children's needs and rights are respected. Professionals who choose to work as coadvocates are typically welcomed and appreciated. Advocacy is not a threat to professionals and should not be so perceived. Indeed, it presents an opportunity for those professionals troubled by the obvious class, race, and geographical differences in children's services and opportunities to work with others for a more equitable allocation of resources and services.

Many children and families are not receiving desperately needed services that are available to them, or they are receiving inappropriate services. This is often because of ecological realities, within both the direct service network and the larger political structure. There are numerous reasons for inefficiency or exclusion procedures, some in which professionals are directly involved and can alter by the choices and decisions they make. The individual professional must accept the ethical responsibility of ensuring that children actually do receive the services they need, whether she provides them herself or makes the necessary links. Not to do so may be considered "the professional abuse of children" (Polier, 1975). The traditional boundaries of the professional role thus must be broadened to include the obligation to see that individual children do not "fall between the cracks" as well as the responsibility to directly or indirectly participate in the child advocacy movement.

Case Presentation for Problem Solving

You are a psychologist in a community mental health center. You are also chairing an interagency board, appointed by the county commissioners to propose a plan for the equitable use of the federal Title XX monies available to the county. You have recently been asked to assume the role of consultant to the local child welfare unit of the public welfare office. Both the community mental health center and the child welfare agency serve a county of about 80,000 people, most of whom live in great poverty in the areas surrounding the one major city.

You receive a phone call from the case supervisor of the child welfare office saying that she is very upset and would like to talk with you as soon as possible. She adds, "There is some advocacy group on my back, trying to interfere with my caseworkers, and I need your help." You have a slightly uncomfortable feeling when you hear this, because you know the local Junior League is in the process of conducting an advocacy project on foster care in your county and two adjacent counties. In fact, at their request, you have just scheduled a meeting with them to discuss both advocacy and the practices toward children removed from their own homes. (You have recently attended a conference on child advocacy, and they are anxious to hear your report.)

You arrange to meet with the supervisor that afternoon. She greets you by telling you how well the interagency board is going, that she thinks you are doing a fine job as chairperson, and she is looking forward to working with you both on the board and through the consulting arrangement. Then she tells you that one of her caseworkers has just made a decision to remove two boys, ages five and seven, from their aunt who has been informally caring for them. The aunt was very upset by the decision, saying that all she wanted from the child welfare office was approval as a foster parent, that she didn't want her family separated, that she only needed more money to manage. In fact, the aunt had called the supervisor to protest, and the supervisor commented that she seemed almost irrational. But the supervisor was particularly upset because the aunt had also called a Junior League member to complain, and the Junior League was trying to make trouble. She said, "I just met with some of their representatives to give them information about our problems in the county around foster care, because I think they can do important work, but this is ridiculous." After a bit more discussion, in which you learn that the aunt already has two children of her own, is a part-time student, and has cared for the two boys for four years on and off by simply stretching her welfare payments, the supervisor says she wants you to evaluate the aunt's psychological state and write a report with a placement recommendation. As further background, she tells you that the caseworker had commented, after the last visit, that the aunt seemed to get more toys and clothes for her own children, that her health has been a problem, and that she simply cannot handle the added responsibility.

You leave very troubled by the case and by the many different allegiances you feel. You also remember that in your brief conversation with the Junior League they expressed great concern because so many foster children from the county were either being placed in foster homes in other counties (supposedly the rates are cheaper, although the League had not been able to document this) or that they were being sent to institutions.

Some problem-solving questions that could be asked in this case are: (1) Would you agree to do the evaluation? Why or why not? (2) Which of the following people, if any, would you try to see: the caseworker? the Junior League representative who spoke with the aunt? the aunt? the two children? your supervisor (the director of the clinic)? (3) Would you cancel the meeting you arranged to talk with the Junior League as a group? Why or why not? (4) In this instance, who is your client: the two boys, the aunt, the supervisor? (5) What are the different concrete actions you could take? What other information do you need? What difference would it make if you decided to be "an advocate"?

Chapter **6**

Consent as a
Cornerstone Concept

Douglas Biklen

What you are about to read in the first few pages of this chapter is documentation drawn from the records of a person who has spent his childhood in an institution for the retarded. Names, places, and even the sequence of events have been changed to protect the person's anonymity. The case has been chosen as an introduction to a discussion of the concept of consent because it is instructive about the unenviable fate of a child who has lived through the abuses of an institution. It instructs us all, by implication, to create alternative services to the institution. But above all, it instructs caution to those who make decisions about children's lives. In the latter regard, this case example leads us to seek answers for the key questions: What is consent? When and how does a professional obtain consent? Whose interests are served by the concept?

On May 18, 1972, at 6:09 P.M., John Abrahms Antigues, age sixteen, a profoundly retarded resident living in the Behavior Shaping Unit, Building 3, at Jefferson State School, was found lying on the ground outside the building by two institution employees. He apparently fell, jumped, or was pushed from the third-floor window. Institutional records indicate that there were no witnesses to the apparent accident. Medical examinations revealed that John had sustained a fractured pelvis, a fractured leg, distortion and fracture of one wrist, and multiple superficial abrasions on the left side of his chest, trunk, hip, and frontal areas. The records cite John's "overactive and unpredictable" behavior as the cause of his fall. He had broken his arm twice before in other accidents. In the present instance, two attendants were on duty in the ward trying to work with other residents. "Evidently Johnny eluded their attention and jumped from the partially open window of the bathroom," a report states.

This incident yielded the worst physical trauma of John's institutional career. But it was by no means unexpected or surprising. John's parents brought him to the Jefferson State School in 1960 at the age of four. Admission documents labeled him as an "overactive, noisy, crying little boy who runs about and is controlled with difficulty." His parents cited his uncontrollable ways as cause for institutionalizing him. They reported that he frequently broke windows when he became upset. He would open doors and run outside if they were not kept locked. He screamed when he did not get his way. When he was admitted at age four, he was not toilet trained, and he could not or would not dress himself. The parents stated simply that he was difficult to manage. According to the admitting officers, his parents brought several nursing bottles and nipples, along with his clothing, which was dirty and shabby.

This is not to imply the parents did not care for him. They traveled by bus from their home to the institution to visit with him. They wrote him letters once or twice a month. They took him home some weekends. Ironically, several times when the parents sought to take him home, the institution refused. The staff psychologist wrote, "We do not give permission for your child to go home overnight except under most unusual circumstances. I cannot give you permission for this overnight visit." Two staff members felt John might have been struck by his father on an earlier visit, although on the records there is no indication that this allegation was investigated. The following year, the parents were again refused. "In reply to your request to have your son for one week's vacation, I would not recommend his going at this time. He is still quite active, is not easily controlled, is quite untidy, and is a feeding problem at mealtime. If he should show improvement within the next year he may be tried at the end of that period."

But John did not improve, and the frequency of family contacts diminished. It seems that the longer he stayed in the institution, the worse he got. The records provide a chronology. Upon admission, John was classified by the institution as "severe, idiopathic, mentally deficient." On his second day at Jefferson, he was given a tranquilizer, Thorazine. During the course of his career in the institution, other medications were tried, including Mellaril, Haldol, phenobarbital, amphetamines, Stelazine, Serentil, Noludor, Navane, Dalmane, and chloral hydrate. The amounts increased with the length of his hospitalization. Early reports on John's intellectual ability are sketchy and probably unreliable. Before he was institutionalized at age four, testing in a children's hospital showed his IQ to be 60. Later that year, another state school obtained an IQ of 33. When he was admitted to Jefferson, the reports indicated that he had an IQ of 15 and, later, at age nine, an IQ of 9. When John was five years old, the institution reports identified John as his ward's "greatest problem regarding care and supervision." That same year, in the summer, he was reported found outside the basement entrance of his building on the cement at 5:45 A.M. According to the "brightest boy" on the ward, he had been thrown out of the window.

At age nine, John was not in any school program. "He is very untidy, restless at meals, abusive to other boys, grabs food from others, and has bitten employees." At this point, he was still receiving mail and visits frequently from his family. At age ten, John had some language ability. He was capable of saying a few words. In a few years he lost this language. Since he was nine years old, he had stopped going to the bathroom in his pants. But he did not use the toilet; he used the floor.

He was able to feed himself but, if he did not like the food, he would throw it on the floor. His record states, "His eating habits haven't improved. He tries to put his own food and what he grabs from other boys on the floor near the radiator. If attendants don't get to him instantly, he will eat off the floor. If we try to prevent it, he will go into a fit, scream, and turn and bite one of the boys. He really gives them very bad bites. When we try to get him away from the boys, he turns on us, hits, kicks or smashes us."

At age twelve, he was judged almost uncontrollable. The report reads, "He is so strong that anything attendants have isn't strong enough to contain him. He tips the bed over sometimes after all the rest of the boys are asleep." Far from learning or changing in more socially acceptable ways, John was becoming more and more bizarre or, to use a common term, institutionalized. The records reveal the making of a back ward resident. By the time he was twelve years old, he was being called "animalistic." The records become increasingly graphic. "The attendants wanted him to go to the toilet because he had started to eat his soil [feces]. He came out of the room, then pulled away from attendants and ran into the dining room, threw chairs all over, tipped a table over, and came at the attendant like an animal trying to bite. He was snarling and acting like a mad dog. When he soils on the floor, before attendants can prevent it, he paints with it and eats it. This is something new; he never did it until the last three or four weeks."

A month later, the only additional information of note was that he was banging his head on hard objects. In institutional parlance, he had become a "head banger." At times, the staff would resort to putting John in an exclusion cell. At age fourteen, he had ceased talking with even the few words he had previously used. At age eighteen, John was still throwing furniture and lunch trays. On March 7, 1974, when an attendant tried to restrain him from throwing things, he fractured John's arm.

John's environment was stark. He slept in a large room with other male residents. There was very little furniture in the dayroom, other than a few specially made "indestructible" chairs and a television mounted high on the wall in a metal frame with unbreakable glass protecting the screen. John had been given a separate alcove off the ward dayroom, a place he could consider his own.

A psychologist described his first introduction to John. "Johnny really has a reputation around here. He is known as the 'wild man.' And the description is pretty appropriate. My first contact with Johnny was when I'd been working here three days. Johnny was in the dining hall and had ripped his shirt off and was tearing the place apart. So, of course, what do the staff do in a situation like this? They send for the psychologist. Here I am, a rookie, and I walk in. Johnny bites me. And I get a tetanus shot. It was a great first experience," he concluded sarcastically.

All in all, sixteen years of institutionalization had left John an emaciated (86 pounds), strong, scratched and bruised, feces-eating, violent young man. A memorandum prepared for the institution's chief psychologist summarizes his state at the time he was twenty years old, the time that most retarded young people are graduating from special education programs:

To: *Chief Psychologist*
From: *Unit Director*
Date: *January 1976*
Re: *John Antigues*

1. Brief Statement of Behavior:
Bites to the point of bruising and puncturing skin both clients and staff and frequently for no apparent reason. He scratches, pushes, kicks, and hits. He digs and smears feces, rips his clothes off, rips his mattress, rips sheets off his bed. Throws his meal tray at least once a day, tips over tables. Johnny cries frequently for no apparent reason. He is self-abusive by hitting and biting himself but never to the point of hurting himself. When staff persons attempt to restrain him, he will quickly dart away or will bite and hit the staff person.
2. Frequency of Behavior:
Bites, or attempts to bite, each time he has an aggressive episode. Episodes occur an average of five out of seven days per week; there is usually more than one episode a day. Episodes can last from one hour to, more frequently, an entire day. This involves all three shifts, and it is not unusual for John to be up all night.
3. Intensity of Behavior:
Very high intensity. Bites are usually quite serious, requiring medical attention. Due to his size and strength, he almost always will hurt his victims. There are only a certain few people who alone can effectively control Johnny. He is dangerous to both clients and staff but slightly more so to clients. Johnny has also been known to attack objects rather than people (for example, cars, chairs, and so on).
4. Chronicle of Behavior:
Johnny has been a behavior problem since admission in 1960 at age four.
5. Present Programming Efforts:
It is felt that we do not have the capability to deal with Johnny on much more than a maintenance level. We provide one-to-one attention at least eight hours a day and have prepared guidelines to enable the third shift to deal more effectively with John. We have not been at all successful in creating behavioral changes in Mr. Antigues. We attribute this primarily to a less-than-adequate environment.
6. Brief Statement of Functional Skill Level:

John has good receptive language. His expressive language is poor although he can sign food. He is capable of toileting himself, dressing himself, and feeding himself when he wants to. His behavior usually inhibits him from doing it. (A recent Title XIX evaluation is available.)

7. Statement of Behavior When Not Aggressive:

When he is not being aggressive, he is still hyperactive and socially isolated from peers.

8. Present Medication:

Navane (4 mg) t.i.d. (3 times per day); Festal tablets—2 each meal; Dalmane—30 mg at hour of sleep; Cascara Sograda one tablet at hour of sleep; Chloral hydrate (1 gm) one at hour of sleep along with Dalmane 30 mg; Chloral hydrate (1 gm) ½ hour after initial dose if he is still restless.

9. Closing Statement

Johnny has a huge appetite, drinks a lot of water, responds poorly to people, and manipulates positive reinforcement. He also responds poorly to uncomfortable climates (for example, humidity). Both the staff and residents of Cardinal House are frequently terrorized by the presence of Mr. Antigues. Dealing effectively with John will require specially trained staff. He has to be restrained with regularity in his present setting, and it is not possible to isolate him from the rest of the clients. Mr. Antigues has been responsible for many injuries to both staff and clients, and we do not feel capable of dealing effectively with him any longer.

Institutions are not healthy for children; they are not even healthy for adults (Blatt and Kaplan, 1966; Blatt, 1973; Goffman, 1961; *Wyatt* v. *Stickney,* 1971). Consequently, there are serious questions as to the legitimacy of placing children in institutions rather than providing support services to parents and, if parents fail, to serve their children adequately even when provided necessary supports, foster care, adoption, and small group home settings. Yet, even today, states vary greatly in their deinstitutionalization philosophies.

But our most immediate question is who gives consent to admit a child to an institution, and to what do they think they are giving consent? Who gave consent for John Antigues? Can anyone, even parents, rightfully consent to place a child in such a hostile and nonnurturing setting? We can ask the same question in relation to a whole range of professional treatments and decisions that affect children, whether the effect is presumed positive or not. Must someone give consent before a child can be administered tranquilizing medication? Must someone consent to have a child enter a special class program? Must a parent consent to a child's participation in behavior modification that involves the use of cattle prods or other forms of aversive conditioning? Must someone consent before a child can become a subject in an experiment, whether an interviewing situation, the testing of a new curriculum, or even hepatitis research? The answer for each question is *yes*.

But is consent for any of these treatments justified? Is it, in fact, legal for professionals to do almost anything, provided consent has been sought and obtained from a legal guardian? Is consent given fairly; that is, does the person giving consent have the *capability* to give consent? Is consent given with full knowledge of its implications? Is consent offered voluntarily?

These questions form the focus of this chapter. The answers suggested may provide some helpful guidelines for professional behavior and a decision-making framework for the consumers of service—namely, children and their parents.

Consent affects everyone. We give consent for our children to go on a field trip. We give consent to a doctor for surgery. We give our implicit consent when we board an airplane, even if we fail to read the small print on the ticket. And we offer consent every time we enter into a contract, whether in buying insurance for a car or selling a piece of land. Professionals, parents, and sometimes even children are involved in seeking or giving consent regularly throughout the duration of childhood. Parents consent to go to a particular hospital or have a particular doctor deliver the baby. Later medical treatments also require that doctors obtain consent from parents. Consent is required at the time a child enters any human service program or setting, including day care, school, or occupational training. For disabled children especially, consent is usually sought and given for diagnostic, evaluative, and screening services. Similarly, consent should at least be considered for certain decisions about behavioral and educational treatment. It is required for human experimentation, including most forms of behavioral research and some kinds of social research. Consent should be obtained if a child must be represented by a surrogate. Also, the release of information from a child's records should be accompanied by consent. Finally, families, children, and professionals must grapple with consent when decisions are made about custody of children in divorce, releasing children for adoption, and the securing of birth control devices or information.

What is consent, and how is it used to alter the lives of children? Particularly, how can professionals use the concept of consent to protect and enhance children's rights and interests? Many professional and parental decisions involving children can have a lasting, even irreversible, impact. Even indecision can have a major impact. Indeed, indecision (whether implied or carefully stated) is a kind of consent, consent to do nothing. Failure to provide special education services to a child who has significant learning problems may ensure the child's failure to develop his potential. Similarly, a positive decision to operate on a child who has acute appendicitis can save a child's life. In the case of John Antigues, the decision to institutionalize him seems to have had a disastrous effect. How might his life have been different had his parents been provided adequate support services to keep him at home or had the professionals and parents consented only to a foster placement rather than the institutional one? Of special concern for this book are the numerous times during John's residence at Jefferson State when professionals might have used the concept of consent differently.

Consent has become particularly crucial as professionals and consumers (parents and children) consider how to improve, secure, and ensure quality human services. The normalization principle (Wolfensberger, 1972) suggests that people should have an opportunity to receive human services in the most culturally natural setting possible. If a child can benefit from a home environment, then she should not be placed in an institution. If a disabled child can receive health care in a regular hospital, such a setting may be more normalizing than a separate hospital for the disabled only. Consent to a given program or service is a decision on behalf of a child. Consequently, the giving or withholding of consent marks the point at which parents and professionals should attempt to ascertain whether the proposed treatment is normalizing or not. A recent outpouring of revealing books about children's services document the nonnormalizing, even inhumane, nature of many human service practices for children (see Schrag and Divoky, 1975, for example).

Similarly, recent litigation and federal legislation (Abeson, 1974; Abeson, Bolick, and Hass, 1975; Gilhool, 1973), most notably the Right to Education for All Handicapped Children Act, Public Law 94-142, requires that children with disabilities be served in the least restrictive setting possible. It is a companion concept to normalization. A child should have his special needs met in a regular school classroom if at all possible. The next least restrictive setting may be the provision of resource assistance or another form of special tutoring supplement to the regular class placement. Then, a self-contained special class may be considered. In each case, the guiding principle for serving children is "least restrictive alternative possible." The time when professionals and parents discuss consent is the time of decision. According to the new law, a parent must be informed in writing of a school district's decision to provide special education services and to classify a child as handicapped. The parents have the right to insist upon *no* change in placement until they have had an opportunity to hear all of the school's reasons for such placement and until they have had an opportunity to exhaust their appeal rights. In other words, parents are given extensive opportunities to withhold consent and to negotiate before a decision can be made that supersedes their own wishes. A child may not be placed in a different special program until the parents have consented or until all appeals have been exhausted.

Consent can serve the interests of parents and children. It is a concept that provides a vehicle for protecting individual interests and rights. One need not consent to inadequate, risky, or inappropriate services, for example. Consent procedures can prove useful to consumers who want to ask questions about a placement, experiment, or diagnostic procedure. One can withhold consent until answers are offered. Consent, if properly handled, can place greater decision-making power in the hands of consumers. It can also be viewed as a way of ensuring, or at least enhancing, a consumer's understanding of a particular decision and its implications.

Similarly, consent procedures can serve the interests of professionals. Although it is true that some professionals may fear the extra responsibility, paperwork, or liability associated with careful consent procedures, the concept proves enormously helpful and reassuring. The greatest benefit, from the professional's vantage point, is that consent procedures provide a way of placing the primary decision-making power, the right of self-determination, in the hands of the consumers. If handled appropriately, a professional's use of consent procedures can help to extricate professionals from the powerful but dangerous and possibly victimizing role of making all the decisions for the client. At the same time, professionals have great responsibility to ensure that clients understand to what they are giving consent. It would be naive to suggest that professionals will cease to explain most of the ground rules in treatment. On the other hand, consent procedures can help professionals work more cooperatively with consumers. Decisions about treatment and service are, hopefully, mutually agreed upon by the professional and the consumer.

Thus far, we have talked about consent without defining it. We have discussed its potential importance and usefulness for individuals as a vehicle to ensuring greater normalization and adherence to the principle of "least restrictive alternative," and as a way of transforming the client–professional standoff into a more cooperative and informed relationship. Yet there is a need to fully explore the concept itself. What is consent?

We have purposefully not used the term *informed consent*. That term misrepresents the nature of consent. It suggests that the key element of consent is the provision of information to people who are giving consent. But that is only part of what comprises the concept. Consent is a legal concept that has been referred to and implicitly defined in court cases and in legislation. It has three major aspects: *capacity, information,* and *voluntariness*. All three elements are equally relevant to any consent procedure or decision. Simply stated, one must have the ability to give consent in order to do so; one must have adequate information to do so in a knowledgeable way; and one must be free from coercion or any other threat to one's voluntariness.

Capacity is defined in several ways. *Capacity* means the ability to receive and process information—that is, to acquire and retain knowledge. Courts sometimes declare people incompetent without proper analysis of the case, although this kind of total determination has become less popular as professionals have advocated for more particular determinations. A person may not be capable of understanding and making a decision about a complex business dealing involving thousands of dollars but may be capable of deciding whether or not to get married. When courts make a blanket determination of incompetency or incapacity, it is done on the grounds that a person is thought, and has been demonstrated to be, unable to manage his or her personal affairs. The principle of normalization suggests, however, that we should consider less global determinations so that people can demonstrate their competence to the greatest extent possible, even if by normal standards that is quite limited.

Capacity may also be defined in terms of one's age. Children are generally considered incompetent before the law. Until a person reaches the age of majority, usually eighteen, he is considered incompetent, although there are exceptions. Many states permit children who are sixteen years old to drive or even own an automobile. Also, in the case of divorce proceedings, it is not unusual for a judge to interview even young children about their experiences with the parents and to try to assess in whose custody the children would most want to be.

A third way of defining capacity relates to criminal insanity. The issue here is whether the accused person understood the nature and consequences of her action (Burt and Morris, 1972). Was the person in possession of her faculties at the time of the murder?

For the purposes of this chapter, we are most centrally concerned with the first two ways of defining capacity, the ability to acquire and retain knowledge, and age. Since we are concerned with the professional's relationship to children and families, it is important to know that children cannot legally make most important decisions for themselves with respect to how they are served. Although a child's own perceptions should be taken into account, which is simply good professional practice, a professional must turn to a parent or guardian to obtain consent for a particular procedure or treatment, and in so doing, the professional must be reasonably certain of a person's capability to acquire and retain knowledge pertinent to the situation at hand. It is important for professionals to reject the "all-or-nothing competency test" and examine whether the parent or guardian is capable of making a decision in the particular. If there is some question about the person's competence, the helping professional should consult a lawyer or court.

The final element of capacity is one's ability to make choices on the basis of information obtained. Can the person make choices among alternatives? Again, if there is some question about this aspect of a person's performance, legal assistance may be required. It should be noted that professionals and courts increasingly recognize that a person's actual developmental and behavioral performance provide the best indications of capacity. All retarded people are not alike. All "mentally ill" people are not alike. A person's label may not reveal the person's capabilities with respect to a particular decision area. Consequently, professionals, whether physicians, psychologists, educators, lawyers, or other human service people, need to focus on observable performance.

The second major element of consent is information. A person's consent to something, whether medical treatment, human experimentation, or an educational placement, has no meaning unless the person giving consent has been afforded all the relevant information. Of course, the information must be presented in a way that will be understood by the parent or guardian. Since parents or guardians may be laypersons in regard to medical, psychological, educational, or other professional information, the burden is on a professional to explain the information in a readily understandable fashion; it should also be explained to the child whenever possible. How many children, for example, are told of the possible side effects of a tranquilizing medication? Even though most states do not require a child to give consent until age eighteen, good professional practice, if not legal responsibility, requires that doctors explain the risks of a prescribed medication to both parent *and* children.

But what is relevant when it comes to providing information? In the context of medical treatment, relevant information may be defined differently than in the context of educational programming. A medical procedure involves greater risks to one's body, whereas an educational program may have deeper psychological effects. Both areas have the potential to alter the course of a child's life. Consequently, the determination of what is relevant will be guided, in part, by the nature of the procedure being considered.

Obviously, the requirement that adequate information be

provided for a consumer to make an informed decision to give or withhold consent can raise problems for the professional. For an admissions officer in an institution, usually a psychologist or psychiatrist, to provide information about the dangers of institutional life may be regarded, at least within the circles of professionals who work in institutions, as unprofessional or even insubordination. Similarly, providing information to a child's guardian about good *and* bad aspects of a prospective foster placement may cause the guardian to withhold consent from the placement decision sought by a welfare agency. These are just a few examples of how the requirement to provide full and candid information can create practical problems for those seeking consent.

What of clients who understand and speak a language that is unfamiliar to the professional? It is easy to say that a professional has a responsibility to explain the relevant information in the language that the person can understand. For example, if a family speaks Spanish, a school district must provide information in Spanish about the child's placement in a special education class. Hopefully the professional can do this but, if not, he must collaborate closely with someone who can.

Although a particular situation will require certain kinds of information and not others, the professional should consider each of the following kinds: the nature, duration, and purpose of the procedure; the method or means by which the procedure will be performed or offered; the potential inconveniences and hazards implied by the procedure; the possible effects that the procedure may have on the person; the benefits to be derived from the procedure; information concerning the person's option to withdraw at any time or at specific times; the desired outcome of the procedure; the least desired outcomes of the procedure; alternative procedures; and any uncertainties about the procedure or its possible effects.

Suppose, for example, that a family of a retarded adolescent girl seeks to have her receive a birth control device; a physician thinks a coil would be the best device. The physician should provide information about the nature of the implant, the risks associated with the procedure of implanting a coil, the methods used for implantation, the potential inconveniences to the young woman, and possible effects that this device may have on her physical and psychological well-being. Also, the physician should explain the benefits and the difficulty or ease with which the device may be removed. The physician should also provide information about other forms of birth control—the pill, for example—and should provide similarly complete information about each method. It is simply not enough to say, "This is a coil. It will serve as a birth control device. I can implant it next Thursday. Please sign here to give your permission for the procedure." There are other safeguards often applied to such situations. Many family planning clinics have human rights boards to review any cases involving people who have disabilities or people who are under the age of majority.

To take an example with which almost everyone is familiar, how often do medical professionals explain to patients the risks associated with x rays? Hospitals, doctors, dentists, and others frequently request series of x rays as a routine procedure. A form may be presented for a patient's signature. Few medical professionals who request or administer x rays ever stop to explain the research findings concerning their dangers. For children with chronic medical problems that require regular attention, the risks associated with radiation become a matter of considerable importance. It is not sufficient for medical professionals to assume that the client could not understand the research data.

The method of how information is disclosed is as important as the nature of the information supplied. The professional must be confident that the information is communicated, acquired, and understood. She must attempt to provide information at the comprehension level of the client—in this case, the parents. It must be provided in their own language in either oral or written form. If information is provided in written form, professionals should avoid the use of small print. For risky or otherwise questionable procedures, the professional should use a two-part consent form (Miller and Willner, 1974). The first part of the form discloses relevant information; the second part of the form asks a series of questions to ensure that the person has understood the information.

The third element of consent is voluntariness. People are assumed, under the law, to act voluntarily until it can be proven otherwise. But professionals should have a moral interest and certainly a personal interest—no one wants to be proven wrong later—

in ensuring the voluntariness of those from whom they seek consent. Voluntariness means that a person is able to make free choices from among alternatives without being coerced, tricked, or hoodwinked. This requirement seems a fair and easily administered one. Indeed, it is fair. But it may be more difficult to do than one would presume.

Are poor people acting voluntarily when they participate in a psychological and biomedical research project that compensates them with cash? Do parents act voluntarily when they allow their institutionalized children, for whom programming has been scarce, to participate in a behavior modification program that uses basic amenities, such as dessert after a meal or permission to go on a field trip, as rewards? Does a parent who cannot afford to buy services in the community act voluntarily in placing a disabled child in an institutional setting? Did John Antigues' parents act voluntarily? Is a parent's agreement to have a child educated in a self-contained classroom made voluntarily, or is it coerced by the lack of options for mainstreaming? Do parents voluntarily allow their children to be placed in foster care upon social services recommendation? Does a parent act voluntarily in allowing a range of professional agencies to evaluate his home as part of a diagnostic workup on the child? Or is this kind of evaluation simply endured in hopes that the child will receive something in return?

Several cases of coercion stand out in the history of human services. A woman on welfare was forced to consent to sterilization as a precondition to her receiving future welfare support. A similar practice accompanied the placement of teen-age girls from mental retardation institutions in the community during the early twentieth century. A number of states still have laws that permit institutions for the retarded to sterilize teen-age girls in similar situations.

Another notable case involved human experimentation to find a cure for hepatitis. Willowbrook State School, now called a developmental center, was the location of hepatitis research in the 1960s. Parents who could find no community services for their retarded sons and daughters and who wanted to secure institutional placement of the children were faced with the fact that the state had a waiting list of more than 400 children. This often meant that a family would have to wait several years to place the child. In part, the decision to place retarded sons or daughters at Willowbrook was coercive because of the lack of community options. These were children for whom admittance to day care, preschool, and school programs had been denied. But there was another kind of coercion at work. Parents found that if they agreed to place their children "voluntarily" in the hepatitis research program, they could jump the waiting list and obtain immediate admission. Their children were injected with hepatitis. It was thinly veiled coercion.

The test of voluntariness requires that professionals ask themselves, "Are the parents making a free choice, or are they being coerced by the lack of options, by a fear of speaking up against a professional, by the provision of inducements?" It is important for professionals to examine issues of power and authority, too. Would parents agree to anything the professional suggested simply out of respect for the professional's authority as a representative of an elite profession or of a state or private agency, or even out of faith in the professional as an individual? Does the parent give consent for fear of challenging the professional's presumed or actual power? There are no simple answers to these questions. Rather, they are warnings for professionals to consider.

We have discussed the nature of consent and, most importantly, its three elements. But who may give consent? Can a school principal consent to have the children in the school participate in a psychologist's experiments or a sociologist's surveys? Again, the answer is not clear. If the experiment or study is part of the normal course of events in the school and in no way will identify a child publicly, a principal might legally permit a psychologist or sociologist to enter the school setting. For example, a psychologist or sociologist might be permitted to observe a variety of classrooms to obtain data to assist the school and to obtain data for her own research. Such a situation might not require a parent's permission. But access to a child's records would require parental consent. Freedom to use the child's full name should be agreed upon by the family. Freedom to photograph the children should be preceded by parental consent. All of these activities are either specifically protected by legal requirements for consent, or else they represent diversions from normal school functions.

In each of the major areas where consent would be an issue —medical treatment; contracts; admission to programs and settings;

diagnostic, evaluation, and screening services; human experimentation; research projects; and records—parents and legal guardians have the right to consent for children. In those instances where custody of a child has been legally conferred upon the state, as is often the case for children in protective and foster placements or in institutions, the state—namely, an institutional superintendent or a social services director—has the power to give or withhold consent. These are the legal requirements. Good professional practice suggests that in the latter case, where a child's service agency and guardian are one and the same, professionals should ask that the courts appoint a *guardian ad litem* to represent a child's interests in certain situations, such as adoption proceedings, psychological and educational assessment and planning, medical surgery, and human experimentation; that is, in situations where there is risk and irreversibility associated with the procedure, a child should always have an impartial advocate to give or withhold consent. Unfortunately, this has not always been the case in social services' dealings with children, where one professional often is expected to function *in loco parentis* in a subjective sense and at the same time look out for the agency's best interests (such as budget).

There are a few exceptions to parental and guardian rights to consent for children. These involve those procedures or services that society requires for all children. For example, compulsory education is required for every child, regardless of a parent's desire to withhold consent for that service. A child must receive an education. It is the parent's choice, however, to consent to the particular educational program among many that are approved by a state. Similarly, certain kinds of medical treatments or diagnostic procedures do not require parental consent, such as tests in infants for phenylketonuria (PKU) or hypothyroidism. Certain inoculations may also be required by the state. Parents may succeed in a few instances to withhold consent for particular medical treatments that the state has generally regarded as in children's best interests—for example, the parents of Karen Ann Quinlan chose to have doctors *not* provide continued life support systems for their comatose daughter (*Matter of Quinlan*, 1976), and Seventh Day Adventists and Jehovah's Witnesses have refused permission to have their children inoculated against smallpox. Most situations of this nature, especially those that involve life-and-death matters, have devolved to the courts for decisions; that is, parents' or guardians' right to give and withhold consent is usurped by the courts when attorneys for the state are able to argue that a parent's decision does not serve the best interests of a child. The state has even encroached upon parental prerogatives that do not involve life-and-death matters. In the Commonwealth of Pennsylvania, the state has developed an administrative hearing procedure to monitor and sometimes refuse parental decisions to institutionalize retarded children.

Finally, it should be remembered that when consent is given, it is rarely ever given permanently or on a blanket basis. A parent may give consent to have a child placed in a group home or in a particular therapeutic program and retain the right to withdraw consent for the placement or service at any time. Also, if a parent gives consent for placement of a child in either of these situations, that consent for placement should not be regarded as blanket consent to permit the professional to apply any additional procedure or treatment without further consent. Consent should always be sought and given for specific purposes, not global ones.

Consent can serve as a critically useful way for parents to obtain greater self-determination for themselves and their children. In this sense, it becomes a tool for advocacy, albeit one that has not been previously articulated in the advocacy literature. The right to give or withhold consent is the right to decide. The availability of consent procedures means that parents have a process by which they may enter into meaningful dialogue with professionals about the future of their children. Consequently, the application of consent to particular situations should be regarded as a welcome opportunity for professionals who also regard themselves as the protectors of children's interests.

We have discussed the three primary elements of consent: capacity, information, and voluntariness. Application of consent revolves around these three elements and several other considerations. Principally, any decision on behalf of a child that may pose significant risks for the child, that may intrude physically or psychologically on the child, or that may have an irreversible effect on the child deserves careful scrutiny. Such situations demand the greatest attention to the obtaining of consent. Sometimes even rather ordinary decisions, such as the decision to allow a child to participate in a routine psychological experiment, must be given careful consideration and the safeguard of a more elaborate consent procedure. This is the case if the child is institutionalized and thereby in a potentially coercive situation, if the family is in some way not capable of considering and acting on the available information, or if the family's voluntariness is in question.

A general rule for applying consent procedures is that the greater the risk, the more intrusive, or the more irreversible the procedure or proposed activity, the greater one's concern must be to afford the parents or guardian a more formal consent process. In situations that involve little risk, intrusion, or problems of reversibility, an implied consent or a simple oral or written consent would be adequate. But in those situations in which these conditions do apply, the two-part consent form mentioned earlier may be more appropriate. It might even be advisable for a professional to record the consent procedure on tape or to submit the consent form and procedure to an independent review body established within a human service organization for that purpose. Of course, the starting point for any professional should be those consent guidelines established by professional associations. The Department of Health, Education, and Welfare has developed a useful list of factors to be considered within consent procedures relating to research that involves the use of human subjects. Similarly, the American Psychological Association has established specific ethical guidelines for psychological research (1973), and the American Association on Mental Deficiency has published a book on consent as it applies to professionals' interactions with and treatment of the retarded (Turnbull, 1977).

Consent must be applied on a continuum. Medical treatment is an example. One would not seek parental consent to apply a bandaid to a child's bruised arm at the local elementary school. But no one would perform surgery on a child without obtaining formal consent. And if that surgery is extremely risky, intrusive, and irreversible—neurosurgery, for example—the procedures for obtaining consent should be reviewed by an appropriate review board within the hospital. In such a situation, parents may not be able to fully understand the possible complications, no matter how adequate the explanation.

The same kind of continuum must be applied to the area of education. Although it is true that education is compulsory and therefore not a matter about which parents must give consent or for which professionals need to seek consent, there are decisions within schools and school systems that do require attention to this concept. Educators need not gain the consent of parents for their children to enter a public school, and parents do not have the right to decide which text books a teacher or school will select for the classroom. A parent does not even have the right to decide which style of teaching a school will offer the child. Although parents can try to influence such decisions and in many schools may be encouraged to participate in them, they do not have the right to give or withhold consent. Furthermore, it is generally presumed that most school programs, whatever their design, are not so risky, intrusive, or irreversible that one need pay any attention to securing parental consent prior to providing a child with the program. School boards make decisions about curricula, and parents are informed of those decisions. But the fact still remains that consent is not or should not be an alien concept for educators and parents. Some decisions very definitely require careful scrutiny and adequate provision of consent mechanisms. The exceptions to the general no-consent rule within schools involve any programs or educational approaches that deviate from standard educational practice. For example, if an educational program involved the use of aversive stimuli, if the procedure involved was to segregate all children whose IQ was less than 50 into a separate class, or if the procedure involved labeling children as handicapped in some way, then parents must be brought into the decision-making process. Ideally, parents should be asked for more than their consent; they should be active participants in reaching a conclusion. It is true that the courts can ultimately decide that the state's interest in pursuing a particular educational procedure or strategy may supersede a parent's withholding of consent, but parents do have the initial opportunity to give or withhold consent in such matters. The separation of children into special classes or even the labeling of children as handicapped can have a stigmatizing effect, hence, the requirement that consent be sought and that such decisions be made with utmost care.

Public Law 94-142 requires school districts to provide prior written notice to parents or guardians before a change in a child's placement to a special program can be made. This law also provides a mechanism for impartial arbitration when a parent or guardian will not consent to a school's decision. Although this law applies the consent mechanism in the form of what the law calls due-process rights to special education placements, good professional practice suggests the desirability of applying similar consent procedures to any educational program that deviates significantly from standard operating procedure.

Finally, some situations in educational programming are exceptionally risky, intrusive, and even possibly irreversible, yet they do not require consent because they are simply unconstitutional (for example, the use of isolation cells for extended periods of time as punishment). One cannot give consent to something that is against the law.

Another example of the application of the concept of consent to the human service professions may further explain the flexibility with which the matter of consent must be approached. Many human service professionals engage in research that involves interviewing, testing, observing, providing training and habilitative programs for primarily research purposes, and analysis of aggregate and psychological data. Human experimentation has received more attention from federal agencies and from the courts than has behavioral and social research. Yet many of the same issues pertain to both areas of research.

Some kinds of behavioral and social research require no formal consent on the part of the subjects. For example, a researcher does not have to obtain the consent of a public official in order to probe the official's background and daily behavior, unless, of course, the research will bring some sort of risk to the person or intrude unusually on the official's rights. Researchers may also observe without permission those people who frequent public places. Thus, researchers are relatively free to observe the functioning of bureaucracies, public recreational programs for children, and even public schools. It is even permissible for researchers to photograph people, including children, in public settings but not in schools since this activity is not part of the normal educational program. Researchers can also use aggregate data, census statistics, or agency data that do not identify individuals by name or traceable number, without obtaining consent. Such information is usually available as a matter of public right.

Other kinds of social and behavioral research require only implied consent. Most interviewing, including polling, does not call for formal consent. A person need not say, "I consent to be interviewed." A person need not know the purpose of the interview. Rather, it is presumed that when a person answers another's questions, consent is implied. In the case of children, it is probably legal for a researcher to ask children, in public places, questions without receiving parental consent. Good professional practice, on the other hand, would suggest that a researcher seek parental approval before interviewing a child.

At the other end of the continuum, researchers must seek express consent of parents. Whenever the research involves risks, is intrusive, or may have some irreversible impact, a researcher should obtain a parent's consent. In order to determine whether consent should be sought formally, a researcher should ask the following questions: Will a child's participation in the research in some way stigmatize the child? Does the research involve harmful treatments or denial of basic services, such as education? Is the environment within which the research will take place free of coercive forces? For example, will involvement in the research or refusal to participate affect one's status in a program? Will the research inconvenience the subject? Will the research in some way, marginally, or in no way benefit the proposed subject? Could the research be accomplished without involving children? If the answer to these questions, or even to some of them, is yes, then the researcher should seek consent formally.

The application of consent to a research situation calls for concern for each of the three elements in the consent concept. Concern must be taken to ensure the capacity of the parent, the disclosure of relevant information, and the voluntariness implicit in or absent from the situation. A researcher must also provide the same level of concern and, in appropriate situations, consent procedures, for any experimental control group. Obviously, there are dilemmas inherent in a researcher's role as experimenter *and* protector of a child's rights. For this reason, most research organizations—for example, universities—maintain review boards to scrutinize a researcher's experimental and consent procedures.

The concept of consent has tremendous potential for professionals and consumers. Consideration of whether consent should be sought by a professional in reference to a particular activity will certainly enable professionals to become more acutely aware of the impact of their actions. Moreover, consumers can use the process of giving and withholding consent as a vehicle to becoming more informed about human services and activities, as a time for entering into dialogue with professionals, and as a way of becoming more centrally involved in decision making that will affect the lives of children. Both professionals and parents can use consent as one of several strategies for safeguarding the interests of children. Consent, if properly considered, sought, and given or withheld, can highlight people's awareness of crucial ethical and moral issues.

But consent is a tool, not an answer. Despite the seeming clarity of the concept—we know its three elements—decisions about whether to seek consent, how to seek it, and whether to give consent cannot be prescribed with a simple formula. The situations in which we must consider consent vary greatly; people and their needs vary greatly; and the outcomes of activities for which consent is considered or applied vary greatly. Hence, there is ample room for dilemmas.

Case Presentation for Problem Solving

Researchers are often interested in evaluating how children respond to different situations and treatments. Psychological research methods often require that in order to secure "good" data, the subject must not know the method, the purpose, and the possible outcomes of the research. These are all conditions that would seem to contradict the prescribed requirements in seeking consent. For example, consider the study by Rosenthal and Jacobson (1968) in which teachers were informed that certain children in their classrooms were late bloomers and could be expected to progress more rapidly than other children. In fact, the researchers had chosen children at random. They had no evidence that these children were late bloomers. The real subjects were the teachers. How would the teachers respond to this information? Would the late bloomers start doing better than their control peers? The results are widely known. In fact, the teachers did demonstrate higher expectations for the children so identified; and the bogus late bloomers did justice to their name. They scored better. But was the research ethical? Was it fair to the other children in the class?

You are now asked to deal with a similar dilemma. It is not a dilemma for researchers but rather for teachers. Similar, if less dramatic, situations occur for any professional who works directly with children. It has become popular to introduce children's literature and exercises into the classroom that will help sensitize children to the nature of racism, to sexism, and to the problems of the handicapped. In one such exercise the teacher divides the class into the "brown eyes" and the "blue eyes." The teacher then criticizes one of the two groups unfairly, always pointing to the color of their eyes as the cause of their problems and poor performance. One group— say the blue eyes—receives constant praise, which, like the other group's punishment and derision, is related to the eye color. The exercise is designed in such a way that the participants, in this case children, are not privy to the teacher's motivations. Perhaps if they understood the nature of the exercise, they would not feel so intensely proud of their blue eyes and ashamed and downcast about their brown eyes. But, also, perhaps if they actually knew what was happening, they would not take it seriously at all. Then they would not have such an intense experience and would perhaps learn much less from the activity.

The exercise is designed in such a way that children take it seriously indeed. Some taunt those who have eyes of another color. Others are reduced to tears. Some are kept after school as punishment for something they do not feel responsible for. The next day, however, the sides change. The brown eyes are in control, receiving praise at every turn, watching their blue-eyed rivals submit to a barrage of criticisms that the day before would have been unthinkable.

Some questions that could be asked in this case presentation are: (1) Does any teacher have the right to engage in such an activity? (2) Should the parents of these children have been asked for their consent to do this exercise? (3) Should the children have been informed of the purpose associated with this experience? (4) And if everyone had been informed and consent been sought and given, would the experiment be the same? (5) Should the parents or children be allowed to withdraw at any time? One can fairly say that if consent were sought in this situation, the exercise would lose its impact. Children would not learn such a powerful lesson about prejudice. (6) Are the costs in individual liberties worth it? It is replicated in virtually every teaching or treatment situation where the child does not share the teacher's knowledge of an activity's purpose until the exercise has been completed. Humanistic education activities which have been developed as a technique for teaching sharing also sometimes keep the learner in the dark. Similarly, some behavior modification programs are designed in a way that the subject does not know the actual behavior that a behavior shaper has chosen to modify. (7) Should all such curricula, however successful, be saddled with the requirement that teachers and therapists seek and obtain consent, even if it means disclosing information that will undermine the exercise's effectiveness?

The dilemma arises from competing values. On the one hand, the teacher wants to expand the children's understanding of racism, other forms of prejudice, or similar concepts. And the teacher wants to create a real experience, something akin to *Gentleman's Agreement* (Hobson, 1947) or *Black Like Me* (Griffith, 1961) so that children can understand in very personal terms what it is like to know and endure prejudice. Yet the teacher presumably holds another value or goal as well, that of protecting the individual rights of each child. (8) Should consent be sought from the subjects? Or are there justifications for ignoring consent? (9) A final question to consider—is there a way the same research goal could have been reached without subjecting the children to so much potential trauma?

Chapter 7

Dilemmas in Standardized Testing

Constance T. Fischer

Today, the phrase *ethical dilemmas in standardized testing* appears straightforward but dull. Less than ten years ago it would indeed have been dynamic because of its apparent contradiction: The primary ethics of testing *were* standardized construction of tests, standardized administration, standardized interpretation, standard report writing, and closed filing. Ethical issues had to do with deviating from these procedures, intentionally or unintentionally.

Of course, the goal of standardized testing has been to obtain measures of the child that could be compared against those of his age group. A standardized test, whether for use with groups or individuals, has been scientifically constructed and demonstrated to be reliable and valid under specified circumstances. Graphs and tables indicate the range of scores that were obtained. Testers are trained to judge whether these norms are appropriate for new test takers and to keep abreast of emerging research. They also are trained to administer the tests according to the manual's explicit instructions, so that each test taker has been exposed to the same testing circumstances, and the resulting scores can be interpreted in the standardized way. Historically, the testing movement rightfully has taken pride in its scientific character: No matter which test administrator gave and scored a test, the measured result would be as similar as possible for a given child (this is the definition of *objective test*).

Today, it is just this allegiance to standardized procedures that raises ethical questions. Ethics are the formal, well-established standards that a profession follows in order to protect and promote the welfare of its clients and society. Dilemmas arise when a client's welfare seems to bring established standards into conflict. Such conflict is most likely when scientific knowledge and/or social consciousness evolve beyond a profession's established ethics. The Karen Quinlan case is an example: Medicine now can keep bodies alive even when all other human capacities are gone. Today's doctors must decide individually whether it is best to uphold their pledge to maintain life.

Partially because of changes in the philosophy of science, partially because of humanistic psychology's teachings, but mostly because of protests by minority groups, users of psychological, developmental, and educational tests find themselves in conflict about whether clients' welfare is best served by standardized testing. In particular, we are increasingly aware that tests are subject to discriminatory use, that rather than being value-free, they inevitably reflect cultural and scientific values, that we have given test technology's reality more credence than directly observable behaviors, and that we have transformed children's lives into a few cognitive and usually unsituated "variables." In short, we have given location on the bell-shaped curve priority over individualized understanding and helping.

I have found that today's ethical dilemmas in standardized testing can be grouped, overlappingly, as struggles of new consciousness against continued respect for earlier versions of "objectivity," "professionalism," and "efficiency." For this chapter I have selected three dilemmas representative of each cluster from instances presented to me by graduate students in field settings and by practicing professionals. After presenting each cluster, I will explore the implicit historical assumptions that no longer need be part of objectivity, professionalism, and efficiency but that still seem to be at the heart of conflicting concerns for clients' welfare. I also will describe my own resolutions and continuing concerns.

Let us consider the dilemma of objectivity first.

Often, even as I gain clinical skill, I find that standardized administration of tests gets in the way of working effectively with personal material. To obtain objective scores and to ensure that a child's energy is concentrated upon responding to the test items before she becomes fatigued, I am supposed to proceed systematically according to the manual, but I'm just sure that sometimes the scores aren't as helpful to the youngster as my immediate response might have been. For example, just yesterday during a Wechsler test, a fifth-grader began to elaborate upon the fact that the bigger boys pick fights with him; but I felt that I had to move him along to the next Wechsler comprehension item. When I brought it up later, he wouldn't talk about the fights. I had lost a chance to explore part of the referral issue—"Mark's social wariness." On the other hand, it was also important to get as valid an IQ as possible, and I wasn't sure that this would be possible if he became emotionally involved in the fight discussion. I just don't know where my greater responsibility to the child lies, so I usually take the conservative course of sticking to the standardized procedures. Yet I'm not certain if that's the right thing to do.

My supervisor says our job is to provide accurate measures on the children and to indicate to which established categories they belong, since other people who work with the children and also locate services and funding for them best understand their needs in terms of categories. He says that it's up to the child care workers to use that information responsibly. But sometimes I think that for the child's sake it would be worth the risk of overstepping professional boundaries, to add my comments about possible misinterpretations or about ways to best use our measures for a particular child. He says that would just be my subjective opinion, which has no place in objective records. I see his point, but somehow it still seems like a "cop-out" from an opportunity to be more helpful to the child.

Well, I personally think it's unethical to objectify a client

*through overly rigorous standardized assessment. You can't see the kid
as an individual if you treat him like all the others. And standardized
results can't say anything about his uniqueness; they just say how many
standard deviations he is from an average. But I'm in a bind here,
because I also don't think it's ethical just to go in and make decisions
based only on my own impressions without test scores as supportive
data. And I guess for the scores to be useful they have to be valid,
which, according to the manual, means derived in a standardized
manner. There must be a middle road, but I don't see it.*

It seems to me that the issue in all three cases is whether
the professional can be *objective and involved* at the same time. The
answer is yes, and the dilemma dissolves when we reexamine the
meaning of *objectivity*. In general, objectivity assures that observations are not merely subjective, that referents and procedures can
be readily agreed upon and shared by different people. That is what
standardization provides for tests. In a still broader sense, objectivity
is the assurance that many perspectives on empirical touchpoints
have been taken into account and have converged in a consensus.
What we sometimes forget is that the test score is only a summary of
(age-based) right–wrong judgments of specific behaviors. True, the
score is an averaging across *many* behaviors, and contrasted to
natural observation, it is more difficult to imagine the testing environment as it might have been experienced by the child. But this
distanced, general, and abstract quality should not be mistaken for
a sign of a reality more basic or valid than firsthand observation of
the effectiveness of particular behaviors. Averages are no more than
generalizations, and they do not generalize beyond the specific kind
of circumstance in which the data occurred. This is true for the
individual child as well as for group norms. Test scores represent a
sample of a particular set of problem solvings. In the case of the
traditional intelligence tests, for example, that set of problems was
put together by middle-class academic whites in a capitalistic society. The tests value efficient production, one-truth answers, and
Aristotelian logic. In short, tests do provide us with objectivity via
their standardization, but that objectivity is inescapably a limited
one: Tests necessarily call for particular values and only selected,
decontextualized aspects of the test taker.

The assessor is obliged to provide not only publicly available—that is, potentially objective—grounds for his testing conclusions but also correctives to the limited perspective of the standardized test. That may require assessment of areas not found on the test. Sometimes the assessor intervenes during testing to explore how the child is missing certain items or to investigate the circumstances in which the child performs more happily or effectively. Often the assessor must assist score users to understand the limits of the particular scores and the necessary place of additional information. In short, assessment is more than testing; the assessor must be more than a servant of technology. The assessor must be *involved*.

So in the above dilemmas, I would amend technological objectivity with broader involvement. In Mark's case, I would talk with him about those bigger boys when he introduces that problem for two reasons. First, the ultimate purpose of applied testing is constructive intervention—helping the child toward fulfillment. Why not begin that process during testing by tailoring the assessment and helping him to be a part of it? Second, for most purposes, an estimate based on additional items or other subtests will place the child in the same range as the precise IQ, and ranges or percentile bands are more reliable than a specific number anyway.

As for including unsolicited assistance in interpreting scores: I am all for it. We are partially responsible for the uses and abuses of our assessments. Score consumers should be helped to use scores in a less absolute way. Accompanying information on the circumstances of testing, information on limitations of the test for particular uses, and additional observations on the child help the recipient make more reflective use of scores.

Standardized findings can be set apart from personal or speculative observations by labeling the latter as such—for example, "Assessor's Comments." In these ways we can provide other workers with data they request but in ways we believe best benefit the client.

By now, the third dilemma seems artificial; we do not very often have to choose between strictly standardized procedures and personal impressions. Neither is adequate by itself. Each is a way station, not a final destination. Both objectivity and the client are best served where different perspectives (for example, the tests' and the clinician's) are specified and integrated by the assessor,

However, I personally feel that any impressions should be documented so that they, too, become available for examination. For example, concrete behaviors, interchanges, or the assessor's responses could be described. This kind of involvement also moves toward individualizing the assessment, which, in turn, goes a long way toward encouraging the child's helpers to see new possibilities. Otherwise, score receivers tend to see "individual differences" as sameness and scores as ceilings or limits rather than present locations or starting places. This is especially true where classification by score replaces team conferences. The same danger occurs when the report is written in third-person, objectifying terms as though there were no historical context for the tests in general and no specific situation for this particular assessment.

The second dilemma is one of professionalism.

*The medical doctor in charge of our unit in the hospital routinely makes out a referral for "*WISC *IQ and* WRAT*" (Wechsler Intelligence Scale for Children and Wide Range Achievement Test). He seems to think that numbers in the child's record fulfill his obligation to be sure every child has been assessed. My problem with this is that, as an assessor, I know that this referral is often inappropriate; other tests are often more useful for a particular child. But our director of psychological services says that our obligation is to provide the doctor with what he needs for his own purposes. At first, I tried to give the tests the doctor wanted and then add whatever else I felt was helpful for the particular child. But there just isn't time to do both. Besides, with most of our children, attention span and interest preclude extensive testing at any one time. Anyway, in my opinion the scores themselves aren't all that helpful for treatment planning; they usually don't add to what the ward staff already knows from interacting with the youngster. And yet, the ward staff seems to feel that the assessor's basic contribution into the multidisciplinary team is test results. They feel more secure about their own judgments if they jibe with my scores.*

I don't know what to think about something that happened last week. It's still bothering me. I was supposed to do a "standard battery" on a five-year-old orphan whose foster parents of six months had brought her back to our agency complaining that she just didn't "fit in" and that they'd rather have a lively boy instead of this quiet girl. In order to give us time to investigate the situation, my boss had promised the foster parents that he would not yet tell Marie why she was being tested; she was told instead that she was being brought in for a "doctor's check-up." But respecting confidentiality in regard to the foster parents meant that I had to be devious with Marie, and I think she knew something was wrong and probably felt that she was defective. I wish I could have been honest with her to help her cope with what was going on.

How would you answer this? Some parents came in and wanted to see their son's counseling file. I explained that this file included the psychiatric consultant's notes as well as the school psychologist's results and that the Buckley Amendment did not apply. They argued that the writer's profession should not limit parents' access to documents that were influencing their son's welfare. So I also explained that laypersons would be confused or misled by the language, scores, and concepts written by and for professionals. I also felt that it would be damaging to both the youngster and the parents to see some of the labels and psychologisms in the record. I know I had both law and ethical standards behind me, but then why do I feel uneasy and defensive every time parents question me about access to the counseling files?

The major assumption in the previous instances is that professionalism requires uncritical adherence to intra- and interprofessional traditions. It is true that traditions embody a certain working wisdom and that client welfare requires cooperative relations among professionals as well as a judicious approach in innovation. But it seems to me that the above examples involve protectionistic rather than responsible professionalism. In each case the clinician has neglected to examine the grounds for established practices and to clarify his understandings of the meaning of tests. The responsible professional places the client's welfare first, with personal confidence in his procedures—confidence that comes, in part, from reflection on the historical situations out of which particular practices evolved.

So, in the above examples, as part of my *professionalism* I would *take the initiative* in the following ways. I would assume the position that it is the psychologist who carries primary responsibility for the selection and use of tests developed by his profession, and I would, in fact, begin to use whatever developmental/educational tests I thought would best serve the child. But also I would have to take further initiative—namely, addressing the situations of the other workers. I would have to take into account their need to feel as competent and comfortable with the new measures as they were with the old ones. Therefore, I might continue to provide WRAT and WISC estimates at first, while gradually familiarizing the staff with additional measures. Through my ways of speaking about tests and through my valuing of direct behavioral observations, I would help the staff to deabsolutize scores. I would help them develop their own senses of how scores are peoplemade aids or tools rather than states of nature or final results. We become servants of the tools rather than the other way when they cover over more of the individual child than they reveal.

The example of foster child Marie illustrates how easily we can forget about the individual child and about our personal responsibility when we think in terms of professional roles. The assessor in this case has created an unnecessary bind; one does not have to pit allegiances against each other. Instead, I would matter-of-factly explore with Marie her concerns about being brought in, and I would help her to face the possibilities of the foster parents' wondering whether they were a good fit for each other. I would explain that I am not a doctor (physician), that I am not looking for things that are wrong, but that I want to get to know her to see if that might help her foster parents to do the right things. In short, I would take an honest middle ground. Later, I would explore with my boss whether our office might formulate a policy of not confronting youngsters prematurely but also of letting guardians know that neither they nor we should deceive their children.

About the problem of closed files: I do think we are obliged to abide by laws and formal policies. But I do not believe that psychiatric or psychological records should be exempt from disclosure, and I have worked within the system for change. In the meantime, I would advise the parents in this case of their options. For example, they could request that an independent practitioner evaluate the files and advise them about whether anything should be challenged or studied for additional assessment. Of course, I am assuming that the school staff has already discussed the general relevance of the file for the student's progress with the parents. Parents should also be advised about the status of any relevant court cases and of the existence of interest groups.

It may well be that the historically ethical practice of closed files with their stark scores and labelings not only impedes maximal child welfare but sometimes is detrimental. If so, unself-critical ethics are morally wrong. For example, the recording of scores without notations about the assessor, about the daily correlates of test performance, the ways the child went about answering the questions, and other situational data falsely leads the reader to believe that the score is independent of these essential constituents. The reader may then assume that scores are limits of capacity rather than starting places. Moreover, even when records are available to parents and children, they often cannot question scores. If they could see reports of specific behaviors, they would be able to put into context what the assessor said. Similarly, the assessor's growth and development is restricted when such challenges and dialogue do not occur.

The responsible professional examines the rationale for closed files and works to change protectionism from within the system. For example, I stamp my reports "Contents have been, and may be, shared with the subject." I can do this because my reports contain no jargon (unless parenthetically explained), no opinions that have not already been shared with the client, and no scores that have not been translated into classroom or everyday behaviors. In other words, I recognize that jargon, conceptions, and scores are tools that I have to use but that my results should consist of concrete suggestions for working with a particular child in his particular situation. Reporting on tools and conceptual efforts is to report unfinished business. If the school or agency has no intention of finishing—that is, of finding out what actual behaviors, experiences, and interventions the tests might point to for a particular child—the records then should be kept only for research, with the children's names removed, or for occasions when genuinely individualized assessment is undertaken.

Finally, I talk to assorted staffs and to school boards, lecture to my students, and write chapters like this one about alternatives to closed files. In this process I not only influence others but I develop and adapt my own ideas, learning from others' efforts. I believe that some such interchange is necessary for genuine professionalism. In sum, the responsible professional person questions traditional ethics and looks for constructive means of meeting the underlying intention of protection of client welfare.

So far, we have not looked directly at instances in which one worker believes another is misusing tests. There are a number of examples. The inexperienced special education teacher interprets House–Tree–Person (HTP) drawings literally from a manual ("dark lines equal hostility"). The pediatrician, not trained in a test's standardization, does not take into account that parts of the test were developed at different times with somewhat different implications; perhaps, too, he gives credit on the test for the first emergence of a behavior, before it is clearly developed, falsely raising scores and expectations. The nurse administering the Denver Developmental Screening Schedule does not evaluate whether the parent is answering according to what she thought should have been the case or to what actually was the case. The school psychologist interprets statistically insignificant scale differences as primary evidence of learning disability. An audiologist's technician administering the Peabody Picture Vocabulary Test falsely concludes that a deaf child is retarded when, in fact, the technician had not seen to it that the youngster was attending to the visual instructions. Incidents like these are all too frequent.

It is our moral and ethical obligation to go directly to such colleagues and share our experience with these complex instruments. Sometimes it is helpful to refer them to textbooks on psychological testing or to specialized works such as Palmer's *The Psychological Assessment of Children* (1970) and Sattler's *Assessment of Children's Intelligence* (1974). If necessary, we must then go to that person's supervisor or (eventually) even to her association's ethics or peer review committee. Professionals are responsible not only for their personal competence but for that of their profession at large (see your own association's code of ethics on this matter). They must also be concerned with the competence of members of other professions if the child's welfare is in question. Yes, one must be tactful and helpful rather than negative. I notice that as I become older and look older—and presumably more mature—my interventions are better received! And yes, in each case, one must balance the welfare of the present client(s) against that of future clients. For example, the former may require a good working relation between you and the problematic professional. Nevertheless, future children can often be helped by working through the dilemma involving the present child. The goals usually are not so mutually exclusive as to justify taking no action.

Now let us consider the dilemma of efficiency.

I know that assessing twenty pupils a week does necessitate one- or two-page, often test-oriented, reports. I've learned much more about each youngster than I have time to write up. And I know that the brevity of the reports makes the findings seem so absolute that they may be misleading. It's demoralizing to all of us, knowing that there is usually so much more we should check into and report. But I don't see any other way. These kids have to be processed, and the county is not about to pay for more assessors.

We run a standardized screening program for developmental disabilities. It's really quite sophisticated, and we've been able to identify and help many disabled youngsters. Since we have this technology available, I think we are morally obliged to use and even to extend it. But many of the teachers and many of the ethnic families strongly oppose the whole program, protesting that our tests are racially biased, that labels and developmental classes hold their children back. Granted, there are always a few false positives, but the numerous correct identifications seem to justify the program. Moreover, even the so-called false positives could use some help, or they would not have scored so poorly on the tests, even if they do perform better in other situations. My dilemma seems to be that although I can make a strong case for the program as a whole, I do feel somehow responsible for the youngsters who perhaps would be better served by some other kind of specialized screening or norms.

We're required by state law to keep records of each student's potential and present achievement. Standardized tests are considered to be the fairest way to compare children, so no one can complain about teacher bias. But I often feel that our records are too test-oriented. They're good for tracking progress or pointing out possible motivation problems, but I wonder if the lawmakers realized that our careful records don't help teachers or parents to develop more effective programs for the individual child. It seems to me that the students would be better served if we sacrificed group testing and just concentrated on developing constructive individual programs for children identified by their teachers as not keeping up or moving as well as they could in the classroom. But our director says that this wouldn't be efficient and wouldn't meet the state law.

Efficient recording of mass data seems to be winning out over *service to individual children* in all three of these examples. Other ways of saying this are that records have become more important than education or intervention and that scientific form or appearance is more important than practical function. How could we have taken such a position? The historical reason is that in our earlier positivist, operationalist understanding of science, we thought of scores as more objective and even more real than actual experience and behavior. But now we find ourselves in dilemmas because we also are beginning to recognize that scores are derived data secondary to behavior and experience. We are realizing that assessment is more than testing, that it requires person-to-person evaluation of the child's perspectives, situations, and options, as well as abstracted end products (scores) from contrived tests. Moreover, service requires going beyond assessment of the present to individualize suggestions for the child's future.

Therefore, my resolution to these dilemmas is to look for ways to deal more directly with the lives of children, reminding myself and others that scores and categories are unfinished beginnings rather than satisfactory assessment or record keeping. True, we still have to be as efficient as possible, especially for monetary reasons.

For example, we might use scaling devices into which we could enter brief phrases describing behavioral instances that illustrate or contradict a child's score equivalent on the scale. I can envision a couple of sheets of paper with a full range of scales including such neglected areas as comportment outside the institutional or clinic setting and, perhaps, self-responsibility. Where life examples had not been filled in for various acceptable and unacceptable reasons, the reader of these records would see that he had, indeed, only a partial record. This contrasts sharply with the more typical assumption that a few test scores tell the basic story.

A national project on the *Issues in the Classification of Children* (Hobbs, 1975b) led to Public Law 94-142 regarding handicapped children's special needs. Schools now are being required to write out an individualized program for each child with such special needs. Thus, a child's record would go beyond traditional diagnostic categories to include, for example, that he requires dental work, extra reading assistance for a year, and a big brother. Reconceptualizing overall classification schemes so that they preserve the individuality and specialness of each child remains a challenge for children's services professionals.

Many assessors are already developing ways both to render evaluations more relevant and to bring in more personnel by serving as consultants to the critical adults in children's lives. Brief interviews with parents and teachers, for example, can provide concrete life instances of test performance as well as the opportunity for mutual development of specific suggestions for these persons. Perhaps we could extend Brown's (1975) procedure of bringing parents into the assessment setting to participate in administering tests. We might train groups of parents to participate in the assessment process at home. Behavior modifiers are doing this now in a specialized way. Besides being time saving and relevant, such procedures go a long way toward returning responsibility and initiative to parents and children. Again, I believe that we are obliged to present fellow workers, the public, and our legislatures with piloted alternative practices and conceptions, with specific suggestions for implementing them. Granted, the changes suggested above require greater skill and reflection than does score-oriented testing but no more than should be expected of a professional. Nor have I encountered any competent students or professionals who have been unable to develop such practices, albeit usually with considerable *initial* time-consuming struggle with the problems of working efficiently while still respecting the individuality and complexity of the child.

Before concluding this section I shall single out for comment the dilemma concerning screening. Despite a historical sense of how we have gotten ourselves into our current binds, I am repeatedly amazed at how blind we have been to the manufactured nature of our tests and to the restrictive, destructive effects of behaving as though these tests were handed down to us by a Grand Scientist who constructed them to be appropriate for all humans at all times. In particular, I am amazed at the continuation of testing programs that have been clearly demonstrated as inappropriate for certain minorities. At the very least, professionals are responsible, as individuals and as associations, for keeping up with research and issues and for refusing to carry out testing programs that both science and ethics present as deleterious to the child. After all, courts and legislatures traditionally have respected the authority of professionals when the latter have presented a unified opinion.

I have often found that as long as I presented useful data and suggestions, even as an individual, many situations have not required scores and sometimes not even categories. When all efforts to change another worker's overreliance on scores to the detriment of the child have failed, I have found that personal, direct proposals to take the problem to our area's peer standards review committee have sent the offender to our assorted standards publications for clarification. In the process he discovers that technological efficiency is not adequate to assure professional and ethical comportment, and change ensues. However, I should acknowledge that my interventions have been effective partially because of my reputation as a person familiar with developments in research and standards and involved in my professional association's governance.

If this sounds a bit abstract, let me remind the reader that Mercer (1973; 1975) showed how California Chicano children have been shunted into relatively unstimulating classes for the retarded on the basis of IQs, even though most of these same children were found to be functioning at nonretarded levels when evaluated in their communities. Also, until recently, deaf children were expected to be intellectually below average. Today, they are not, and the total dynamics of their language disabilities are more fully understood and handled. Other handicapped children continue to be misassessed. For example, boys with Duchenne muscular dystrophy are frequently diagnosed as retarded when, in fact, they may be reflecting a limited learning environment or reacting to the emotional components of the disease. Even when the dystrophy diagnosis has been made, the psychological assessment too often neglects to explore the related dynamics. Perhaps, as we look beyond scores to the complexities of the overall life situation, we may discover that the historical supposition that Duchenne dystrophy boys can be expected to be intellectually deficient has been in error. At least we should not assume reduced mental functioning to be a component of the dystrophy before we discover the etiology of the disease itself.

There are two points in these examples: (1) Test conditions are necessarily artificial and may have little bearing on the profundity of a child's resources or on his effectiveness in his everyday life. (2) The American Association on Mental Deficiency (AAMD) and many state standards formally require that adaptive social and emotional accomplishment be included in determination of retardation. We know this, but often practice as though we do not, despite well-publicized articles such as Bersoff's (1973) presenting rationale and procedures for psychosituational assessment. Through our IQ-oriented technology, we have created and perpetuated many cases of retardation. To function as mere technicians is not only unethical; it is destructive.

In sum, although I may have to work within restrictive policies or laws for a while, I insist upon deabsolutizing scores by such practices as adding clarifying life events to the record or even exchanging scores for life events alone. Meanwhile, I work with colleagues to develop systemwide alternatives that meet the spirit of regulations and thus allow the latter to be changed. Efficiency and scientific form are not worthwhile in themselves; we are better off without them if they are not in the service of children's individual welfare and growth.

Procedures that work against the best interest of the child as an individual are unethical. Standardized testing can work against the child; it becomes unethical when scores are taken as more real than daily behaviors and experience and when these are presented as though they were independent of dimensions such as cultural values, historical context of test construction, the specialized, contrived nature of testing, the personality of the tester, and the child's sense of the situation. The danger is that scores will be seen as underlying causes rather than as being extracted aspects of the child's complex, total existence and that they will thus be taken as levels of capacity rather than as sampled areas for investigation or encouragement.

The dilemmas presented in this chapter showed workers

caught between older traditions and emerging changes in our understandings of science and social responsibility. Ethical resolutions
are ones that acknowledge new developments and that strive to develop practical procedures based on those developments.

My own resolutions involved acknowledging the inevitable
human involvement in testing and encouraging innovative intervention in the interest of service to the individual. All of these resolutions in one way or another rejected subservience of the assessor
to tests and sought to promote recognition of the child's life events
as the primary data and concern.

Case Presentation for Problem Solving

For years, the teachers, counselors, and school psychologists
of the Dobson School system had been distressed that students could
continue even as far as high school before finally being identified
as developmentally disabled. It was not just that these youngsters
had been deprived of special instruction that could have helped
them to benefit much more from their school years; perhaps more
disturbing was that family, teachers, and peers had assumed that
these youngsters were simply stupid or, more often, that they were
lazy or otherwise perversely motivated not to learn. Worse, these
students often wondered if such assumptions might be true. They
developed assorted defenses that were not particularly adaptive
either to school or later life: They became class clowns. They dis-
dained academics. They associated with dropouts and delinquents.

Although the problem diminished somewhat after inservice
training was provided by the community mental health consultation and education service, it persisted. So the Dobson Schools
leaped at an opportunity for preschool screening even though the
federal funds covered only the hiring of one school psychologist who
was to screen kindergartners and follow up questionable cases with
further evaluation himself.

John Ockar was hired as the screener. He constructed a
behavioral check list for preschool teachers and aides, emphasizing
attention span, ability to follow directions, motor skills, counting and
color naming, and peer relations. He mailed these out to the teachers

with instructions to collect a human drawing from each child, and to feel free to add comments or to call him for clarification.

Five-and-a-half-year-old Joanna Pace was selected for followup. The teacher explained to Mrs. Pace that Mr. Ockar had noted remarks about Joanna's fast tempo and roughhouse ways and, in combination with her self-drawing, which included a furry puppy—indicating needs for warmth and security—he had felt that perhaps Joanna would not be ready for first grade. Both the teacher and the Paces were a bit dubious but agreed that the best thing was to give permission for the follow-up testing.

About a month later, Mrs. Pace asked Joanna if she had yet taken the tests from Mr. Ockar. Joanna said she didn't think so, although a man had taken her to another room "to play some games." But he did not really play and even slapped her hand away from his box of toys. She had become frightened and was glad to get back to her room. Mrs. Pace then obtained Mr. Ockar's number from the teacher and left messages for him to call. Two weeks later, the secretary called with an apology from Mr. Ockar, whose testing schedule of twenty children per week had not yet allowed parent conferences. The next day Mrs. Pace called back to request a change in her scheduled meeting, which had turned out to conflict with a dental appointment. In turn, Mr. Ockar's secretary later requested a second change since he would be on the other side of the county that day. While waiting for a return call of suggested times that would meet her schedule, Mrs. Pace complained of the situation during her psychotherapy session. Her psychiatrist suggested that, as a mental health professional, he could request a copy of the report, which he could then interpret for her. After his review of the report, the psychiatrist pronounced it incompetent and recommended that the Paces make arrangements for a private evaluation. He sent the report to Dr. Irene Taylor, a psychologist. The report:

> *Tests:* Bender-Gestalt, House–Tree–Person, Rorschach, Wide Range Achievement Test. *Intelligence Test:* Stanford-Binet, Form L-M.
> *Results: Binet: CA:* 5-11, *MA:* 5-5, *IQ:* 91.
> *The building principal should make this report available for the information of other concerned school*

*personnel. Special care should be taken in orally inter-
preting report information to parents. Under no circumstances should the report be given or read to the parents. Mental ability may be explained in general terms
(above or below average, etc.) but no specific MA or
IQ should be given.*

Joanna is currently in kindergarten and scholas-
tic progress has been slow. Reaction time to directions is
slow. The child appears to be unhappy and expression-
less. This evaluation is part of preschool readiness testing to determine feasibility for entrance into first grade.

The Stanford-Binet Intelligence Scale, Form
L-M was administered to Joanna at this time. She
passed all items at year level 4-6 and failed all items at
year level 7-0. This gave her a mental age of 5-5 at
this time. This certainly appears to be sufficient mental
capability for entrance into first grade.

On the Wide Range Achievement Test Joanna
had extreme difficulty in identifying letters of the
alphabet. It is also noted that Joanna had extreme
difficulty in speech with certain sounds. She had difficulty responding verbally to the examiner, and she
looked somewhat anemic. I noticed that she bites her
fingernails. Her reproductions on the Bender-Gestalt for
young children appeared extremely poor. This would
tend to support visual discrimination problems at this
time. It was also noticed that on several occasions
Joanna had a nervous twitch of the eyes.

Joanna is an extremely large child and repeat
of kindergarten would not appear to be in the interest
of this child socially. Although she obtained a mental
age of 5-5 and is eligible for entrance to first grade, it
is felt that she will continue to have learning problems
in first grade. Nonetheless, I am recommending entrance to first grade.

A parent interview was required in this case
so as to assess background information, both socially
and medically. Parents could not come in at this time
for an interview. Some resistance on the parents' part
was encountered here.

John W. Ockar, M. Ed.
Clinical Psychologist

In October, Dr. Taylor met with Joanna for two-and-a-half hours, during which she repeated the Bender, drawings, and WRAT, and substituted the Wechsler scales for the Stanford-Binet. Joanna scored well within the average range on the WISC and on the reading and spelling portions of the WRAT. She was below first grade level on arithmetic. Her WISC scores and Bender-Gestalt figures vacillated; for example, the former varied between four- and eight-year-old levels. She appeared neither anemic nor large. The referral section of the four-page (single spaced) report included the following: "However, Dr. Meyer [psychiatrist] felt that the report's brevity rendered its predominantly negative and finalistic tone misleading to those who might have had prior hopes of helping Joanna to develop fully. Hence, at Dr. Meyer's suggestion, Mrs. Pace requested that I attempt a fuller psychological evaluation—hopefully one that might provide some understanding of the ways in which Joanna functions rather than primarily reporting her levels of achievement. Presumably, such an understanding would go beyond the prior prediction that 'she will continue to have learning problems in the first grade,' to suggest a basis from which parents and teachers might better aid Joanna's development."

The report went on to describe the ways in which Joanna had gone about working on the tests. An excerpt from "Conclusions":

"Thus, although she scores predominantly in the average range on the intelligence and achievement tests, it appears that there is indeed cause for concern about Joanna's future progress in school. Specifically, her current ways of handling new demands drastically curtail learning. She seems to vacillate between two extremes of an activity–passivity continuum: when passive, she withdraws from the new task, refusing to try herself out; when active, she turns her attention away from the problem and involves herself instead with familiar things. Neither course is conducive to learning, especially learning of school-type concepts and reasoning. Joanna's difficulty with arithmetic may be an example." The concluding paragraph began: "Although this report has thus far focused primarily on the youngster's difficulties, it is obvious that they are the reverse side of otherwise promising gumption, assertiveness and sensitivity to others." Concrete suggestions for working with Joanna followed.

Both Mr. and Mrs. Pace met with Dr. Taylor, each reading a copy of the report, which included illustrations of the assessment activities but on which IQs had been blocked out. They requested that copies be sent to Dr. Meyer and to Joanna's past and present schools. Six months later, a telephone follow-up indicated that Joanna was in her class' accelerated reading group, keeping up in arithmetic, and being a bit of a *Peanuts* Lucy with her peers but otherwise doing well socially.

In the meantime Dr. Taylor had enquired informally of colleagues in one of the local university's school psychology programs whether they knew of John Ockar (they did not) and whether school psychologists could refer to themselves as "clinical psychologists" (at that time they could if they wished). She debated going to the director of school psychology in the public schools to discuss Ockar's report which she saw as incompetent and destructive. Eventually, she decided just to hope that through her report personnel in the two schools would be alerted to future incidents and would manage to inform the right people about this one. She was fearful that, as a newcomer to town and as a clinical rather than a school psychologist, any personal action at this point could be resented and might jeopardize her later professional relations. In later years, she felt that her judgment had been correct but her decision wrong.

Some questions that could be asked in this case presentation are: (1) How would you have handled Mr. Ockar's responsibilities for screening and follow-up? (2) What are your reactions to Mr. Ockar's report? (3) What do you think of the excerpts from Dr. Taylor's report? (4) If you were Dr. Taylor, would you have contacted Mr. Ockar? Would you have contacted the kindergarten teacher or the principal? If so, what would be your reasoning in each case? (5) Would you have given the parents the IQs in the conference if you were Dr. Taylor? (6) What is your evaluation of Dr. Taylor's handling of the issue of the competency of Mr. Ockar? What are the various factors you would take into consideration?

Chapter 8

Potential Errors in Clinical Practice

Jane W. Kessler

The period between 1960 and 1970 was marked by dramatic revolutionary movements spearheaded by youth and minority groups. In a more quiet way, the revolution has continued in the mental health field, as Morse notes in Chapter One. It is no longer assumed that mental health professionals "help" people; in fact, the contrary is often asserted. The first line of the report of a round-table discussion on responsibilities of individual professionals at the Annual Meeting of the American Orthopsychiatric Association in 1970 reads: "Professionals should blame themselves for the ineffective and unfair state of the helping services today" (Mearig, 1970). More recently, writing on the subject of professional abuse of children, Polier (1975, pp. 358–359) questions professional practices and policies determining whether services are to be withheld or granted, and what services are to be delivered to children and their families. She states that "disposal of human beings by professional classification based on scraps of paper is symptomatic of the all too common alienation of professionals that spells abuse."

There have been two developments that are designed, in part, to check the mental health professional's abuse of power. One is the child advocacy movement, which was first introduced in the recommendations made by the Report of the Joint Commission on Mental Health of Children (1969). In the Report to the President of the 1970 White House Conference on Children (1971), the forum dealing with the child advocate attributed the notorious inadequacy of services to children to professional biases as follows: "First, agencies emphasize program descriptions more than implementation and evaluation. The search for status, prestige, and empire building by following the latest fad or catchword in professional circles leads to many 'paper programs.' Secondly, agencies tend to be dominated by one particular profession or guild whose concerns are less child-oriented than territorially dominated. Too many programs are written to expand a guild's territory rather than to give relevant and needed services. Thirdly, agencies use their expertise in diagnosis and classification of children as a means of excluding children from services. Rigid definitions of who can be treated often exclude children who need the service the most or send them on endless rounds of diagnosis in lieu of giving help" (pp. 389–390).

This same forum report described the child advocate as a full-time salaried individual to be a spokesperson for individual children who do not have a concerned parent to speak for them or to secure needed services. The forum also recommended a high level, independent office of child advocacy and, indeed, a National Center for Child Advocacy in the Office of Child Development of the Department of Health, Education and Welfare was established. Nevertheless, individuals specifically designated as child advocates have seldom appeared; instead, there has been much discussion regarding the child advocacy role of professional persons employed in other capacities. Most of the real work of the child advocacy movement has taken legal form and has been concerned with issues of child placement outside the home (*Gary W. et al.* v. *Stewart et al.*, *Kremens et al.* v. *Bartley et al.*). In these cases, serious questions have been raised regarding the legitimacy of professional decisions or parental decisions in providing for the best interests of the child.

This leads to the second development—namely, the demand for accountability. The idea of written treatment contracts, with specified goals agreed upon in advance by the consumer, and "goal attainment scaling" (Kiresuk and Lund, 1976) indicating the degree of success of treatment, are part of the Standards for Providers of Psychological Services adopted as official policy by the American Psychological Association (1975). Written documentation of the treatment plan is the prime vehicle for peer review and even appears in legislation requiring written habilitation plans for the mentally retarded and mentally ill individuals placed in institutions (Ohio R. C. Sect. 5122.27) and written individual education plans for handicapped children (Public Law 94-142). It is no longer sufficient for a professional worker to be educationally qualified and in possession of the necessary license or certification; she must continue to demonstrate competence and responsibility in the real world.

Against this background of doubt, professional persons continue to ply their trade in the delivery of human services. Faced with a dazzling array of options, mental health workers try to help children and families with problems. And however depressed and doubtful the individual professional worker may feel, the public continues to believe that professionals are people with special expertise who can effectively help people in need. The dilemma can be great when a professional attempts simultaneously (1) not to disappoint the public or herself concerning the expertise image, (2) to acknowledge honestly lack of certain skills or power to help, and (3) to comply with a variety of accountability procedures, some of which take time away from what the public thinks a professional should be doing. Assuming that the professional worker incorporates the public image as part of her self-concept, it is imperative that she also consider her fallibility. In this context, it is instructive to review mistakes we professionals make and why we make them.

Sometimes it is our knowledge base that is at fault. Errors are made because of *collective ignorance*. A personal example concerns the diagnosis and treatment of a girl with Prader-Willi syndrome. Laura was first seen at the age of three years. She was one of twins and had had a very difficult birth. Early feeding was difficult, and her very survival was in question. Development in all areas was slow and, at the age of three, she tested in the mildly retarded range. Over the years, the mother consulted our Mental Development Center occasionally about educational placement and her serious behavior problems, particularly her insatiable appetite, which was, indeed, phenomenal. She stole food and ate everything from pet food to garbage. In addition, she was selfish, demanding, and even sadistic. Because of her constant eating, everyone connected with the center, whether we admitted it or not, operated on the assumption that Laura had been deprived of maternal affection and attention as an infant. Although we tried to absolve the mother of guilt, it was assumed that Laura had been "starved for affection" in comparison with her competent, healthy twin brother. When Laura was eleven years old, a staff member suggested that she might have Prader-Willi syndrome, a relatively rare condition but one which had been diagnosed in another Center case showing similar behavior. Because it was thought to occur only in boys, this possibility had not been considered. When the diagnosis was confirmed, we all felt humbled and chagrined as we rethought the hypotheses we had used to explain, and treat, Laura's problems. Of special concern was the perception of maternal deprivation, which the mother may have obtained from us. At least we were honest with her about our previous lack of knowledge. This kind of mistake can happen to anyone, but it should warn professionals not to assume that the facts are inviolable or the theoretical assumptions untouchable. As new knowledge appears, today's facts may turn out to be tomorrow's errors.

Another reason for professional mistakes can be *ignorance on the part of a single individual.* I am acquainted with a ten-year-old girl named Sandy, who was placed in a residential facility for children with psychiatric problems when she was three years old. Before the admitting psychiatric examination, her mother had died and she was not sleeping, refused to eat, and regressed to soiling herself. The psychiatrist wrote a report full of careful observations, describing her as bizarre and out of contact with reality. He gave the specific example that she was constantly talking to her mother, when everybody knew that her mother had died. Clearly, the psychiatrist did not know normal three-year-old children and how much they fantasize. It is not an uncommon trap for professionals to overgeneralize the breadth of their expertise, seduced by the fact of their degree or certification. Psychologists have made similar errors with their tests by assuming that test data are objective and independent of situational factors. Perhaps the most distressing aspect of this kind of error is the passive acceptance of "expert" pronouncements by other professionals. In the seven years that Sandy had been in residential care, she continued to be diagnosed as schizophrenic because someone had once said she was psychotic.

This brings us to a third source of professional mistakes—namely, the professional's *need for certainty.* This leads the professional to make pronouncements and decisions that are more sure and more simplistic than the facts justify. Many common mistakes are understandable on the basis of the professional's feeling that he is expected to make the definitive statement, particularly to the parents. The parents search for a categorical explanation, even a label, for their child's problems, and it is tempting to comply. The fact that the same child may be variously labeled does not mean that most of the diagnosticians were in error, because each label may represent part of the whole. The error is made when a diagnosis is reduced to a single factor to explain the manifold aspects of a child's development and behavior. In the past, it was common practice to request psychological testing to determine if a given problem was "organic" or "functional." Although this is now considered less crucial, the same issue lurks in covert form when one is asked to determine if a child has a "learning disability" or an "emotional disturbance."

My experience can illustrate an error based on oversimplification. Jay was a bright child, brought for help when he was five years old because of out-of-control behavior, hyperactivity, temper outbursts, aggressiveness, and many fears. He had been viewed as a very difficult child since the time of his adoption in infancy, and his parents were at a loss to control him. He was badly mismatched for his family in terms of temperament, and their child-rearing practices had been at times harsh and punitive. His problems were interpreted in terms of psychodynamic factors intrinsic in him and in the family dynamics. After two years of psychotherapy and family counseling, his behavior was somewhat improved, but, on the basis of an observation by the father, the family sought neurological consultation and an electroencephalogram was done. This proved to be seriously deviant, an abnormality confirmed by another electroencephalogram two years later. Amphetamine medication was recommended, and the benefits were immediate and impressive.

Our first reaction was one of shock and disbelief, followed by guilt and rejection. Since Jay was an "organic" hyperactive, we thought we had grievously erred in offering psychotherapy. Suddenly, he became the responsibility of the neurologist. Finally, when we became accustomed to the fact of his having a "really" abnormal electroencephalogram and some measurable neurophysiological difference, we found that there was still much to do psychologically if we could only synthesize the two aspects of his problems. There are a lot of combinations in treatment that we find difficult to tolerate because the one seems to vitiate the other. Intellectually, we may appreciate the fact that almost all behavior represents some kind of interaction of organic and psychological–experiential factors, but few practitioners are prepared to work with both simultaneously. In this respect, the clinician is like a six-months-old infant who cannot hold a block in both the right and the left hand at the same time—one or the other is dropped.

The organic–functional issue is not the only one that can illustrate errors of oversimplification. Another issue is the extrinsic–intrinsic one that explains behavior solely in terms of its external consequences. In behavior therapy terms, one often reads that behavior is "attention-seeking." This suggests that the child is motivated by nothing except the immediate reactions of the people around him and, of course, the "cure" would be to ignore, punish, or reward alternative modes of behavior. A particularly poignant example concerns the behavioral treatment of a five-year-old, mildly retarded girl placed in a regional residential center. She spent her weekends at home and, on returning to the institution, would cry and carry on in the cottage. In order to stop this behavior, the staff hit upon the idea of placing her in a large cardboard packing crate as a "time-out" procedure. This particular error of oversimplification was partly the result of theoretical bias and partly the result of frustration. The child care staff, given a crying, screaming child, was helpless in trying to comfort her. If the staff had empathized with her separation distress, their guilt feelings would have been intolerable. So they did the only thing in their power to do; that is, they manipulated immediate external conditions in the name of behavior therapy.

In addition to unfounded certainty in diagnosis and treatment, there are many errors of this type in prognosis. Everyone has had the experience of reading old reports that are definite—and definitely wrong! Hindsight, of course, is always better than foresight, but individual predictions, usually based on the diagnostic labels, are often given with a certitude that is truly amazing. Not so long ago, if a child fell in the range of "educable mentally retarded" (that is, with an IQ between 50 and 70), it was said that he would never surpass an academic level of fourth grade, and if the IQ were between 35 and 50, that "he will never learn to read." This is a good example of stereotyping the individual who, in fact, may do either worse or better than the expectancy, which is only an average for a large group of individuals sharing some single characteristic. If clinicians could help consumers to understand probability, it might be safe to make predictions, but many reports are couched in absolutes.

The fourth category of reasons for professional mistakes may be labeled professional *denial*. This familiar mechanism of seeing what one wants to see is not restricted to laypersons. Sometimes we do this by isolating our area of interest. There are many special therapies available that focus on one or another developmental aspect. Therapists are easily seduced, particularly if they work with young children. For example, I know of a two-year-old boy who achieved a Bayley Mental Development Index of 70 after a number of visits and observations. In addition, he had a specific language disorder, both expressive and receptive. He used only a half-dozen single words, and he did not respond to any verbal instructions or use any pointing responses. He was referred for language therapy but, two years later, his mother returned. She reported that the speech therapist had said that now her son was "just fine." He could enter a regular nursery school, and her worries about his development should be over. She remarked, "But I am not so sure that, compared to my other children, everything really is all fixed up." The child's language was markedly improved; he was using sentences and responded to simple, one-level verbal directions. However, on retesting, his Stanford-Binet IQ was 70—again. The language therapist had done an excellent job, and it was no longer possible to detect a specific language disorder, but his reasoning and perceptual–motor skills were not at the level of a normal four-year-old. Although the recommendation of "regular" nursery school seemed appropriate, it was also useful to suggest some supplementary activities. And the mother was right in her observation.

Many other illustrations could be used, particularly in the field of developmental disabilities. We are now in a period where early identification and intervention are stressed, and some workers have almost a rescue fantasy about what they can do. However, it is an uncomfortable fact that we have no hard data regarding the long-range effectiveness of early intervention with handicapped children, particularly those with an identified organic condition (Brassell, 1977). This should not deter us from trying all we know, but we should do so with proper humility. The current stress on early identification is the present "up" side of the decision-making coin. Formerly, diagnosis was postponed because "there is nothing that you can do." But in our zeal to counteract this attitude—still prevalent in the medical profession—we must be cautious not to oversell our product. A similar attitudinal reversal is occurring in the push toward "mainstreaming" handicapped youngsters, now that we have proven the limitations of self-contained special classes. To date, comparable data are not available for alternative forms of special education. A very real dilemma for the conscientious psychologist concerns recommendations for educational placement for a specific child when factors such as teacher selection, peer group response, and supportive services are unknown.

A final example shows dilemmas, as well as mistakes, in dealing with the mechanism of denial on the part of both parents and professionals. David, whom I have known since he was four, was very slow in development in all areas. At the age of four, he was still bottle fed and no effort in toilet training had started. He had virtually no speech, was very dependent, and clung to his mother. However, he tested between 80 and 90 on intelligence tests and definitely showed more potential than his behavioral achievements suggested. After family counseling, he entered public school, was

classified as a "learning disabled" child, and received special help
from a learning disabilities-trained teacher. Gradually he became
more independent, less fearful, and more outgoing. But he progressed slowly academically and continued to disappoint his mother,
who tried every kind of special therapy that she chanced to come
across in her extensive readings. When he was eleven, David was
reevaluated and all the tests concurred in indicating an IQ in the
65–70 range. Suddenly, the school personnel saw him differently
and requested his immediate placement in a program for the retarded. Some even expressed resentment that they had been "fooled
into wasting their time" with him as a learning disabled child. The
mother, too, was indignant and disbelieving. Despite the counseling,
she had continued to believe that he was going to be a "late
bloomer," and she interpreted the evaluation as indicating that his
educational and psychological treatment had been remiss. She
redoubled her efforts in dietary treatment, occupational therapy,
and optometric programs. In the meantime, this child's frustrations
and feelings of failure became even more painfully obvious in his
questions about what was really wrong with him and why the children teased him. Understandably perhaps, the mother left our
counsel and sought help elsewhere. Her denial would not be of concern except that it blinded her to the child's feelings and made it
impossible for her to appreciate any achievements that he made. He
could never do well enough. At the same time, the school's haste to
transfer him seemed to reflect the disappointment of the learning
disabilities teacher rather than the academic or social needs of
the child.

A general comment is in order about professionals who devote their lives to serving only children, and thereby invoke a time
limitation on their span of interest. There is a tendency to deny the
future and to ignore the problems faced when these same children
reach adulthood. The only cure is to have some mechanism for following children throughout the years—even after the magical age
of twenty-one. Then one encounters many surprises, both happy and
unhappy. Not everything is worse than we expect. I am well acquainted with a young man whose early test scores were in the
retarded range. Over the years, his mental growth rate slowly accelerated, and he completed a difficult academic curriculum at the col-

lege level with good standing. This case is particularly instructive because he had no special help of any kind, so there is nothing to pinpoint for credit beyond the persistence of the boy himself.

The fifth category of reasons for professional mistakes might be labeled *projection*. The most common form is to project responsibility onto some factor beyond our control—often the parents. Laura's case is an instance where the parents were blamed on the basis of theory and without direct evidence. We have all been appalled by professional judgments that the child's condition *must* be the result of parental neglect. It is easy to understand why parents often feel so guilty or have such negative feelings about professional workers. There are other targets of projection, such as insufficiencies in the school program, poor medical care, and lack of resources. The danger is in using outside factors as a rationalization for inaction. It also is truly tragic if a professional worker projects an explanation into the situation and follows it with a recommendation that is not feasible. Child psychoanalysts were very much guilty of this in the past, recommending analysis as the only possibility of treatment when it simply was not available to the parents. This practice is not the present-day style, but the same problem exists when an unavailable special educational therapy is recommended as the "only thing to do."

The sixth category—*displacement*—somewhat overlaps with both denial and projection but deserves separate mention. In this category the clinician may act as if "out of sight, out of mind." The solution is always in a referral. The examples offer reprehensible illustrations of professional errors. A seventeen-year-old black girl named Joan came from a large, multiproblem family, so her fate was decided by professional agencies. Her younger sister died in a convulsive seizure in Joan's presence, and Joan remained very upset with the fear that she was "haunted" by this sister. Things went badly for her, and she ran away from home after accusing her stepfather of improper advances. In the juvenile court process, it was recommended that she be sent to an out-of-state residential treatment school. Many glowing things were written about this school, none of which were, in fact, true. The workers had a fantasy place in mind and were very pleased with their disposition of this very difficult case. This attitude can also be seen in the ease with which some professional workers recommend special class placement with no direct knowledge about whether expectations bear any relationship to reality.

We also often see instances of what might be called professional "form blindness"; forms are used as a quick way to solve problems. A thirteen-year-old boy, who had been in an out-of-state residential school for emotionally disturbed children since the age of eight, showed me a letter from his home-state social worker in which he was asked to "state your goals in regard to your family, school, and a job. You may ask a counselor for help in stating what you need. Mail the form back to me so that I can try to help you with your goals." In light of the fact that he had been pronounced "cured" and was on the waiting list for foster home placement for two years, this form request seemed ironic, as well as very impersonal.

Finally, professional errors sometimes occur out of simple *frustration*. It is not necessary to offer specific examples, but I mention it as a reminder that professionals are simply people trying to earn a living on the basis of their knowledge and good will. There are many situations that they cannot change or change as much as they would like, either because they do not have the knowledge or because of factors beyond their control.

This account of professional fallibility has not been intended to discourage professional activities but as a reminder of our vulnerability to cognitive and emotional misjudgments. In spite of mistakes, helpful suggestions are made and acted upon, and therapeutic interventions have made a significant difference in many children's lives. Although the public is more skeptical now than it has been in the past, requests for help still come in large numbers. Having dethroned the professional, we now offer a positive way to look at professional practice. For the purposes of this discussion, we will assume that the professional person is autonomous and empowered to make decisions independently. It is easy to blame the organization (whatever it may be) and disown personal responsibility, but one of the more significant changes in the latest code of ethics adopted by the American Psychological Association (1977) is a new sentence added to the principle of responsibility: "They [psychologists] accept responsibility for the consequences of their work and make every effort to ensure that their services are used appropriately" (p. 13). When psychologists are, in fact, hamstrung by their employing institutions, they face a crucial decision about conflicts that arise among values, good practice, and employer demands. However, it is imperative that the psychologist first think clearly about his own personal values—where they come from and what their effects may be on others.

Professional practice consists of a series of decisions, starting with the decision to accept a case or to provide a requested service. The next decision is the one about appropriate procedures to determine further action, then the one concerning recommendations. If the client moves into continuing service, the decisions are continuous—or should be—culminating in the final decision regarding termination. The number of decisions faced by the professional person would be paralyzing except that there are many guidelines. We will briefly review these, both in terms of their helpfulness as well as their limitations.

In the first place, the professional person looks to the official "rules and regulations" provided by the ethical statements, licensing and regulatory boards, and standards adopted by professional organizations for specific purposes. These codes represent some kind of group consensus; compliance at least guarantees that the professional person can remain in business. Although codes are a place to start, a closer look shows that they are not sacrosanct and are subject to revision as times change. A comparison of the *Revised Ethical Standards of Psychologists* (American Psychological Association, 1977) with the previous version (1953) shows many changes in what is defined as ethical practice. The issue of test interpretation provides a concrete example. In the standards considered official from 1953 to 1977, Principle 14 states that "Test scores, like test materials, are released only to persons who are qualified to interpret and use them properly" (p. 59). This was generally interpreted to mean that "IQ's are regarded as numbers that should rarely if ever be reported as such to students or to their parents" (Psychological Corporation, 1959, p. 2). Far more openness is encouraged in the latest revision of the standards: "The client has the right to have, and the psychologist has the responsibility to provide, explanations of the nature and the purposes of the test and the test results in language that the client can understand" (p. 14). Still, the access to records is a controversial issue; some practitioners argue that the client should know what is being said or written about him, and other professionals argue that the record should be tempered by the professional's opinion of the beneficial or harmful effect on the client. At present, the rules on disclosure do not cover every situation, and, in many instances, the psychologist is left to make his own decision.

Another set of guidelines is provided by "leaders," such as instructors, trainers, supervisors, and authors. However, any graduate student who has attended more than one class or read more than one book has discovered a wide variance in expert opinions. To mention only a few relevant to work with children, views differ regarding the choice of criterion-referenced or norm-referenced assessment techniques and how much assessment is needed before starting therapy. The selection of the mode of therapy is highly variable, depending more on the therapist's training and preferences than on the specific needs of the case. Family therapy, behavior therapy, chemotherapy, and psychotherapy are used for cases that appear much the same; and comparative outcome data are not available to assist the novice in making a choice in a given case. Finally, guidelines are provided by examining what is "usual, customary and reasonable" practice among one's peers. This criterion has been applied particularly to the problem of setting fees for services but can also be used in evaluating type and frequency of treatment.

All these guidelines have some value, and every practitioner should be well acquainted with codes, expert opinions, and common practice. But there are many exceptional situations in which the professional must go beyond the guidelines and make decisions based on personal conscience and her own professional judgment. It is my contention that the professional must recognize these are exceptions and weigh the risks to herself and to the client against the potential harm if the risks are not taken. Most of the examples of dilemmas in professional practice that have been offered here have dealt with diagnostic issues, partly because they could be described briefly. The two cases that follow illustrate dilemmas in treatment that led the psychologist involved to go beyond all the guidelines.

Karen ran away from home when she was fourteen years old and was located by the police in another state several weeks later. Her parents arranged for her hospitalization in a private psychiatric hos-

pital where she was very uncooperative and noncommunicative. The psychiatrist suggested the diagnosis of schizophrenia, a diagnosis the parents often quoted. Nonetheless, she was discharged to the care of her parents who, seeking a residential school, came to the Mental Development Center for recommendations. With a female worker, Karen was more responsive and had a great deal to say regarding her feelings of rejection in the home. It was this worker's opinion that she was not psychotic and could be treated on an outpatient basis. With some reluctance, the parents agreed to keep her at home and allow her to continue her education in public school.

Karen was willing to see the psychologist once a week, but the parents were dubious and did not agree to pay the fee that fit their income bracket. They also did not wish to see the psychologist themselves and tried to discourage continuation of treatment for Karen. This presented one dilemma since the Mental Development Center, as a community mental health agency, was publicly supported and expected to bill clients according to their ability to pay. It also presented the professional dilemma of treating an adolescent against the expressed wishes of the parents. In addition, one might well ask how successful the counseling could be if the family situation remained unchanged. The psychologist elected to treat Karen, to set a fee according to her own income (from babysitting), with the proviso that the parents at least knew that she was continuing to come.

During the period of treatment lasting over two years, there were only two contacts with the parents in which they complained their daughter was a prevaricator and expressed concern lest the psychologist believe her stories about them. They felt that she was a hopeless case destined to end up in a mental institution. Indeed, Karen had many stories to tell and complaints to register about her parents' neglect and humiliation of her. The details, of course, could never be checked for veracity. A particular dilemma arose when she described her plans to run away again on a certain day and to a specific destination. If she had carried out this plan, the psychologist might well have been considered liable since she did not warn her parents.

Diagnostically, there was a problem of how far to go to investigate the possibility of neurological factors. According to school reports, Karen's behavior changed dramatically between the seventh and ninth grades. Karen reported that she had blacked out and fallen from a tree and hurt her back. She reported other falls occurring without loss of consciousness. The school reported instances of strange behavior. On a math test, she turned in two pages of poetry, and it was reported that other teachers felt that she gave incoherent and irrelevant answers to questions asked of her. Her school performance deteriorated, and she showed angry outbursts. When these various episodes were reported to the parents, they took this as confirmation that she was "crazy," as they thought. Indeed, her behavior at times seemed "out of contact with reality," and a therapist might also legitimately have requested a psychiatric opinion or special testing, such as the Rorschach. With some trepidation, Karen's therapist avoided any specific diagnostic investigations, on the basis that these would confirm Karen's fears and suggest that the therapist agreed with the parents. There was a risk that Karen would prove to be psychotic, but the potential danger to the therapeutic relationship seemed to be the greater risk.

The final dilemma occurred when Karen applied to colleges and several wrote asking us for a report of her diagnosis and course of psychotherapy. She was no longer in therapy at that time (because she felt she no longer needed it), so it was difficult to decide what would be relevant to the college admissions officers. Although this case was happily resolved, many decisions were made contrary to the usual guidelines, for which the psychologist needed special justification.

The case of seventeen-year-old Jeff was even more exceptional. He lived alone with his mother and cared for her during a terminal illness. After her death, he lived briefly with a number of relatives, but no permanent arrangement could be made. He was attending special classes in public high school when he was referred to the district office of the Department of Mental Health and Retardation for placement. The placement was to a private forty-bed institution, mainly for older and more retarded clients. He was resentful, angry, and uncooperative, and the staff requested a counselor from the Mental Development Center. Particularly they complained that he "did not accept his mental retardation" and would not comply with the rules. There was a critical episode a few months later where he verbally threatened the staff and brandished a knife. When he was scolded and restrained, the excitement escalated, police were called, and he became totally out of control. He was taken to jail and his counselor was called in. The institution refused to accept him again, and he was returned to the custody of the district office, which declared him to be in need of treatment for mental illness rather than retardation. Everything seemed to fall to pieces; Jeff was particularly excited because he felt that he was "going crazy" and would be committed as was his father, who had been in a mental hospital for many years. The counselor, of course, knew that this was a long-standing fear of Jeff's and was appalled by the probability that Jeff would now be placed in a mental institution himself.

At this point, the counselor invited Jeff to stay with him in his home until he calmed down and some other arrangements could be made. Jeff asked, "What are you doing this for?" He came to live with the counselor and his wife, who eventually proceeded with the necessary legal requirements for temporary guardianship. This action, although approved in the name of "child advocacy," goes far beyond "usual, customary, and reasonable" and was viewed with suspicion and even disapproval by professional colleagues and agency representatives.

Jeff's case raises many questions. First is the matter of changing roles. Is it possible or advisable to continue as therapist when one is also personal guardian and sharing a home? Was the therapist correct in assuming that the governmental bodies would proceed toward commitment and that this would have a permanently damaging effect on Jeff? It is interesting to speculate on the reasons for official disapproval. Was it only because of the irregularity of the move, or was there some feeling of being put to shame by the unselfishness of the action? Perhaps the greatest question has to do with the sheer impracticality of this kind of intervention. Although it was feasible for Jeff and his therapist and was a reasonably successful placement, therapists have limited resources for such advocacy and cannot afford to take the place of friends and relatives for every client. The immediate problem faced by Jeff was solved, but professional responsibility extends beyond the single case.

The final case illustrates a dilemma that has yet to surface as a major problem in the literature but that can be anticipated as the by-product of increased use of third-party payments. Funding agencies, private as well as public, are demanding accountability, not only to prove that services were rendered as billed, but also to prove their effectiveness. For example, the Cuyahoga County Community Mental Health and Retardation Board of Ohio requires that participating programs specify five measurable impact objectives that will have direct bearing on the client's everyday life. These, of course, are couched in terms of demonstrable change in the client's social, school, or work adjustment. This represents a problem when one is dealing with chronic situations in which the client has achieved a kind of marginal adjustment.

The Smith family has many problems. The father is chronically depressed and holds a job with much effort. The mother is also depressed in addition to being phobic and guilt-ridden about the family situation. One grown son, moderately mentally retarded, was placed in a community residence where his continuance is always in some doubt because of his behavioral disturbances. The group home staff attributes much of his trouble to his mother's over-protectiveness and has decided that there should be no direct contact in the form of letters, telephone calls, or visits between the family and the young man. This is very hard for the mother, although she complies with their requirements. In addition, a younger daughter, Betty, has not been able to keep a job after graduating from special classes. Betty is very touchy, moody, and fearful of new experiences. Many direct efforts have been made in counseling Betty and offering vocational rehabilitation services, as well as indirect efforts through the parents, but with no demonstrable change. She prefers to remain at home where she helps with the housework, runs errands, and takes occasional babysitting jobs. She is socially isolated, has one or two friends whom she sees very infrequently, and does a lot of fantasizing about boy friends. The mother continues to request appointments, however, and seems to find comfort in coming in to review her frustrations. There probably has been no "demonstrable change" in the past three years.

One might ask if continued service should be provided under these static circumstances. Is this anything more than the purchase of friendship? In the therapist's opinion, there are real possibilities that the situation could get worse, including even the possibility that Betty could become psychotic. For this reason, the therapist has continued to offer support even though it is primarily on a maintenance basis. In a large program where the objectives are stated in terms of 80 percent success, one can afford to carry a few such cases, but clearly the record would be better if the "no-change" cases were closed. But if mental health professionals start to choose their cases on the basis of having good success, we may well come full circle to the situation of the early 1960s when only a privileged few gained access to mental health services (Gordon, 1965). Another question that the Smith family raises is the possibility of referral to a new agency that might succeed with a fresh approach. However, the mother does not want this change and would be very much upset if such a suggestion were made to her. The long-term relationship means a great deal to her, and the therapist's motivations in taking such a step would have to be very carefully considered.

What seems like a long time ago, Schafer (1954) discussed the interpersonal dynamics of the psychologist in the test situation. His comments apply equally well today to the psychologist as therapist. "The needs and problems of the tester in the testing situation are defined by his historical and social position as a particular type of professional man, by his spontaneous and imposed assumptions as to his professional and scientific responsibilities, by the additional responsibilities he assumes and gratifications he seeks because of his personality make-up, and by the behavior of the patient and the particular conflicts in the tester this behavior stimulates" (p. 7). Schafer goes on to describe the anxieties and defenses of psychologists as testers and the pushes and pulls toward grandiosity, hedging, propitiation, rebellion and withdrawal. These also plague the mental health professional in her role as therapist. The solutions, such as they are, to our dilemmas reside in constant self-examination, checking old facts and looking for new ones, reexamination of guidelines, looking at each client as a unique case, and the courage and energy to take risks in exceptional circumstances. Those in the mental health field may take comfort in knowing that our moral dilemmas are shared by our colleagues in the field of physical health: "There is an inescapable need for . . . moral sensibility, or the exercise of good judgment, morally speaking. We must have some way of applying general principles to particular cases, and we cannot do that by rule. For if we had rules for the application of the general to the particular, we would still need sensibility and judgment to decide which rules to apply where" (Kaplan, 1968, p. 163).

This chapter notes the contemporary challenges to professional power and effectiveness and reviews sources of potential mistakes and dilemmas in clinical practice with children and their families. Individual professionals must be concerned with recent emphases on accountability for their work. At times the expectations for, and pressures upon, them may seem unreasonable, but it is important that they examine their fallibility as well as their responsibility to make ethically sound choices for children.

Seven sources of mistakes professionals make in children's lives are identified: (1) collective ignorance, (2) ignorance on the part of a single individual, (3) the need for certainty, (4) denial, (5) projection, (6) displacement, and (7) frustration. There also are many opportunities in dilemma situations for individual professionals to demonstrate their ethical commitment to children. It is important that they become fully familiar with all ethical codes and other professional standards available, but the dilemma situations referred to here require going beyond the guidelines and depend most upon personal conscience and individual professional judgment.

Case Presentation for Problem Solving

Lee was first seen when he was four years old because his mother was concerned about his temper outbursts, nightmares, hyperactive behavior, and his pretending to be a girl. Some suggestions were made regarding sex education, reducing the amount and kind of television viewing, offering him more opportunities for play, and time-out procedures for discipline. A year later his mother returned because Lee was continuing to have difficulties. He was a major problem in kindergarten and was even more entrenched in his female identification. At this time the recommendation of twice-weekly psychotherapy with concurrent mother guidance was made.

In therapy, Lee proved to be a very excitable, fearful, confused boy who often got out of control, screamed, and threw things around. Besides setting limits, the therapist tried to discriminate between fantasy and reality and to identify his feelings of anxiety. The therapist understood Lee's pretending to be a girl as a defense against his fear that something was going to happen to turn him into a girl. As these questions were explored with the parents, the therapist learned that Lee had been threatened for playing with himself, that his mother believed his bad temper was evidence of his "being possessed by the devil," and that she felt physical punishment was the only way of discipline because "he is too young to reason with." She was adamant in these beliefs and found confirmation from relatives and her pastor. When she heard Lee carrying on in the therapy room, she punished him and warned him about "the devil in him."

Lee's confusion, excitement, and anxiety seemed, if anything, to increase during two months of psychotherapy. The therapist concentrated on behavior control and minimized verbal explanations or interpretations which usually ran counter to what he was told at home. Despite alternative suggestions offered to the mother, she continued to use physical punishment, not abusive, but certainly harsh and inconsistent. She felt that the only way to subdue him was to frighten him. He did become somewhat quieter in school but was not learning well. The nightmares continued; he referred to himself as "Laura"; and he developed frequent stomach aches.

Some questions that could be asked in this case presentation are: (1) How long should the therapist continue in the light of the mother's practices? (2) What should the therapist say to the school personnel when they express concern about his not learning and ask for a report? (3) Is it possible to apply a strictly behavioral approach if the mother does not concur in what is to be expected from a five-year-old boy? (4) If the case is to be discontinued, what kind of statement should be given to the mother? (5) What are the limits of parents' rights in disciplining their children? (6) Is there some approach with limited goals which would be acceptable to both therapist, as child advocate, and the parents? (7) Should the probability of future homosexuality be a matter of concern to the therapist?

Chapter 9

Strategies in
Bureaucracies

Brenda G. McGowan

Most professionals like to think of themselves as independent, dedicated, knowledgeable practitioners. Students in professional schools often envision themselves as carrying out the proud tradition of such professional forebears as Jane Addams, Bruno Bettelheim, Tom Dooley, and Anna Freud. Yet, increasing numbers of children's service professionals work as salaried employees in agencies and institutions where they cannot function autonomously and must constantly weigh children's interests against organizational interests. Therefore, despite the professional commitment of many individuals, a more accurate self-image for the average practitioner would be that of the loyal bureaucrat.

The twentieth century has witnessed a rapid bureaucratization of children's services, and historical evidence suggests that this trend is likely to continue for two reasons. First, any group desiring to attain specific social goals must have leadership and an authority structure, and it must give continued attention to the problem of organizational self-maintenance. Second, whenever a third party pays the costs of professional services, some type of formal organizational structure is essential to ensure fiscal accountability. Hence, the very goals of the children's rights movement, which include the provision of necessary services to all regardless of ability to pay, make increasing bureaucratization inevitable.

Despite the anarchist fantasies we all share occasionally, it would be counterproductive for professionals simply to fight the growth of bureaucracy. Instead, they must learn how to shape organizational structures so they do not interfere with the attainment of professional goals, and they must discover how to monitor and use bureaucratic policies and procedures for the benefit of their clients. This chapter will explore the dilemmas confronted by a professional working in a bureaucratic setting and examine alternative ways to ensure that organizational interests do not take precedence over children's needs.

Bureaucracy and professionalism, two of the major structural elements of American society, converge in many modern children's service organizations, and the professional working in such settings must understand the strengths and weaknesses of these two forms of organization and their interrelationship in order to serve children effectively. It should first be noted that bureaucracies and professions share certain common characteristics. Both require some type of community sanction, which is provided because of the societal benefits that may accrue from specialized use of knowledge and technical expertise. They are both expected to provide services in an equitable, impersonal manner. It is assumed that neither professional status nor organizational rank will be granted because of an individual's social characteristics or personal relationships, but, rather, they must be earned on the basis of knowledge and performance. These shared characteristics all have consequences for client service. For example, because of specialization in professions and bureaucracies, there are many gaps in service; efforts to treat the total person are frequently inhibited; and affective neutrality often results in dehumanizing treatment. However, since the ethical issues confronting all professionals are discussed elsewhere in this book, this chapter will consider only the practice dilemmas that are peculiar to the professional functioning in a bureaucracy.*

Some of the significant differences between professions and bureaucracies, which have specific consequences for client service, are: (1) Bureaucracies are based on a hierarchical authority structure, whereas professions employ a self-monitoring model. (2) Professionals are expected to put client needs first, whereas organizational loyalty is a priority for bureaucratic employees. (3) Organizations are goal-oriented, whereas professions tend to emphasize process or proper use of knowledge and technique. (4) Responsibilities of bureaucratic employees are carefully delineated and staff are expected to separate work obligations from personal life, whereas professionals are expected to place professional obligations above personal needs. (5) In bureaucracies, separation is made between policy making and administrative functions, whereas these roles are not distinguished in professional behavior.

Let us consider each of these differences in turn insofar as they may affect client service and create ethical dilemmas for the professional working in a bureaucracy. The traditional bureaucratic model is built on the assumption that the person occupying the superior position not only has greater authority but also has greater expertise and is therefore able to make better decisions than the supervisee. However, this type of hierarchical control may be inappropriate in professional situations for two reasons. First, promotions in bureaucracies are frequently based on seniority. Yet, as Merton (1958) has observed, because of what Veblen termed "trained incapacity," the longer someone is employed in an organization, the more likely he is to translate means into ends and to apply solutions that were used successfully in the past indiscriminately to new situations, which may require different responses because of changed conditions. To illustrate, a school principal may deny a teacher's request for a mental health consultation for a hyperactive child because her practice is to suspend every child who disrupts a class-

---

* See Litwak (1961) and Blau and Scott (1962, pp. 60–74) for further discussion of the similarities and differences between bureaucracies and professions.

room in order to demonstrate the seriousness of the situation to the child's parents; yet, in this case, the parents may already be involved and asking for professional help. The other reason that a hierarchical authority structure may be an inappropriate means of regulating professional behavior is that professional decisions must be based on a thorough assessment of all the factors in an individual situation, but since so little is really known about human behavior, professional interventions often require an element of art as well as science. Therefore, the supervisor, even if she has more experience and greater theoretical knowledge, may not understand the needs of an individual client as well as the practitioner whose assessment is based on extensive interpersonal contact. For example, a social worker may "know" that a foster home with which she has worked previously would be a better choice for a particular child than the one that her supervisor prefers on the basis of the description in the home study.

One of the distinguishing characteristics of all professionals is that they are bound by ethical codes prescribing a service ideal in which client interests are expected to come before personal interests. Although service organizations are also expected to benefit their clients, they are not bound to place individual client need above organizational interest; and as Gouldner (1963) has suggested, one of the best-kept secrets of service organizations is that the primary goal is often that of organizational self-maintenance. Aside from blatant abuses of power, which can occur in either professions or bureaucracies, this distinction regarding primary responsibility is likely to be most obvious when individual interests must be weighed against benefits for the total client population. For example, a private pediatrician might argue that the parents of one of her hospitalized patients should be permitted to visit mornings since they are unable to come during regular visiting hours. The hospital administrator may agree that this would be better for the individual child but decides that she cannot approve this request because it would set a precedent and create problems with the other patients. Similarly, professionals are obligated to use whatever resources are available to provide the services that are needed by their clients, whereas agency employees are often expected to limit current expenditure of resources so that their organizations will be able to meet the needs of future clients.

Another difference between bureaucracies and professions is that organizations have explicit goals and are expected to achieve measurable results, whereas the professional emphasis is on process rather than results. Because professional goals are so global, it is often more feasible for professionals to evaluate how knowledge and skills are used than to measure results. Many authors have documented the profound service delivery problems that are created by the professional tendency to emphasize process rather than product (Vinter, 1959, 1963; Cloward and Epstein, 1965; Freidson, 1970; and Mackey, 1964). In fact, one of the unanticipated benefits of increased governmental funding for human services is that professionals have been forced to accept some independent monitoring of their results and are developing better accountability procedures, such as problem-oriented records in social agencies, standardized testing of students in different school systems, and utilization review teams in hospitals. However, overemphasis on bureaucratic goals can create other ethical dilemmas for the professional. First, organizational goals often have a strong social control component so that professionals in school, court, or welfare settings may be expected to help their clients conform to societal norms rather than to help them determine their own goals. Second, bureaucratic goals are often very narrowly defined so that professionals may be inhibited from providing the full range of services that would benefit their clients. For example, a child welfare agency may limit homemaker service to families in which there has been documented child abuse rather than offer this service to all families in which children are not receiving adequate care. Third, an overemphasis on results may lead to a selection of clients who are most likely to succeed rather than provision of services to those most in need. This pattern, which has been termed *creaming,* has been clearly documented in services to the blind (Scott, 1967). Finally, effective results can often be achieved through questionable means that raise ethical dilemmas for the professional. For example, some of the new behavior modification programs for delinquent adolescents have reported successful results from the use of negative reinforcement techniques that totally violate the concept of client self-determination.

A fourth difference between bureaucratic and professional patterns of organization is that the responsibilities of bureaucratic staff are carefully defined and circumscribed, and since staff are expected to refrain from interfering in anyone else's area of expertise, it becomes very easy to "pass the buck." In contrast, professionals are expected to take total responsibility for their clients and to place professional responsibilities above personal interests. The dilemma for the professional in a bureaucracy is the degree to which she can overstep boundaries in order to meet client needs. For example, a special education teacher may feel that a child is ready to be transferred back to the regular classroom; however, efforts to effect such a transfer may jeopardize future relationships with the classroom teacher and the school principal. Similarly, the professional may feel a responsibility to work late in order to help a particular child, but in a bureaucratic setting such efforts are often defined as a form of "rate busting," and the professional may be subjected to strong informal pressure against being too eager.

Finally, bureaucratic personnel are expected to implement policies determined by the governing body in a uniform manner; although professionals may have policies that they use as general guidelines, they are expected to modify and adapt preestablished policies whenever necessary in order to meet the needs of an individual client. This difference can create tremendous tensions for the practitioner. To illustrate, a psychiatrist in private practice usually charges for services, but if her client is at risk and unable to pay, she can decide to waive the fee. However, a professional in a child guidance clinic may be told that she cannot see her client until the fee is paid, or a patient in a psychiatric hospital may be discharged or transferred because her insurance has expired, although her physician does not think she is ready.

As this brief discussion suggests, the professional functioning in a bureaucracy may confront many situations in which organizational needs conflict with, or overwhelm, the professional commitment to client interests. If these conflicts were always resolved in favor of the client, there would be little reason for concern. Certain tensions are inevitable and may serve to highlight problem areas and to stimulate productive change. However, because of the relative power of organizations, professions, and clients, such conflicts tend to get resolved, first, in favor of the organization and, second, in favor of the professional group. Client interests usually come last. This is illustrated by Billingsley's study (1964) of bureaucratic and professional orientations in three family and child welfare agencies. When asked under what conditions workers should give the needs of their clients priority, only 25 percent of the sample (N = 110) said professionals should do this if it required violating stated professional standards. Similarly, 61 percent said workers should carry out agency policy even if this required violating stated professional standards, and 97 percent agreed that the workers should do this even if it required violating community expectations. On the basis of these findings, Billingsley concluded: "Workers have been found to be relatively more oriented to carrying out agency policies and professional standards in that order, than to meeting client needs or community pressures" (p. 407). This study was conducted in the early 1960s; it is possible that respondents would display a somewhat different orientation now because professionals have become more sophisticated, at least in principle, about the vested interests of agencies and professional groups. However, in view of the current tight job market for human services professionals and the increasing concentration of power in large bureaucracies, it seems unlikely that actual behavior would be very different from that described in the Billingsley study.

It is useful for the emerging professional to be forewarned about some of the pressures in a bureaucratic setting and to understand the sources of these tensions. However, the urgency of these dilemmas becomes apparent only when she is confronted with an individual child in need and feels constrained from meeting that need. At that point the individual professional must decide such questions as: What is my obligation? What would be the most equitable solution? How can I intervene most effectively? Will I have any support? What will happen to my client if I "blow it"? Determining the answers to these questions can be a very difficult and lonely process. This chapter will consider next the organizational models that may alleviate some of the pressures on individual professionals. Guidelines for professional intervention to effect organizational change will be discussed in the final section.

Children's service professionals are generally quite sophisticated about the need to develop differential treatment plans to meet the needs of individual children. However, they often fail to recognize that organizational structures, like treatment techniques, are

162   Working for Children

tools that must be adapted for use in particular situations. Instead, organizational structures are usually viewed as givens to which professionals and clients must adapt. Yet, the traditional Weberian model of bureaucracy, which is employed in public schools, welfare departments, and some of the other major children's services agencies, is an inefficient and inappropriate mechanism for coping with the idiosyncratic problems presented by human services consumers. The therapeutic community model, which has been adopted in many residential settings, is an equally inefficient and inappropriate mechanism for handling routine tasks such as payment of fees in a child guidance clinic or laundry and meal preparation in a large institution.

As Litwak (1961) has suggested, a rationalistic bureaucracy with rules, division of labor, and hierarchical authority structure is the most efficient way to organize behavior in situations that require expert knowledge, yet demonstrate a fair degree of routine and predictability such as record keeping and payroll. On the other hand, a primary group model of organization with diffuse communication patterns and flexible role allocations is the most efficient means of handling nonroutine situations that require sharing of information and quick response such as intakes and psychiatric emergencies.

Most children's service professionals have had contact with parents who attempt to organize family life according to rigid rules, clear-cut division of labor, and a strict authority structure; they are quick to recognize the pathological consequences for children who belong to a family in which few spontaneous decisions or communications are permitted. However, this bureaucratic pattern may have an equally pathological effect on organizational dynamics. Similarly, as it is difficult for children to master certain maturational tasks in families in which there are no consistent rules or structure, so professionals cannot function efficiently in settings in which there are no procedures for handling routine tasks. It is not that any one form of organization is good or bad but rather that organizational structure should reflect the goals and tasks of the agency. Since any one agency may serve several different functions and client groups, it may have to use different organizational models at different times or in different sectors of the agency. The organizational structure should be considered a tool to be used and modified in relation to client needs.

It is not possible to discuss alternative organizational models in depth in this one chapter. However, there are certain essential factors that the professional should consider in evaluating whether the organizational model employed by her agency is appropriate for meeting client needs. First is the degree to which the organization is structured so as to permit professionals to use their knowledge and skills to the fullest. For example, does the structure permit full exchange of information among different professional groups? Are professional staff free to respond quickly and flexibly to individual client situations requiring immediate attention? Are routine tasks handled efficiently by nonprofessional staff? Litwak (1961) has suggested an appropriate model of organization for what is termed a *professional bureaucracy.*

A second factor that must be considered is how the agency acquires information about what is happening in the social environment and makes decisions about future directions that take these changes into account. In order to remain relevant to client needs, a children's services organization must be attuned to changing social values and mores; acquire adequate knowledge of current research bearing on their client population; and stay informed about economic, political, and legal changes that may affect future agency policies and resources. Therefore, it is essential that the agency's organizational structure be designed in a way that makes provision for gathering information from all relevant sources and for utilizing decision-making processes that incorporate all these sources of information. To illustrate, many child welfare agencies in New York City were unprepared for the recent, rather dramatic shift in the types of children needing foster care; yet, if they had been attuned to changing demographic trends related to the increased availability of contraception and abortions, they could have anticipated a sudden decline in the number of infants and a relative increase in the number of teen-agers requiring foster care (Bernstein, Snider, and Meezan, 1975).

The third—and perhaps most important—factor that must be considered in relation to an agency's organizational structure is the role assigned to clients. As Eliot Studt (1965, p. 49) has commented in an article on fields of social work practice: "As social workers in direct relationship with an individual or a group, we have emphasized the dignity of the client as the primary problem solver. But we have generally ignored the impact on the client's life of the organizational role provided for him by the system to which he becomes related because he needs service. If we examine many of our problem management systems, especially those with extensive public responsibility for large populations, we can observe that the organizational role provided for the client is that of a low-status subordinate whose chief function in the organization is to be a 'good' recipient. Because we have ignored the importance of the client's organizational role for the service process, we have often permitted that role to express primarily the community's devaluation of the person who needs service." Certainly, this comment is equally applicable to many other kinds of human service professionals.

There is no one correct organizational role for clients because this depends entirely on the age and needs of the child and the function of the organization. Adolescents can be asked to assume more responsibility than younger children; the organizational role of clients in a residential setting has a very different impact and must be designed more carefully than that of clients in a family life education program. However, as recent studies on the tutoring by children of older children have demonstrated, even relatively young children can experience significant personal growth and provide an important service to others when they are assigned responsible organizational roles. Therefore, it is important for professionals to consider how children can be involved in policy determination, direct service provision, community organizing efforts, and consultation to agency staff. This, of course, may require a change in professionals' traditional psychological set, which evolved in settings in which the professional always occupied the dominant position. However, if the professional's primary goal is to maximize client growth and well being, this should ultimately be a more effective approach.

Related to the issue of organizational roles assigned to clients is the question of agency provisions for safeguarding accountability to clients. Probably the most important action professionals can take to ensure that organizational interests do not take precedence over children's needs is to develop strong consumer protection mechanisms in their agencies. There are many different ways this can be done, depending on agency function and client population. It is not possible to discuss the full range of consumer accountability mechanisms in this chapter. However, with imagination, professionals can design appropriate consumer protections for every type of setting. Accountability devices such as ombudsmen, client grievance committees, fair hearings, consumer evaluation surveys, and citizen advocates have been used successfully to protect client interests in a range of children's services agencies. What is important is that some formal mechanism be established to ensure that clients obtain the services and resources to which they are entitled. No matter how well-intentioned the staff and administration are, problems are inevitable in any service bureaucracy; and given the sometimes conflicting interests of the organization, professional staff, and consumers of service, it is essential that mechanisms be devised to protect the interests of children.

Even in organizations carefully structured to serve client needs, situations will occasionally arise in which the professional feels constrained from serving children's interests because of some bureaucratic policy or procedure. At that point, the professional must decide whether or not to take any action and, if she decides to intervene, what is the most effective way to proceed.

The professional's first step when confronted with such a situation is to assess the problem. First, what is its source or location? Does it reflect a larger social policy issue, such as inadequate level of welfare benefits, or some deficiency in the community service network, such as lack of homemaker or daycare services? Is it an intra-organizational problem, such as a discriminatory admissions policy or poorly trained staff? Or is it an individual problem that cannot be solved by existing professional knowledge, such as violent assaultive behavior in the classroom?

Understanding the source of the problem will help the professional to decide whether it can be resolved by any action she might take at the organizational level. For example, if her client is denied needed mental health services because community resources are inadequate and there is a long waiting list, the professional might eventually want to work with a community planning agency to document the need for additional resources. But if her client is not accepted for treatment because the agency policy requires parental cooperation, then the professional would want to challenge this policy immediately. Professionals certainly have an obligation to engage in social action around major policy issues, such as inequitable distribution of income, and to conduct research in areas in which current knowledge is inadequate, such as treatment of violent youth; however, these are long-term endeavors that are unlikely to benefit an individual child with whom the professional is currently working.

If the professional concludes that an organizational problem is interfering with her capacity to meet her client's need, it is essential that she define this problem carefully and secure as much evidence as possible in order to understand the extent and severity of the problem and to document this adequately. This is especially important when her definition of the problem is likely to be different from those of others in the organization.

The manner in which the problem is defined will depend in large measure on the professional's orientation. For example, in a mental health clinic, one therapist's explanation for a client's withdrawal from treatment might be that the type of therapy provided was not appropriate for a low-income client overwhelmed by financial and medical difficulties, whereas another might argue that client withdrawal reflects an unresolved problem in the transference relationship. Professional ethics would seem to demand that we first consider the possibility of some organizational or professional deficiency before concluding that whatever problem arises is the client's fault. However, the professional who takes this stance may find herself in frequent conflict with her organization because of the widespread tendency to "blame the victim."

Once the professional has defined the problem carefully, she is ready to decide whether or not she should intervene. There are three factors that should influence this decision: the sanction for her intervention, the extent and severity of the problem, and the feasibility of effecting desired change. The most important issue for the professional to consider is *sanction*. What right does the professional have to intervene? How does she know her assessment of the problem is correct and that her objective is justified? What gives her the authority to challenge the authority of the organization, which may have a long history of effective service to children and enjoy strong community support? Certainly any true professional will approach such a decision judiciously and will decide to go ahead only after careful thought about the potential costs and benefits and thorough self-scrutiny about her own motives and biases.

However, there are several possible sources of sanction for the professional's intervention. The strongest sanction derives from law. Briar's suggestion (1967) that the social worker's primary obligation is to the civil rights of his client is applicable to other professions as well. If an organization is in any way violating a client's legal rights, the professional has a clear mandate to intervene, knowing that, if necessary, she can achieve her objective in court. Similarly, a professional has a clear right to intervene if her client is denied any administrative entitlement because regulations of public agencies have the force of law.

When there has been no violation of law or administrative entitlement, it is much more difficult for the professional to decide whether she has the right to intervene. However, sanction can derive from several other sources. First, the organization's own written statements may provide sanction if the problem involves some violation of the agency's explicit objectives, policies, or procedures.

A second important source of sanction is the professional's code of ethics. Professional codes are designed to protect the public from unethical conduct by members and to provide grounds for sanctioning members who violate ethical prescriptions. However, the codes of many professions are written in such global, abstract terms that they do not provide specific behavioral guidelines for members. In practice, it seems that their primary function has more often been protecting professional groups from outside regulations. Nevertheless, ethical codes can provide some guidance to the professional who is uncertain whether she has a right to intervene in a particular situation; and because some of these codes, such as the recently revised standards of the American Psychological Association (1977), have increased their consumer orientation, the individual who wishes to engage in some action to protect her client's interests can often use the code of ethics as a source of sanction. For example, the Code of Ethics of the National Association of Social Workers and the Standards of the American Psychological Association both make provisions for client confidentiality. Therefore, a school social worker or psychologist might want to challenge her school principal's directive that mental health staff give classroom teachers a full report of all contacts with children in their classrooms, on the grounds that this would violate her code of ethics.

Another type of sanction derives from what has been termed value power. As Patti and Resnick (1972) have suggested, professionals who articulate and represent values to which other of their colleagues are committed often possess informal power within their organization, and this power can be used to build colleague support for organizational change efforts. Staff consensus regarding an organizational problem that is interfering with the capacity to meet client needs can serve as a strong catalyst for change. The sanction derived from shared professional values is especially important in interdisciplinary settings. For example, the social worker in a private psychiatric hospital who is concerned about the agency policy of discharging patients as soon as their insurance expires will probably be able to accomplish little on her own. However, if she can persuade her colleagues in various departments to challenge this policy on the grounds that it violates the treatment contracts they have established with their patients, she will greatly increase the likelihood of effecting some change.

A final and crucial source of sanction is provided by the client. Because of the principle of client self-determination, there are very few instances in which a professional would be justified in undertaking an advocacy action on behalf of her client without the client's explicit agreement. Occasionally it is impossible or inappropriate for the professional to ask the client's permission because of time constraints (for example, emergency hospitalization), the nature of the reason for the professional's involvement (investigation of a child neglect complaint), or the type of client (severely retarded or very young children, for example). However, professionals should approach such situations very cautiously and, if possible, should at least discuss their plans with someone who can be presumed to represent the client's interests. Client sanction is not as strong as some other sources of sanction. Because of the relative power of organizations and clients, it alone is usually not sufficient to guarantee success. However, client sanction is an ethical necessity and may help the professional to decide how to proceed in ambiguous situations. For example, when a professional is confronted with a situation in which action on her part might produce long-term benefits but risk the child's immediate well-being, or when she has to decide whether to intervene in a way which might benefit a larger group of clients or to limit his action to advocacy for an individual child, the client's wishes should determine her decision. Although the professional may feel that a particular situation offers a good opportunity to effect institutional change or that this child's needs are not as great as those of other clients, the professional has a responsibility while working with a particular child to put that individual's needs first.*

A second important factor the professional must evaluate in deciding whether to intervene is the *extent and severity of the problem*. Like the boy who cried wolf, the professional who overreacts to every minor problem is likely to lose her capacity to be heard and may not be effective when a serious problem arises.

Finally, before deciding whether to intervene, the professional should assess the *feasibility* of any proposed action. Some organizational problems require professional action because of the severity of the problem and the clear violation of client rights. In less serious, more ambiguous situations, however, professional action is discretionary. In these cases, in addition to considering the nature of the problem and the sanction, the professional should evaluate the likelihood of success. Since it may be counterproductive, or at least wasteful of professional time and resources, to undertake what is probably a futile cause, professional wisdom—not cowardice—would dictate that feasibility be considered in discretionary situations.

Once the professional decides to intervene, the first task is to define her objective. This is determined in large measure by the nature of the problem. However, it is essential that she assess what she realistically can and cannot hope to achieve. For example, the

---

* Other authors have argued the contrasting position that professionals should try to evaluate the greater good. See, for example, Ad Hoc Committee on Advocacy, 1969; Brager, 1968; Panitch, 1974; and Gilbert and Specht, 1976 for a further discussion of this point.

professional may conclude that the agency's admissions procedures have a discriminatory effect because of the type of testing used routinely. Rather than tackling the problem of biased tests directly, however, she may decide that all she can accomplish at this point is to obtain an exception to policy for one particular child or to persuade the organization that different criteria should be used to evaluate one group of potential clients. If she is successful in an individual instance, she may later be able to effect change in the entire admission procedure. When engaged in an organizational change effort, it is often essential for the professional to work first for intermediate or short-term objectives; once these are achieved, she may be able to move toward the long-term goal.

There are two critical decisions that the professional must make in regard to her objective. First, she must decide whether the goal can be achieved within the organization as it is presently structured (policies, procedures, personnel, technology, resources) or whether some structural change is necessary. Second, she must decide whether the desired change should benefit an entire group of children or whether individual benefit is sufficient. Trade-offs must be considered at this point because it is usually easier to attain an objective for an individual child that does not require structural change than to effect structural change that will help a larger group of clients; however, the long-term benefits of the latter approach may justify the increased professional effort it will demand. Certainly, if everything else is equal, it is appropriate to work for structural change, but the professional's primary responsibility is to her client. Therefore, when establishing objectives, the individual child's need must be the primary consideration.

Before selecting a strategy for intervention, the professional must make a careful assessment of all the factors that may promote or inhibit the change desired. This should include the environmental, organizational, professional and client characteristics affecting the situation.*

Two critical factors that must be evaluated at this point are: (1) the likely response of organizational decision makers to the

---

* The force field analysis is a useful tool for making such an assessment. See Jenkins (1949) or Brager and Holloway (1978) for a full description of this technique.

proposed change, and (2) the resources the professional has available to effect the change desired (Brager and Holloway, 1978). Consideration of these factors together with the nature of the problem, objective, and sanction for intervention should enable the professional to select an appropriate strategy.

The professional's strategy may be collaborative, mediatory, or adversarial. A collaborative strategy is ordinarily used when there is no disagreement about the problem situation and when the professional hopes to elicit the change desired from the organization by using techniques of intercession or persuasion. A mediatory strategy is often used when the professional and the organization disagree about a particular situation, but the professional hopes to be able to achieve a compromise through negotiation because there is some agreement about underlying values. An adversarial strategy should be used only when there is a serious disagreement about the basic values underlying the problem situation. A collaborative strategy relies almost exclusively on the use of communication skills, whereas a mediatory approach employs implied use of power in combination with communication skills. An adversarial strategy relies primarily on the use of power.

As some of the community organizing literature has suggested, change strategies can range from consensus to conflict, but most change efforts demand a mix of different types of interventions during the change process. The primary modes of intervention include intercession, or pleading on the client's behalf; persuasion, or convincing by reasonable argument; negotiation, or settling by mutual discussion and compromise; pressure, or exerting strong and continuous influence; and coercion, or compelling by force (McGowan, 1973). Any or all of these interventions can be used in an organizational change effort.

As suggested above, the primary factor influencing the professional's selection of a particular mode of intervention is the type of response she can expect from significant decision makers in the organization. However, the professional must also consider what resources she has available. For example, how much time is she willing to devote to this effort? Does she have the support of key colleagues? What is her reputation in the organization? Does she have an informal relationship with any of the significant decision makers? Would any associates be able to advocate more effectively for her proposal because they have better access to organization decision makers? Does she have any special knowledge or skills that the organization needs? How much will the organization be willing to concede in order to retain her?

Analysis of all these factors should take place during the assessment phase. Once the professional has clearly defined the problem, evaluated the factors that may promote or inhibit change, identified her objective, and selected an appropriate and feasible strategy, she is ready to move into what Brager and Holloway (1978) have termed the *preinitiation phase*. During this period the professional continues to reevaluate and plan her strategy; she may also want to obtain additional information, sound out colleagues about her plan, arouse organizational concern about the problem, establish links with organizational decision makers, and generally act in ways that will help to structure the situation so that the introduction of the change idea will be timely and appropriate.

As Litwak and others (1970) have suggested, the first task in the change process is that of drawing attention to the problem. It is at this time that the change idea is actually introduced. Drawing attention to a problem often requires different tactics than solving the problem. Therefore, the professional may have to plan sequential strategies. For example, in order to draw attention to a problem, it is sometimes necessary to dramatize the situation or disrupt routine procedures. But once the major organizational decision makers acknowledge that a particular problem exists, they may take responsibility for mobilizing the organizational resources necessary to solve the problem. In other cases, the professional, especially if she holds high status in the organization, may only have to mention a situation in order to draw attention to the problem with which she is concerned. However, if this problem arose because of basic value differences between the professional and the organization, she may have to exert tremendous pressure in order to negotiate and implement a satisfactory solution. As in all the other phases of the organizational change process, the professional's approach to this final task of solving the problem should be based on a careful assessment of her resources and the likely response of significant organizational decision makers to her interventions.

It is not possible to discuss organizational change strategies in detail in this chapter.* However, there are a few basic principles that should be identified. First, bureaucracies, like other social systems, are in a constant state of change because problems are endemic to formal organizations (Caplow, 1964). Therefore, the professional's task is not so much to precipitate change as to shape and direct the change that is taking place naturally. Since change occurs as a result of efforts to solve specific organizational problems, sufficient attention must be drawn to the problem about which the professional is concerned to make it an organizational issue. Many change efforts fail because of professionals' reluctance to create organizational stress around problem situations.

Second, problems and objectives can be defined in many different ways. The more the professional can describe problems and identify goals in terms acceptable to the organization, the more likely she is to succeed. Similarly, the more specific she can be, the less threatening the change proposal is likely to be.

Third, the stronger the professional's position and reputation in the organization, the greater her chance of success. Therefore, the professional who wishes to engage in organizational change efforts should strive to perform her assigned tasks effectively and should attempt to establish a reputation as a responsible, knowledgeable, and committed staff member.

Fourth, organizations, like people, often display marked resistance to change. Therefore, although change is a constant part of organizational life, the professional should anticipate resistance to any proposal for change and plan ways to handle it. For example, timing and terminology may be crucial. If the objective is introduced in terms acceptable to the organization at a time when the administration is seeking answers to a problem for which this may provide a partial solution, the professional's chances of success are much greater than if the proposal is introduced in unfamiliar terms at a time when critical decision makers are preoccupied with other problems. The professional must also remember that any type of change takes time. This is especially true when there is strong organizational resistance to the proposed change effort. Even revolu-

* Interested readers should see Brager and Holloway (1978) and Patti and Resnick (1972) for fuller discussion of this subject.

tions, which appear to occur so quickly, take place only after a long period of stress in which the forces for change are building. Therefore, the individual professional must often be content with simply laying the groundwork for a change effort that will occur much later and for which someone else will probably receive credit.

Fifth, what has been termed the *principle of parsimony* (Meyer, 1976; Brager and Holloway, 1978) suggests that the simplest, most direct approach is usually the most appropriate. Although the professional may occasionally have to employ an adversarial strategy and use a range of complex interventions in order to accomplish her goal, whenever possible she should attempt to achieve her objective in as collaborative a manner and with as little effort as possible. Not only does this approach save her time and energy, but it also preserves whatever resources she has for use in a situation that may demand a more elaborate, adversarial approach. A recent study of 150 incidents of case advocacy on behalf of children revealed that adversarial strategies were used in only 26 percent of the incidents. These interventions were carried out by persons especially trained in the use of advocacy techniques, which suggests that effective advocates abjure the use of power whenever possible (McGowan, 1973).

Sixth, it should be noted that the professional is as bound by her code of ethics when coping with organizational problems as she is when dealing with individual clients. No matter how "right" the professional's ultimate objective, she has an obligation to observe professional standards such as confidentiality and honest, direct communication with colleagues, while attempting to effect the organizational change desired.*

Finally, whenever the professional is able to involve her client directly in the organizational change process, not only is she likely to increase the probability of success, but she may also enable the client to increase her sense of competency and self-esteem.

This chapter attempts to demonstrate that professionals in the children's services field will inevitably confront organizational

---

* Other authors have argued that use of covert tactics may be justified under certain circumstances. See, for example, Brager and Holloway (1978) and Patti and Resnick (1972).

problems that limit their capacity to provide optimal service to their clients. Therefore, it is essential that emerging professionals learn to identify the strains created by differences in bureaucracies and professionalism and that they strive constantly to shape organizational structures to meet client needs. It often requires personal courage and integrity for professionals to risk challenging bureaucratic policies and procedures. However, the professional commitment to meet children's needs demands nothing less, and professionals who acquire the knowledge and skills necessary to engage in effective organizational change efforts will meet this challenge willingly.

Case Presentation for Problem Solving

Jimmy Young is a bright, appealing ten-year-old who was first referred to the school psychologist, Ms. Evans, in third grade because of "disruptive behavior in the classroom, inability to socialize with peers, and hyperactivity." Jimmy has superior intelligence and performs at an above-average level, despite little or no effort to achieve academically. Because of his all-American-boy looks, small stature, and friendly, slightly cocky manner, adults find him somewhat disarming and initially respond to him very positively. However, this initial positive response quickly turns to anger and frustration because Jimmy is such a difficult child to handle in a classroom setting. He is restless, has frequent temper tantrums, often refuses to do any work, and simply runs away. Moreover, he attempts to maintain a tough façade with other youngsters by using a great deal of wit and sarcasm and precipitating rather constant classroom conflict.

Jimmy is the youngest of three children in a white, middle-class, single-parent family. His parents were divorced a year after his birth, and his father disappeared shortly thereafter. Mrs. Young, a well-educated, articulate woman who holds a responsible position in the community, is very embittered about her husband's abandonment and devotes all of her energy to her work. She finds Jimmy's behavior at home very provocative but is unwilling to consider family dynamics in relation to the problem, preferring to blame his problem behavior on "hyperactivity." Mrs. Young has been faithful about giving Jimmy the Ritalin that the school pediatrician prescribed for him in first grade, but she is unwilling to accept any other responsibility for his behavior. School personnel who attempted to discuss Jimmy with her found her "rude, uncooperative, and antagonistic."

Ms. Evans, the school psychologist, was a recent graduate who had only been in Jimmy's school three weeks when she was assigned his case. His teacher that year was a very experienced woman who had the reputation of being a strict disciplinarian able to handle any child. Therefore, everyone was somewhat surprised when she announced early in the school year that either Jimmy had to go or she would. However, her reaction served to confirm all the horror stories about Jimmy that had circulated in the teachers' room in prior years and provided some solace to his former teachers who had always been told that Jimmy could be managed in a classroom if he were just handled properly. Ms. Evans felt that the referral was a test of sorts for her since the principal was somewhat skeptical about this "therapy business" and told her that the efforts of her predecessor to work with Jimmy and his family had been a total disaster. The principal also said that he felt the only solution now was to transfer Jimmy to a special class because they had tried everything else; however, after some urging by Ms. Evans, he agreed to give her time to evaluate the case and to attempt some direct intervention if it seemed indicated.

After a careful review of the rather sketchy school and medical records and some initial diagnostic sessions with Jimmy, Ms. Evans concluded that Jimmy's behavioral problems were caused by familial rather than neurological problems and that his emotional difficulties were compounded by the fact that Jimmy had been labeled as a problem child at home and at school. Jimmy himself told her that "Everyone around here has hated me since I locked myself in the teachers' room by mistake in first grade." And the little information available about Jimmy's home life suggested that his family was very chaotic. Despite adequate income, Jimmy was always shabbily dressed and had few books or toys. The family seldom had any regular meals and never shared any activities other than watching television. Although Mrs. Young was very strict, her discipline was quite inconsistent, and she left most of the responsibility for his care to his older sisters. Little effort was ever made to structure Jimmy's behavior or to communicate reasons for the rather capricious demands issued by his mother and sisters. Mrs. Young rebuffed all of the previous worker's efforts to work with some of these family problems, insisting that all of Jimmy's difficulties stemmed from his hyperactivity.

Ms. Evans began to work with Jimmy on a biweekly basis with the goal of establishing a supportive relationship in which he could learn to accept minimal but consistent limits and to take some responsibility for his own behavior. In these sessions Jimmy displayed little understanding of cause–effect relationships and little capacity for introspection. However, he responded positively to Ms. Evans, displaying an eagerness to relate and manifesting no discipline problems within the therapeutic relationship. Although he was reluctant to discuss school or family problems, he initiated conversations about his various interests and activities and began to use her as a resource in crisis situations, going to Ms. Evans' office instead of running from school when he had difficulty in the classroom.

During this period Ms. Evans also attempted to establish some alliance with Mrs. Young by demonstrating her interest in Jimmy and her belief that his behavior could change. Because of Mrs. Young's resistance to any outside intervention, she decided that her initial goal should simply be to help Mrs. Young see Jimmy more positively. Later, if Mrs. Young began to see that Jimmy was capable of change, she might be able to work toward modifying her interaction with him. After several months this approach began to have some positive results. Mrs. Young said that this was the first time she felt the school was really interested in Jimmy, and she started to interact with Jimmy a little more consistently.

Unfortunately, Ms. Evans was not as successful in her efforts to help Jimmy's classroom teacher handle him more constructively, and, in March, the teacher demanded that Jimmy be transferred to a special class. By that time Ms. Evans could see that the teacher's attitude toward Jimmy was not going to change and that her increasing frustration was exacerbating his acting-out in class, despite the progress he was making in treatment. However, she did not think he needed to be placed in a special class. When Ms. Evans met with the principal to discuss Jimmy's transfer, he said that none of the other third-grade teachers would take him; moreover, it would be an insult to his teacher to place him in another regular class. And, since it was too late in the year to transfer Jimmy to another school, he would have to place him in the special class for moderately retarded children aged eleven to thirteen.

Ms. Evans initially opposed this placement, pointing out that Jimmy had superior intelligence and was gradually learning to take some responsibility for his own behavior. This placement would only confirm his fear that there was something wrong with him and bolster his mother's view that his behavioral problems were caused by a neurological deficit. However, the principal said there was no choice. Since Jimmy would only be in this class for three months and would have a skilled and dedicated teacher who was not afraid to set limits, the placement could not do him any real harm. Ms. Evans therefore agreed to participate in the meeting at which the transfer would be explained to Mrs. Young. During this meeting, the principal told Mrs. Young that the placement was being arranged solely for Jimmy's welfare and that he was functioning on the same level as other youngsters in this classroom, neglecting to mention that they were older but retarded. Ms. Evans did not distort as much as the principal, but she supported his recommendation; and Mrs. Young readily acquiesced to the transfer.

Jimmy responded well to the attention of his new teacher and was somewhat less disruptive during the remainder of the school year. Ms. Evans was pleased about this and was very optimistic about the help he might receive in the therapeutic camp she had arranged for him to attend during the summer. Therefore, she felt he could probably be returned to a regular classroom early in the fall.

The first day of school in the fall, Ms. Evans met Jimmy outside of school. He immediately screamed at her, "I ain't going into that damn building with a class of —— retards." After some effort, Ms. Evans was able to calm him down, pointing out that if he did better in school he could be transferred back to his regular class. Jimmy told her excitedly about his camp experience, displaying special pride in the fact that he had been taken off the medication; and he eventually agreed to go back to his assigned classroom.

Ms. Evans continued to work with Jimmy that fall and was pleased at the progress he was making. However, she was concerned about his remaining in the special class, as he was bored and had begun to take advantage of the fact his classmates were retarded, teasing them unmercifully. Ms. Evans and the special education teacher both agreed he belonged in another classroom, but the principal refused to transfer him until he received a report from the camp. Despite persistent calls from Ms. Evans, and an enthusiastic verbal report of his progress from the camp director, no written report was received until late November, which was too late to help Jimmy.

In October, in response to a complaint from a parent of one of the other children in Jimmy's class, the principal asked to meet with Mrs. Young and discovered that Jimmy had been taken off Ritalin. He was furious that he had not been informed about this and ordered Ms. Evans to tell Mrs. Young that Jimmy must go back on medication. She refused, pointing out that Jimmy had done well at camp without Ritalin and was doing no worse now than last year when he was on medication. Moreover, the psychiatric consultant agreed with her diagnosis of unsocialized aggressive reaction of childhood and saw no evidence of hyperactivity. Ms. Evans also explained that much of her work with Jimmy had been directed toward helping him to accept responsibility for his behavior and supporting the progress he was making without medication. Therefore, returning him to medication might undo much of the progress he had made. However, the principal was adamant that Jimmy needed Ritalin and told the school nurse to call Mrs. Young and ask her to start Jimmy's medication again. Mrs. Young was surprised at the nurse's call because she thought Jimmy was doing just as well without the medication, but she agreed to call the school pediatrician who had seen Jimmy two years before. He said that it would not do any harm to try the Ritalin again and that if the principal wanted this, it was important that they try it.

Jimmy was somewhat subdued for a few days after the medication started and expressed some concern to Ms. Evans about becoming dependent on medicine again. Within a week or two, however, he began to be disruptive and to tease his classmates again so the special education teacher said that he really must be transferred; and neither the principal nor the teacher would consider trying again to remove Jimmy's medication and place him in a regular classroom.

This time Ms. Evans was prepared with a recommendation

for a special private day treatment center for Jimmy and would not agree to another special class in the public school system. Ideally, she felt that he should be maintained in a small, regular classroom where he could be given individualized attention and consistent discipline without receiving the message that he was sick. However, a private school seemed the best compromise solution for Jimmy's problem at this time. The price of the special placement was that Jimmy would have to stay on medication and to accept a problem label; however, in the new setting the staff would be willing to try and help Jimmy on an individualized basis rather than placing the entire burden for change on him. Ms. Evans reluctantly concluded that no further efforts on her part within the regular school setting would be sufficient to create the learning environment Jimmy needed. Therefore, Ms. Evans discussed her recommendation with Mrs. Young and made the necessary arrangements for the placement. In January of that year, much to the relief of everyone involved except Jimmy and Ms. Evans, Jimmy was placed in a special day treatment program for emotionally disturbed children.

Some questions that may be asked in this case presentation are: (1) Are there any procedural errors you can identify at the various stages? (2) If you were the new psychologist, would you have taken on Jimmy at this point in time? Why or why not? (3) Assuming you had decided to try to help Jimmy, would your procedures have been the same as Ms. Evans'? If not, what else would you have done? (4) What do you think of Ms. Evans' goal for Mrs. Young, the mother? (5) Put yourself in the place of the school administrator. What alternatives do you think he missed? Would you agree with his conclusion about the impossibility of placing Jimmy in a third grade? (6) If you were Ms. Evans, what would have been your stance in the meeting to inform his mother of the transfer to special class? (7) Evaluate all professionals' responsibilities in the medication issue. (8) Would you have made the private day treatment center recommendation? Why or why not? (9) How would you rate the value of the three intervention strategies for the psychologist?

Chapter 10

Issues in Child Custody

Edith Smith

Children temporarily or permanently not in custody of their parents are often placed on a custody merry-go-round, circling with the consent and momentum provided by a variety of professionals and systems, including the legislature, the courts, and the child welfare agencies. This is a merry-go-round with no brass ring for the winners because there are no winners. The children have come to the courts and agencies unwanted or neglected, often traumatized, and may already be deeply troubled. The parents themselves have been victims of personal, family, community, or societal failures. Over the years, well-intentioned professionals, agencies, and those who act as advocates for children have tried to confront the complex economic, sociological, and psychological problems involved in the separation and placement of children away from their natural parents as well as to develop plans and programs geared to the needs of individual children. In practice, they have often had to go beyond the guidelines of accepted child welfare thinking to develop such programs. The problem is that frequently when a good idea is adopted as a general guideline, it is applied to some children inappropriately and loses its original effectiveness. The professional must continue to find ways to individualize decisions and programs for children caught in custody difficulties.

A brief review of thinking about the dilemmas professionals face in custody decisions could begin with King Solomon's rather dramatic way of resolving two women's claims to an infant. Strauss and Strauss (1974) note that this first-reported custody case was, in fact, an easy one because only one of the women had a just claim, only one was prepared to be responsible, and the judge had the advantage of surprise. In cases in which two parents each have a claim and may be prepared to give up their own interests for the child and in which the rules of the decision may be known in advance, it is harder to achieve the right and just answer for the adult and the child. It is even more difficult when there is no one fighting specifically for the child, and custody is sought because of the need to separate the child from his family for his protection or because the parents are no longer able or willing to keep the child.

In their review of the history of the custody of children, Axinn and others (1973) state that the earliest provision for the custody of children in the United States followed the pattern established in Great Britain. Common law and statutory law distinguished between the needs of rich and poor children and between approaches for their welfare. For the rich child who owned property the state focused on a concern for the protection of property rights, whereas for poor children, the state focused upon its own protection against poverty, which was seen as leading to dependency and criminality. The affairs of the rich child became matters of common law and were handled in civil courts; the concerns of the poor child were matters of statutory law and handled in criminal courts. Guardianship proceedings, which are used today primarily when property is involved, grew out of common law. Many of the current provisions for the care of children away from their own homes and the foundations of the juvenile court systems grew out of statutory law.

In the early 1800s, the poor, unattached, or neglected child was indentured by court agreement, so that the person who assumed responsibility for the child's care expected him to work to earn his keep. Concerned educators, clergy, and people interested in the welfare of children encouraged the development of orphanages and group care facilities for children. However, the number of state and privately supported orphanages could not keep pace with the homeless and neglected children resulting from the industrial urbanization of the times, so alternative solutions were sought. A new "child saving" approach was developed, and in the mid-1800s, thousands of children were "saved" by being taken off the streets of large cities and sent to rural foster homes in the West. Institutional and boarding arrangements were developed for the care of large groups of children; child advocates of the day and the developing social agencies called attention to the fact that child care groups must take into account the child's real needs and that real needs include the child's family tie. The logic of this approach permeated the child care field and became the philosophical basis of professional and social accountability for the welfare of children.

The twentieth century has become known as the century of the child in that professional and social awareness has led to child welfare developments that have brought both national and governmental commitments to the personalized welfare of children (Axinn and others, 1973). The first White House Conference on the Care of Dependent Children in 1909 was dedicated to the concept that children be provided with a home, preferably the child's own or, if this was not possible, a foster home. The conference also stressed the need to find ways to make a home for the child financially feasible. Public funds were made available through the Social Security Act, which has been amended and improved to the present. However impressive the intent of the commitment and the legislation, the concerned professional and others who care about the lives of children have had to challenge interpretations of laws and regulations in order to improve the care of children in their own or substitute homes.

Theoretically, the intent of programs and regulations has

been to help the family maintain itself and to enable the children to remain with their biological parents. Financial support through the Aid to Dependent Children Programs (1935) addition to the Social Security Act was designed so that children would not have to be removed from their homes solely for financial reasons. A network of privately funded social agencies designed to strengthen family functioning and to work with the emotionally troubled child was developed. Agencies devoted to facilitating the adoption of abandoned children and the infants of unwed mothers were established and supported, again with the aim that no child be without a home and a family.

Foster family care programs were developed to service the children who had to be removed from their biological families, and were planned as short-term living arrangements for neglected children or children who needed temporary substitute homes because of family illness or disorganization. From its beginning, foster care has been a relatively inexpensive way of providing for children separated from their parents and not placed for adoption. In foster placement, there need not be judicial termination of parental rights; both the court and the agency view the disposition as temporary and the rights of the natural parents are held in abeyance. However, the child placement worker faced the dilemma of helping the child retain the tie to his biological family, while also encouraging the child to feel at home with the foster family. The worker also had the dual responsibility of supporting the foster family's care and concern for the child but, at the same time, stressing that the foster family should not become too attached or want to adopt the child. At that time children were occasionally removed from foster homes because the foster family became too attached to the child. In other cases, the agency received temporary or permanent custody in order to protect the child while he resided in the foster home.

Although the intent of foster care as originally developed was that the child would have continuity of care and the support of living with a family until he could return to his own parents, Katz (1971), Maas and Engler (1959), and Wicker (1977) all note that between 200,000 and 300,000 children are in agency-supported foster homes in any one year, that children remain in foster care longer than had been assumed, and that children are often shifted around and moved from one foster placement to another. Fanshel (1976) reported on a recent five-year longitudinal study of children in foster care in New York that showed that at the end of the five years, 36 percent of the children remained in foster care and that 29 percent of these children had at least two placements, 18 percent had three placements, and 10 percent had experienced four or more shifts of home within the five-year period. In their study on several communities Maas and Engler (1959) stress that unless children move out of foster care within the first eighteen months, the likelihood of ever moving out is sharply decreased.

Concerned child welfare workers and others committed professionally to the care of children, including social workers, psychologists, nurses, psychiatrists, pediatricians, lawyers, judges, and lay advocates, became aware that the intent and design of foster care was not meeting the needs of many of the children placed in foster homes. Mental health agencies and the courts were seeing the resulting upset, maladjusted and sometimes delinquent children. What had been developed to serve the best interests of the child by offering a family instead of institutional care often became a permanent state of living in limbo, particularly for minority, poor, hard-to-place, older, or emotionally handicapped children. The evils of long-term shifting foster placements were well known, and there were attempts at finding alternative solutions within the system. Agencies tried to get custody of children from families who had disappeared or been totally uninvolved for years so that some of these children could be adopted. They tried to locate adoptive homes for hard-to-place or adolescent children. Group foster homes, with foster parents hired as employees of the agency, were developed by many child care agencies. This allowed more control over the children's total environment and, it was hoped, more continuity of care.

Goldstein, Freud, and Solnit (1973) brought new parameters into the field of child placement. Using psychoanalytic theory, they suggested changes in the law and agency procedures concerning all placement and custody decisions and proposed that the traditional biological standards that had dominated child custody law be replaced with psychological ones. Understanding how children grow and develop, how they interact with the environment on the basis of their individual innate characteristics, and the developmental phase they are in is essential for professionals who have any influence in what happens to children. Children are not miniature adults; their mental nature, their behavioral expressions, their understanding of events, and their reactions to them are different than those of adults. In custody cases, the biological parents traditionally enjoyed a specific advantage because they had little difficulty obtaining custody after having placed their children in foster homes. Even in adoption, there was, and still is, usually a waiting period in which the natural parents are permitted to change their minds about retaining custody. These practices fail the child. The child needs the unbroken continuity of an affectionate and stimulating relationship with an adult. The crucial problem is the means by which the law can assure each child a chance to be a member of a family where he feels wanted on a continuous basis. The concept of the psychological parent was defined as one who wants a relationship of enduring character with a child and one who through the course of continuing concern for the child comes to be regarded by him as parent and thus serves as his model of maturation and development. "Whether any adult becomes the psychological parent of a child is based thus on day-to-day interaction, companionship, and shared experiences. The role can be fulfilled either by a biological parent or by an adoptive parent, or by any other adult, whatever his biological or legal relationship to the child may be" (Goldstein, Freud, and Solnit, 1973, p. 19).

These authors also suggested that placement decisions should reflect the child's rather than the adult's sense of time and emphasized that speedy decisions, especially for young children, are essential. When infants and young children are left by their parents, they not only suffer anxiety and separation distress but also setbacks in the quality of the next attachment. When there are multiple placements in the early years, the children's emotional attachments may become shallow and indiscriminate. Courts deciding custody cases traditionally are concerned with the best interests of the child. The law must make the child's needs paramount, but the limitation of existing knowledge makes it impossible to know with certainty what is best. The authors advocate as their solution choosing the "least detrimental alternative." "The least detrimental alternative is that specific placement and procedure for placement which maximizes in accord with the child's sense of time and on the basis of short-term predictions, given the limitations of knowledge, his or her opportunity for being wanted and for maintaining on a continuous basis a relationship with at least one adult who is or who will be his psychological parent" (Goldstein, Freud, and Solnit, 1973, p. 53). Waiting periods in adoption cases should be abolished on the grounds that the uncertainty generated by the lack of finality hinders the development of psychological parenthood in the new home. Foster parents who wish to adopt or retain custody on a long-term basis should be favored over natural parents on the grounds that every change of custody (even back to biological family) undermines the stability that is essential to healthy child development. "Common-law adoption" is the term used by the writers for long-term foster care.

Goldstein, Freud, and Solnit urge that all child placements, except where specifically designed for brief temporary care, shall be as permanent as the placement of a newborn with his biological parents. The use of subsidized adoptions to help families care for the child should be used when necessary. Child placement decisions must take into account the law's inability to supervise interpersonal relationships and that at the present there are limits in our knowledge to make long-range predictions. Ongoing agency or court supervision in adoptive or foster placements would be an interference rather than a help to the child. The child should be represented by counsel in any contested placement that appears before the court. These new proposals can have far-reaching effects on the reconceptualization of the law of child custody and will demand closer cooperation between lawyers and child welfare workers. The concept of the child's need for continuity of care, speed in placement, and the least detrimental alternative will have its effects upon agency policies.

In reality, agencies, social workers, and the courts, although having the best interests of the child in mind, have always operated in terms of the least detrimental alternative. But the choices available have not always been what the worker on the line, the one who actually places the child, considers ideal. There is rarely a long list of loving, caring families waiting to take in the child with significant problems. The current principal and tragic deficiencies in the child welfare system come not so much from the professionals' unwillingness to acknowledge the child's need for love, continuity, and good care. Rather, they result from the limitation of the financial and human resources and an adequate social commitment to provide this care. The professional must work to change attitudes of the community toward a deepening commitment to children in need of families. He can work toward a different relationship with foster and adoptive parents by viewing them more as colleagues than as clients and can support subsidized adoptions, aggressive home finding, and single-parent and older-parent adoptions.

The dilemma professional workers face is how to integrate the knowledge base of the psychological needs of children with their day-to-day agency practice. Professional workers are often employees of a system and are responsible to their agency administrators and governing boards as well as to the welfare of the children they serve. What is expedient for one is not necessarily expedient for the other, a point McGowan has elaborated on in the previous chapter. Agency fiscal accountability is also important. The worker who stands for quality services and reasonable case assignments may not be appreciated by the administration and the board. However, although employees of an agency or system, the workers have the right and the duty to make sure that their knowledge and skills are not subverted in violation of their professional best judgment. Polier (1976) states that workers have the responsibility not only to act as child advocates but also to alert their boards and governing bodies to the gaps in services and the inadequacies of care and treatment.

No matter how uncomfortable the position may be, workers in the field of child welfare cannot escape the role of decision maker. Polier (1976) warns the professional worker to be on guard lest fragmentation of services and ill-considered referrals relieve them too easily from their responsibilities to the child who needs service. Workers should guard against using the results of consultation and classification systems which could result in the abuse of children and their right to appropriate care and treatment. For example, several years ago a young physician and his wife became foster parents for an eleven-month-old brain-damaged little girl, Susie. They had requested a hard-to-place child with the expressed hope that they would in time adopt the child. Five months later, the father accepted a job in another state, and the family petitioned the public child welfare agency to permit them to take Susie with them. The supervisor instructed the worker to get both legal and psychological consultation. Legally, the agency could not supervise the foster placement of the child in another state, and the psychiatrist stated that in the long run these highly educated parents would not be satisfied with this little girl. Rather, they deserved a bright, normal child who could benefit from the advantages they could offer. The parents were denied the chance to keep Susie. They fought the decision for several months, but since they had to relocate, they "gave" the child back to the agency, which placed her with several other handicapped children in a foster home. The social worker was very upset, and she tried to speak on behalf of this child, but the agency administrators used the results of their consultants to overrule her ideas and insisted on retaining custody of the child in their community.

The dilemmas the worker in the field faces are many-faceted. When a family is sent to the agency because they cannot care for their child, the worker must assess the child's need for continuity of care and also evaluate the limitations and strengths of the child's biological family. Workers will have to assess the supports the community can provide to help biological parents care for their children. The caseworker will be in the best position to recognize what gaps in the services preclude this decision. Yet, from the individual case viewpoint, this is a rather arbitrary criterion. If the decision will rest on community resources and if communities within twenty miles of each other offer varied services and have such different gaps in these services, very different decisions for similar cases could result. Workers have to be ready with an infusion of needed services at a time of family crisis, such as a mother's mental illness, in order to avert separation of children from families. Adequate day care, homemaker services, emergency financial assistance, and aid with housing and home management can help keep children with their families.

Jones, Neuman, and Shyne (1976) reported on a demonstration project documenting positive results of massive services that assisted the children remaining with their families. Data from the control group demonstrated that, without such services, children were placed in foster home care. The caseworker may often be the one who will have to decide when the supports offered will enable the child to remain with his biological family in safety and with adequate care and when placement is truly the least detrimental alternative. There is also a great variability in training and education of caseworkers who are involved in such important decisions. In some localities, workers need only have a seventh-grade education to qualify as a child welfare worker, whereas in other areas the majority of workers have bachelor's degrees and social workers in many positions have master's degrees. The dilemma is that often the worker who needs the most insight and understanding of the child's needs is the line caseworker. But he is frequently the least trained and the least experienced. Professionals in the community who are aware of this situation must raise standards for those who plan for and supervise the care of children outside of their families.

When the worker and the court agree that the child would be best cared for outside of his biological family, the dilemmas the worker faces are equally great. It is important to strive for placement that is geared to the child's sense of time and that offers the best continuity of care. There is need for greater communication between the social worker, the lawyer and judge, and the psychiatric or psychological consultant; the ability to work together and respect each professional's expertise is essential. Professionals must reassess agency and community truisms, such as the belief that an educated family will have trouble with a slow child or that no one really wants a teen-age boy. Professionals must reexamine their own prejudices so they will not bias the provision of the least detrimental alternative for each child.

The following example illustrates the provision of this least detrimental alternative for a retarded boy. Brian was originally placed for adoption when he was two weeks old. Soon after placement, he had several seizures, which frightened the adoptive family sufficiently that they requested he be removed from the home. The worker then placed him in an infant home used by the agency for temporary care of babies. The foster mother was in her late 40s and the foster father, who was mildly handicapped, was at home most of the time. Brian was left in the infant home for almost a year.

Medication controlled his seizures, and his development was steady although slow. When the agency began looking for a long-term foster home for Brian, the foster mother requested adoption. The worker pointed out the many problems they would face, such as the husband's handicap and the fact that by agency standards they were too old to become adoptive parents. However, the worker thought about the request and discussed it with the agency administrator, who agreed that Brian had found a family who loved him and accepted him and that he had made a good adjustment to the home. The agency recommended to the court a subsidized adoption for this family, with the added provision that casework assistance be available whenever the family requested it as well as ongoing help in using community resources for their retarded child.

Bernstein, Snider, and Meezan (1975) studied children in New York City and devised a set of comprehensive criteria for foster placement and alternatives to foster care. Although this organization of alternatives, which ranges from community supports to the biological family to long-term institutional placement, can be helpful, each child in the placement system is separate and special. Therefore, it is hoped that individual decisions concerning a particular child will be able to go beyond the written criteria and guidelines. For example, thirteen-year-old Rick, who had been in multiple placements, had to leave his foster home because of difficulties with his foster father and was being considered for a group home. The supervisor was concerned that the boy had made such a poor adjustment, and the mental health consultant used by the agency felt he could not tolerate the close relationships generated in living with a foster family. The move to the group home run by the agency would remove him from his peer group, the junior high school, where he had just begun to make an adjustment, and an older neighborhood couple who had become his friends. The caseworker took it upon herself to visit the older couple and to explore with them the possibility of having Rick as their foster child with agency support and supervision. After talking with the boy and the caseworker, the couple agreed. The caseworker had to counsel the boy to help him understand his contribution to his difficulties in previous placements, and a counseling contract was established with the boy agreeing to work on his problems. The caseworker had to defend her decision with the agency administration, which she did. The boy was able to remain with the couple until he was an adult, and he was truly their psychological son.

Workers must face the crucial social issues and be influential in determining how issues affecting children will be resolved by legislators, courts, and administrators of agencies. They must also be aware that trends in custody decisions, placement alternatives, and adoptability of children reflect larger issues. For example, when there are fewer infants available for adoption because of increased use of birth control, availability of abortion, and the greater acceptance of the unwed parent raising a child, social policy should respond and change. New social trends require flexibility, creativity, and growth. Of course, trends must be examined in light of professional knowledge of a child's psychological needs. Workers must not waver in the face of criticism if they feel the child's best interests will be forfeited if they concede; the least detrimental alternative for the child must be actively pursued.

An example of the major dilemmas professionals now face can be seen in the current search by adopted adults for their biological parents. Starr (1976) points out that, over the years, agencies committed to professional standards concerning adoptions had developed both a philosophy and practice for adoptive planning. Supported by this body of knowledge and the concurrent literature, agencies had moved to a degree of security and authority in this area. In what was considered sound agency practice, workers were committed to protect the natural mother's identity from the adoptive parents and from the adopted child. This plan was predicated on a number of theoretical assumptions. Having made a sound plan for her child, the biological mother would experience a freedom to create a new life for herself, and the child, supported by a loving adopted family, would form close ties with that family as well as come to terms with the reality of his adoption. Agencies anticipated the search for information as the adopted child grew into adulthood; they provided generalized information to questions. The agency also felt it was protecting the adopted family from intrusions of the biological parents.

Then adopted adults began to demand the right to seek out their biological parents. A newly formed organization, the Adoptees'

Liberty Movement Association (ALMA), functions in locating the biological parents of its members and advocates changes in the law that prohibits the opening of adoption files. This leads to many dilemmas for professional workers within adoption agencies: how to respond to these adopted adults, what information to share, to whom this information belongs, and what protection the agency owes to the biological parent who was told anonymity would be preserved. Workers may be able to make decisions based on knowledge of the adopted adult, the adopted family, and the biological family, but there are also legal considerations. What if records are subpoenaed? What is the agency's proper role if it is consulted? More importantly, how should agreements be made in the future with biological and adoptive families concerning confidentiality?

The professionals, led by the adopted adults, have become more aware of individuals' need for their sense of origin and their roots. Such a sense comes about most easily in families with stories, anecdotes, and photograph albums. The adopted adult should have at least an adoption record that could be made available. Foster children, particularly children in long-term placement who have lived with several families, need a sense of history and their own roots. I have met with foster children who have no recollection of their early lives and no idea why they have lived with three or more families. They are confused about their biological parents, the role of the supervising agency, and the ever-changing array of caseworkers who periodically come to visit. Could the agency compile a chronological history for all foster children, complete with photographs of their biological parents and foster parents, the houses they lived in, the reasons for placement, and pertinent information for them to integrate as they become able to do so?

Finally, who is really the advocate for the child not in custody of his parents? If the child is adopted, the new parents fulfill this role. Who is the parent for the foster child? When an agency gets custody, can it really become a surrogate parent? Who actually makes the decisions that are the least detrimental alternative for this child? Even though property is not involved, the child in placement must be given a guardian who would be responsible for him. The foster parent, who would be court-appointed and who would act as long-term advocate, could be the guardian if he had a genuine commitment to the child. Child welfare workers are not good guardians because they change jobs and must also represent the agency who employs them. However, workers can make it their responsibility to tailor the arrangements made for each individual child according to his needs. In custody cases, workers must be willing to testify according to their knowledge and expertise and to represent the child's needs, which include the need for guardianship.

The professional who works with children not in custody of their parents must often take professional and personal risks. These children are ones who may have no other advocates and who frequently remain without permanent homes and families much longer than is safe for their developing sense of identity. Of course, caseworkers should try to keep all children who possibly can remain there in their original families. Most of the dilemmas encountered and decisions to be made have no right answers, but professionals have a commitment to explore all areas of influence on an *individual* child's psychological and physical development and to devise a custody and living plan that will be the "least detrimental alternative" for meeting this child's needs. This plan may have to go beyond traditional organizational guidelines. Individual professionals have to stimulate their organization to keep up with new knowledge and social change indicators as well as to try and evaluate new approaches. An overall goal should be to increase the flexibility of the system to accommodate children's needs. When agency and other official policies lag too far behind what is happening or *should happen* for children in the "real" world, operational practices become ineffective and create dilemmas of their own. Availability of children for adoption and identity of adoptees are two recent examples.

Case Presentation for Problem Solving

Don, who is now nine years old, has been living with his foster family, the T's, for the past five years. He is a small, very active child who is in special education classes for the mildly mentally retarded in his local public school. Recently, a private national adoption agency has opened local offices in the city where

Don lives, has contacted the local child welfare department, which services Don and other foster children, and has offered to place him for adoption. Because of his hyperactivity, learning problems, and destructive behavior, Don and his foster mother have been receiving counseling at the local mental health agency, which was also contacted about his "adoptability."

Don was born to a young woman who was rejected and neglected in her severely disorganized nuclear family. She was considered "somewhat slow" and went to special classes for retarded children. She did not graduate from high school and had a history of short periods of employment in unskilled jobs. Little was known of Don's natural father other than that he was twenty years older than Don's mother when Don was born and, although named as father, he was not involved in any planning for Don. Don's mother was considered emotionally and financially unable to provide a home for him, so a local private child placement agency received temporary custody. Don was placed in a foster home when he was released from the hospital.

Don remained in the foster home until he was two. In retrospect, no reason is given in the record for his not being placed for adoption as an infant. Could it be that Don was considered a fussy child who developed slowly in the first year and was therefore less adoptable? When he was two, he was placed with an adoptive family, the A's, where he remained for two years until he was four-and-a-half. Although the adoption had become finalized after one year, the adoptive parents demanded his removal from their home because they could not "see him as their own." They had many questions about his intellectual and emotional development, and, although the agency tried to reassure them that he was normal, they continued to suspect that he was retarded.

With little preparation, Don was removed and placed in his present foster home. His foster parents were looking for a son to complement their family of three daughters. They were not told of any suspicion that he might be slow or have any problems. At the time of replacement, he appeared hyperactive, sucked his thumb, was enuretic, and seemed anxious and panicky much of the time. After one year, although the foster parents felt he had made a good adjustment, they requested psychological testing to see if he was intellectually retarded. When he was five-and-a-half years old, he achieved a mental age of four, yielding a Stanford-Binet IQ in the low 70s, and the parents were told he was somewhat behind. The examiner viewed Don as an anxious, emotionally deprived boy who was functioning at the borderline level of intelligence. He postulated that although the emotional traumas Don had suffered could have contributed to the delay in his intellectual and emotional development, the evenness of his cognitive functioning suggested that there was an underlying slowness in intellectual functioning and that he would probably perform below an average level.

Don was given a medical examination at the request of his foster mother who considered him very hyperactive, and he was placed on Ritalin to "calm him down." Don talked about the pills which were "keeping him good." Because it now appeared that Don would remain in foster care for a long time, the case was transferred to the county child welfare department. During the next year, Don began regular kindergarten and had difficulty with both the pre-academic work and his behavior. Don was subsequently placed in classes for the educable mentally retarded, but he experienced difficulty in learning up to his tested potential. He roamed the room, asked many questions, and had difficulty concentrating.

The foster family was approached by their child welfare caseworker several times about adopting Don through their subsidized adoption program. The foster parents did not want to do so because they felt that he would have many problems as an adolescent that would require special care. They also understood that the adoption subsidy could only be promised yearly and might be denied any given year. They considered Don a child they could control now but who might grow out of their control and be dangerous to their natural daughters.

The child welfare worker followed agency review procedures, which are now done yearly for each child in foster care, and sent the case to the adoption department for case review. A new caseworker did another home study and again tried to enlist the family in subsidized adoption. The worker implied that if they were not ready to do so, the new private agency that places older and handicapped children would be sent Don's record to review for their home-finding department. At this time Don underwent another complete medical and psychological evaluation. The pediatrician was concerned with Don's slight stature and lack of growth and recommended that he be taken off Ritalin. The psychologist referred Don for therapy because of his severe learning inhibition and impulsive behavior. His foster parents were referred for counseling to help Don with behavior management so that he could achieve greater social and emotional maturity.

The child welfare worker, the mental health caseworker, and the private adoption worker are faced with the dilemma of what is in this child's best interest. On the one hand, the T's refuse to make a long-term legal commitment to Don although they promise him long-term foster care, say they are attached to him, and, indeed, care for him adequately. The adoption agency worker says there are families who would adopt a disturbed, slow-developing child, offer him security, and hopefully continue care until he is an adult. On the other hand, the T's have become Don's psychological parents; he has asked to use their last name; and they have had his legally changed. He relates to his foster parents as his parents and talks about his future within this family. The foster parents agreed to and followed through in the plans for mental health counseling for Don and themselves. The mental health worker knows that Don has had three different "families" and that since his placement with the T's at age four-and-a-half, he has shown many signs of insecurity and fear of loss of people and objects. He is still struggling with his aggressive feelings and often provokes fights. The worker is also aware of Don's ambivalent clinging to his foster mother and his preoccupations which keep him from attending to school work. There is the added possibility that Don's early deprivations and separations will interfere with his ability to tolerate and adjust to adolescent upheavals. He may need a therapeutic residential placement, which would be of further cost to the community. However, the T's would remain the psychological parents for this disturbed, shifted-around adolescent boy. The child welfare administrator has funding pressures to reduce case loads of foster children.

Within this case are many dilemmas for many professionals. The most important one, of course, centers around the questions of where Don's home should be and with whom he should identify. Discuss your recommendations concerning this decision.

Some other questions that could be asked in this case presentation are: (1) What is your evaluation of the initial decision to remove Don from his natural mother? (2) How might the adoptive parents have been helped by the professionals not to give him up? (3) What would have been an ideal foster placement preparation for Don and for the parents? (4) How might the psychologist have played her role differently? (5) What alternatives were not considered by the professionals at each step of the way?

Chapter **11**

Survival of
Severely Impaired Infants

Theodore J. DiBuono

What can one tell the developing professional about the survival of severely handicapped infants? We can cite lowered mortality rates in the newborn period, and we can point to the wonders of medical technology, which may extend life for some children. Such data might convey the notion that today's world is, indeed, oriented toward meeting the needs of the severely impaired. Most parents of such children would say otherwise. That there are many individuals in the helping professions who are sincerely committed to aiding the severely impaired and their families cannot be doubted. But how ready are we to recognize that there are also many respected professionals who exhibit the most devaluing attitudes and actions in regard to these children, that, in fact, the severely impaired are prototypes of those whom society devalues and often destroys? There have been well-publicized instances in which impaired infants (not even necessarily severely impaired) were denied treatment and allowed to die unnecessarily. How often does this occur? How can it occur in the face of available technology? And what does a severely impaired infant who survives have in store? Despite all our resources and high living standards, what have we done to assure a reasonable life for these individuals? They live on the fringes of our society, without priority in our materialistic world. Their parents and those professionals who advocate for them are considered annoyances with unrealistic dedication to a cause that lies outside the mainstream and threatens our own sense of well being. Only recently have federal laws been enacted that guarantee public education to all regardless of severity of handicap and that attempt to bar discrimination on the basis of handicap. The Constitution notwithstanding, severely handicapped persons have been consistently denied full rights of citizenship and are frequently treated as if they had no rights at all. What rights does a severely handicapped infant have? Who will tell us without equivocation and when?

We have constructed a world in which differences are not encompassed gracefully, although we pretend otherwise. The considerable resources we have used on behalf of the severely impaired have assured that they continue to exist apart from us in institutional or other segregated settings. Only a few parents, professionals, or other individuals have had the courage to demand that society provide healthier alternatives.

All of this seems like a heavy burden to place before a developing professional person. It is admittedly a harsh indictment of our handling of the severely impaired. It is a devastating view that does not pretend to balance our achievements against our deficiencies. Injustice exists and flourishes, and the professional who is part of it must either see it or blindly perpetuate it. As professional persons, we must develop a high degree of consciousness about the external forces (both sociocultural and politico-economic) that profoundly affect our efforts. Even more importantly, as individuals we must develop awareness of the internal counterparts of those forces, the often unconscious attitudes in ourselves that compromise our energy and direction when it comes to serving any devalued group.

There is no way to discuss issues relating to the survival of severely handicapped infants without dealing outright with the central value dilemma. Guidelines for professional conduct are meaningless unless we are able to bring to consciousness the ideology out of which we are operating when faced with our responsibilities to such children. Before we deal with technical questions, we must explore further the usually unspoken values that too often impel our actions.

Who should live? How can this decision be made? In every culture, guidelines for such a decision are communicated to all its members. Whether they are interpreted as divinely dictated or socially conceived, such guidelines represent the values the society holds regarding life. However, there are spoken or conscious and unspoken or unconscious guidelines, which often conflict and compete. Most members of a society enact its spoken values. Some who do not may be rebels or even criminals. But they also may be leaders or heroes, since it is sometimes allowable for certain individuals to violate the society's articulated values and to act out unspoken ones. If we turn for a moment to the title of this chapter, "Survival of Severely Impaired Infants," we can examine how our societal values operate. Consider the following scenario.

I am a physician and have at my command technical resources to be marveled at. Should I use them? Should I not use them? The infant who is my patient offers no solutions but, rather, is the problem. It lives. It is in need of assistance if it is to go on living. But it is seriously "defective." The child's parents believe that they wish it to die. Have they the right to command this? Do I have an obligation to follow their wishes? I am committed to preserving life and feel that I should be my patient's advocate, but are the parents not right? Would it not be the "best" thing to allow the child to die?

Let us look further into the nature of this dilemma. We are a society that is for life and that does not deal in death. This position is articulated everywhere—in law, in religious and ethical proclamations, in traditional documents. Yet we do kill, and we justify killing under a host of allowable conditions—for example, in war, for personal defense, as punishment for certain crimes, and to terminate gestational life. We also "let die" when there are no other alternatives. But sometimes when a technical alternative is available, the decision to "let die" is made nonetheless. Consider the following recent newspaper story, headlined "Kill Severely Retarded at Birth: Anglican Study" (Harpur, 1977):

> Putting severely retarded infants to death at birth as suggested in an Anglican Church task force report would be "playing with fire," a leading Anglican scholar said today.
>
> Reverend Reginald Stackhouse, principal of Wycliffe College and a professor of ethics, said in an interview: "We saw what happened in Nazi Germany when they used selective extermination to create a so-called pure race. I don't think Canadian society would ever want to go that route."
>
> The nineteen-page report of ethical problems on death and dying is not a policy statement by the church. It suggests death be considered only in the case of infants usually referred to as "human vegetables."
>
> However, the document—drawn up by an eleven-member group of doctors, nurses, theologians, and lawyers—is creating furor within the church and has sparked bitter complaints from a number of doctors, according to Anglican sources.
>
> "I think we're playing with fire when we claim the right to decide who will live or die," said Stackhouse. "The security of all of us as human beings depends on society being committed to preserving lives of the innocent, the very young, and the very old alike." That is a tradition as old as Hippocrates and has always been the position of the church, Stackhouse said.
>
> The Anglican Task Force on Human Life, commissioned in 1975 by the General Synod, highest court of the Anglican Church, also suggests that means of prolonging life be withdrawn in cases of terminally ill patients in a comatose state. In the brief section that argues the case for killing the "severely defective newborn infant, which has no chance of gaining a modicum of spiritual or intellectual life," the group says that at present "paralysis of thought" is preventing society from taking any such direct action.

"A very black day for the Anglican Church," commented Doctor Leverett deVeber, of London, Ontario. "I'm astounded they even put this forward for discussion. It's another step backward. I don't see how anyone could look at a baby and say that this is one that should be killed."

DeVeber, a Roman Catholic, is a member of the Canadian Physicians for Life—a group of doctors who banded together to oppose "what appeared to be the Canadian Medical Association's position of supporting abortion on demand."

The report quotes both Pope Pius XII and the Archbishop of Canterbury, Most Reverend Donald Coggan, in support of "passive euthanasia"—the cessation or withdrawal of extraordinary means to prolong life—in cases of the terminally ill "when the quality of life is marginal, when the patient is irremediably comatose or when death is already in sight."

On the question of infants, the report says: "The medical attendants may hope that the infant may contract some infection which, without treatment, will cause death, but if such a merciful outcome does not occur, the parents and society may acquire a sad burden for twenty or thirty years."

Pointing out that the severely defective baby may not be human as defined by the authors—that is, able to relate meaningfully with others and with God—the paper says it would be a "fundamental error" to treat it as human. "Our senses and emotions lead us into the grave mistake of treating human-looking shapes as though they were normal humans although they lack the least vestige of human behavior and intellect." Deciding which "human shape" has the continuing potential to become fully human will be difficult, the report concedes, and in cases of doubt "we should err on the side of humanity." Where there is no doubt, however, the agony of parents and the burden assumed by society—especially the diversion of time and services which could be better used elsewhere—have to be considered, it says. Parents would have the paramount say in such active euthanasia, according to the report, and

the church could play a leading part in helping them
deal with any lingering sense of guilt.

Doctor Lawrence Whytehead, a Winnipeg surgeon who is chairman of the committee and edited the
report together with Reverend Paul F. Chidwick of
Walkerville, told *The Star* in a telephone interview:
"It may read as though we're advocating active
euthanasia but our intention was to say that this is a
point of view or option which has to be seriously
considered."

Anglicans in Toronto say there is already "one
hell of a do" over the report and several doctors have
written letters of bitter complaint to the head office
here. One doctor accompanied his protest with a documented series of case histories of children who would
have been eliminated if the recommendation on euthanasia had been applied but who have gone on to
achieve remarkable human fulfillment.

Such decisions are *value based*; that is, we allow ourselves
to make the determination of who should live and who should die
according to the value we place on the particular individual. What
is the worth of a severely handicapped infant? Is it not the general
societal perception that such children are "better off dead," and are
not parents and professionals sometimes asked to play the roles of
conspirators in a drama in which societal prejudices are enacted
and the child dispatched? Do we not think parents irrational who
demand all-out efforts be made on behalf of their severely impaired
child? Do we not damn with faint praise the physician whose treatment of such a child is "heroic"? Have we not, in fact, entrusted
physicians and certain other professionals with the ancient responsibility of "casting out" the unwanted by granting them decision-
making powers for life and death and presumed immunity from
consequence, especially when parents are collaborators?

We could accept the answers to these questions without defensiveness and without pain if we were, indeed, a society that was
plainly death dealing. We are not; therefore, most of us as professionals and as individuals must experience pain and equivocation
every time we are faced with deciding our response to the needs of

devalued individuals. However, because we are indeed also life pre-
servers, we have provided some safeguards (guidelines) that prevent
us from violating entirely our more generous natures. It may even
be postulated that our maturation as a society can be measured by
the extent to which we increasingly develop such guidelines to protect the most vulnerable among us and by the extent to which these
guidelines reflect the coming to consciousness of our currently unconscious devaluations. The fact that the present guidelines and
safeguards are unclear and equivocal reflects accurately our collective equivocation about the value of human life.

The ultimate question is really "Is all human life *inherently*
valuable?" An even more daring humanistic perspective is "Is not
all human life of *equal* value?" A materialistic society that measures
value in terms of health, beauty, wealth, strength, intelligence, and
productivity could not, in honesty, accept or implement an "equal
value" hypothesis. A humanistic society with a somewhat more
cosmic or eternal perspective could. Inevitably, we cannot escape
the logical conclusion that if people are not of equal value it is only
by arbitrary social agreements that they are not.

The person or persons who might decide at some critical
point whether or not a severely impaired infant will be treated or
will live or die should be aware that these decisions, albeit complex,
ultimately rest on a central value choice. Of course, it can be, and
frequently is, argued that it is an expression of humanism to allow a
severely impaired person to die or, conversely, that it would be
"cruel" to assist the person to continue living. However, this point of
view presupposes the materialistic values cited above and the conclusion that life is not worth living if one cannot be the possessor of
those things that we say are good. It also opens the door to discretionary judgments regarding who has enough potential to live the
good life and forces those (usually professionals) who are willing to
make such judgments to act as doorkeepers to death, a role that is
ultimately brutalizing. So, the judgment giver has a twofold value
choice to make—not only what is valuable to keep alive in others
but also what is valuable to keep alive in oneself. To the extent that
there are clear, unequivocal, external guidelines for professional
conduct, an individual is freed of having to make this value-based
choice. But to the extent that external guidelines are unclear, one

must make choices based on internal guidelines and values that are, inescapably, the very values that govern one's own life.

Technology in itself does not provide solutions for essentially moral dilemmas. There was, perhaps, a time when professionals were spared the necessity of making many value-laden decisions because the technology was simply not available to alter a fatal course or to deal with the consequences of a severely impaired infant who survived the neonatal period. The medical technology of today, however, is astounding! It has kept pace with, or has exceeded, technological advances in many other aspects of our culture. We have applied technology toward the alleviation of human suffering with a high degree of consciousness that this was being done in the service of humanistic values, and we have been very successful in the areas to which we have given clear priorities. The field of neonatology is a relatively new but rapidly developing one that has altered remarkably our ability to decrease infant mortality and morbidity. It is no longer possible to take refuge in a fatalism attributable to technologic deficiency. Where we have the technology, the choice becomes simply one of whether to use it or not, and this decision is one based on values. However, if we pursue for a moment the notion of technology used in the service of values, it is possible to conceive of a broadened technological application that would permit us to opt for life-saving measures in a moment of crisis with the assurance that the consequences for a child and its family would not be disastrous. That is, one could plan an immediate and long-range comprehensive series of interventions that would augment the child's abilities and provide all necessary supports to the family. We could envision many technical means to enhance a child's functioning. We could envision the creation of a physical environment that would be barrier-free and that accommodated all. We could envision minimum physical and psychological suffering and maximum life-enriching supports. If we can agree that all human beings have a right to survive, if that guideline can stand as the paramount one, and if the means to survive are already largely available, then the task of technology is to provide the means to thrive. And it becomes the responsibility of society and its individual members to see to it that technology is used toward this end. Helping professionals have a special responsibility.

We teach clinical professionals clinical skills. But clinical skills alone cannot solve complex human problems. We do not usually "teach" social awareness, the politics or economics of human services, or the moral necessity for humanistic activism. Except for a brief encounter with the guidelines for professional ethics in each discipline, it is largely assumed that the professional person who completes a course of training is somehow magically endowed with humanistic instincts and certifiable moral fiber. But professionalism and humanism are not necessarily synonymous. Furthermore, the professional membership may, in fact, harbor values that contradict the stated purpose of the discipline.

The medical profession's purpose is to preserve life, to alleviate human suffering, and to promote health. It does so but not without equivocation and partiality. We have maintained that the dilemmas arising derive, in part, from the physician's internalizing of societal values. Let us examine for a moment how the training process reinforces society's priorities. Few medical schools include in their curricula significant training modules dealing with the problems of the developmentally disabled. The absence of curriculum time devoted to this area is significant. Instruction is overwhelmingly related to medical and surgical interventions in primarily intact persons. The healthy individual who becomes acutely ill and the valued individual whose chronic illness is viewed as a public as well as personal misfortune are its focus. The elderly, the disadvantaged, the multiply handicapped, and the developmentally disabled do not fare quite as well medically. In fact, the developmentally disabled are represented in most curricula as highly stereotyped categories exhibiting definable syndromes. Some of these can be classified in relation to causal factors; some cannot. Classified as "disorders," few of these are curable, and many are untreatable by any known medical intervention. Such individuals are considered interesting curiosities. They simply do not accommodate well to the medical model, which is based upon the assumption that once the cause is found the cure can be applied. Perceiving this, the student of such "disorders" immediately becomes aware of the fact that the physician's skills are not always as pertinent here as they are in other areas. This is sometimes communicated pejoratively by the use of devaluing terms such as "gork" and "F.L.K." (for "Funny Looking

Kid"), or less grossly by the adherence to the professional jargon of classification ("this little hydrocephalic," "that little trisomy"). These are surface defenses that put distance between the medical professional and the "patient," once the professional has realized that failure to obtain a definitive cure is inevitable. The approach also coincides with society's perception that such different individuals are a liability. But since we tend to conceptualize negatively valued differences as "disorders," we have persisted until recently in assigning them primarily to the medical realm. What inevitably follows is that the medical student who wishes to understand how to relate to developmental disabilities must explore other disciplines— for example, social work, psychology, education, and rehabilitation. This course is usually a lonely one, embarked upon by a relatively few medical professionals with special interests, since the medical teaching institutions themselves have been slow to facilitate an integrated curriculum that meaningfully balances what they teach and what the other human service disciplines offer. The complex interrelationships between the handicapped person, his family, the physician, community agencies or programs, and other disciplines are alluded to during the physician's training, but never given the coverage they merit. Thus, the physician emerges from training as a highly skilled diagnostician-technician but ill-equipped to orchestrate the developmental interventions that must occur if the severely disabled child is to grow. Paradoxically, until recently in most states, this latter role is precisely the one that physicians—because of their traditional status as the director of the "team"—have been asked to play. How difficult a task for anyone, let alone those who have not had special preparation for it! Faced with this complex reality, the physician can respond to the demands made of him in several ways. He can openly admit that he does not have the skills to coordinate a developmental plan for the child and can ask to play a more limited role in purely medical areas. He can acquire necessary skills to function as a developmental specialist who also is knowledgeable about the contributions that must be sought from others and can accept the coordinator role with confidence. He can persist in the notion that his medical training and professional status qualify him for this key role. Or, if he is uncomfortable in these areas, he may consciously or unconsciously insulate himself from meaningful involvement in such situations. The latter two alternatives are the dangerous ones! They often result in unknowing judgments, noncomprehensive management, parental abandonment (by the physician), and support for restrictive options, such as institutionalization, that relieve the physician of further responsibility. Those who practice these latter alternatives are in need of consciousness raising and self-awareness far more than additional clinical expertise. There is further danger in the fact that input into policy making, program development, and resource allocation is also sought most frequently from physicians, without due regard for their level of expertise or breadth of perspective. Society indiscriminately places great expectation upon medically trained people. However, this entails great responsibility, and to be seduced into a task or role for which one is unprepared or not fully aware is unconscionable.

Perhaps we can now review our case. We have chosen to view the issue of survival of severely impaired infants as prototypical of the plight of the vulnerable and devalued in our society. Instead of focusing on clinical management issues, frequently discussed elsewhere, we have focused on the central issue of societal and individual values in the belief that creative solutions to human problems flow from value decisions, not technology. We have attempted to understand the medical professional as an individual member of society shaped by its values, which are manifested as well in professional training and ultimately in the conduct of the physician. We have maintained that awareness of external forces and consciousness of one's internalized ideology are both indispensable to humanistic action and the avoidance of sanctioned brutality. And, lastly, we have postulated that guidelines for humanistic action are equivocal in our society, permitting such extreme actions as termination of life and suggesting that we have not yet come to grips with how we feel about the severely impaired and how we intend to address their needs.

How will we address those needs? Consider the following document, "A Declaration on Human Rights and Responsibilities," prepared by a group of residents of Onondaga County in New York state. This group included consumers, services providers representing many disciplines and agencies, and other interested citizens.

I freely sign this Declaration affirming the constitutional right of anyone to make public one's individual beliefs, irrespective of that person's affiliations or the auspices under which that person is employed. I act now as an independent citizen, representing neither agencies nor others but myself, dedicated in support of these beliefs:

- that, as human beings, all people are inherently valuable,
- that all people have essential rights and privileges,
- that, included in these rights, all people must have access to a broad spectrum of services and opportunities to ensure their physically, spiritually, socially, and psychologically optimum development,
- that such development is enhanced in integrated open community settings,
- that among those who have been most frequently detained in segregated settings and who have most often been denied their basic rights are devalued people with special needs—the so-called handicapped (for example, physically disabled, mentally retarded, emotionally disturbed), the elderly, and the disadvantaged.

Therefore, because I support the above statements, I pledge to work to achieve the following goals:

State and local priorities and allocations shall be designed and implemented to encourage the creation of sufficient options to make it possible for all people who are legally entitled to their freedom to lead integrated and purposeful lives.

Relevant agencies and individuals shall provide support for the fullest community integration by working toward a moratorium on the planning, construction, purchase, or endorsement of any segregated or closed settings that deprive people of free access to share in community services. This goal requires enunciation because community priorities and resources heretofore have been primarily designated for segregated facilities.

State and local public and private tax exempt agencies shall feel obligated to present regularly to the people their plans created to ensure the fullest community integration of their clients with special needs. Included with such plans shall be time estimates for the achievement of their objectives, descriptions of special efforts that have been made to promote integration, and evaluation summaries of program progress.

That, because all people have a right and a need to achieve and are guaranteed access to most opportunities by the elements of due process, state and local agencies shall agree that laws are for all people and must be applied justly to everyone, and present discriminatory laws and practices shall be eliminated.

Therefore, because I believe in the natural rights of all people to freedom within just laws and for full opportunities to develop, I will work to achieve the following related provisions, whether such efforts require legislation, litigation, or program implementation:

Human service agencies shall be accountable to their constituents in ways that shall ensure that: In both planning and evaluation there shall be clear and well-marked lines of such accountability; providers of services shall not be the sole planners and evaluators of those same services; the primary sources of program planning and evaluation shall be derived from the local community, with substantial consumer participation; there shall be identifiable mechanisms for monitoring and ensuring quality of human services; agencies shall be evaluated according to their abilities to demonstrate growing responsiveness to the needs of those whom they serve; detailed information on the general operation of human services will be publicly disseminated and readily accessible, with proper protection of individual privacy. Prudence shall be used in limiting access of third parties to confidential materials in personal records while, at the same time, consumers or their specified agents shall not be prevented access to their own records.

Citizens who seek human services shall be provided with a series of accessible and appropriate options, from which they shall be free to select.

Consumers or providers of services who raise questions or criticisms regarding accountability, discrimination, due process of the laws, treatment, or related issues shall not be subjected to retaliatory actions.

Any individual affected by a decision will be involved in the process of that decision making. A person unable to act positively to advance one's own interests shall be represented by a person pleading the cause of the individual as if it was his or her own.

Funding shall be dependent upon the ability of agencies to demonstrate the above principles.

A reasonable proportion of all funding shall be allocated to support innovative programming sponsored by either established or emerging agencies.

Recognizing that we, in our society, too often compromise our human values by treating people unjustly and recognizing my responsibilities to myself and others, I pledge dedication in my daily life to working for the support and realization of these values and goals.

Consider also the following items which are quoted from the United Nations General Assembly "Declaration On The Rights Of Mentally Retarded Persons," which was adopted in 1971. "(1) The mentally retarded person has, to the maximum degrees of feasibility, the same rights as other human beings. (2) The mentally retarded person has a right to proper medical care and physical therapy and to such education, training, rehabilitation, and guidelines as will enable him to develop his ability and maximum potential." And consider this from the constitution of the New York state chapter of the American Association on Mental Deficiency: "Recognizing that all people are of *equal* value, we affirm that citizens with special needs are entitled to the same rights, privileges and respect as is due all individuals. Hence, we (A) recognize that all people with special needs are entitled to appropriate services to meet their specific needs, and (B) we believe that the continuum of services should include access to the same opportunities as those that are afforded our general citizenry." This clause was negotiated in an agreement between a community hospital and a developmental center *after* the death in that hospital of a severely retarded person under questionable circumstances, including the withholding without notification of life-sustaining measures that physician-advocates did *not* consider extraordinary: "Prior to a decision to withhold *extraordinary* life-sustaining measures, the hospital will secure the agreement of the administration of the developmental center and the patient's next of kin. *The hospital agrees to provide medical services to mentally retarded patients without prejudice based on race, creed, color, national origin, sponsor, or degree of developmental disability.*"

All of these statements are guidelines for professionals' conduct. They do not carry the force of law and are, therefore, subject to violation. Nevertheless, they represent a concerted, growing commitment to humanistic activism, which if spread to communities everywhere, can change our collective consciousness and the future of human services.

Humanistic activism derives from a life-valuing ideology from which springs a commitment to bring about life-supporting and life-enriching changes. Devoid of naiveté and romanticism about life, the humanistic activist must see clearly the realities that threaten or compromise it but is also able to envision the evolution of a society that will have confronted its value dilemmas and applied its resources and technology in the service of life. Those who can overcome cynicism and embrace such a vision of society should

see themselves as the agents of change and dare to live accordingly
—not necessarily as revolutionaries but as aware, committed
individuals.

How might this broadly stated humanism manifest itself at
a given critical moment in the life of a professional person? Let us
examine with an awareness of the ideologic issues and the option for
an activist perspective the physician's dilemma described earlier.

I am a physician and have at my command resources to be
marveled at. Should I use them? Should I not use them? The infant
who is my patient offers no solutions but, rather, is the problem. It
lives. It is in need of assistance if it is to go on living. But it is seriously "defective." The child's parents believe that they wish it to
die. Have they the right to command this? Do I have an obligation
to follow their wishes? I am committed to preserving life and feel
that I should be my patient's advocate, but are the parents not
right? Would it not be the "best" thing to allow the child to die?

"I am committed to preserving life" is the key statement in
the active resolution of this dilemma. If our physician has internalized this commitment, then equivocation disappears. The "problem"
is no longer the handicapped infant but, rather, the rallying of
supportive interventions, the overcoming of attitudinal barriers in
other professionals as well as in the parents, and the application of
technical resources toward the infant's survival. Of course, all of this
is easier said than done, but the most difficult obstacle has already
been overcome—one's own crippling doubt about the course to
pursue. Conversely, the most serious error the professional who is
working with severely handicapped infants can make is to underestimate, or to fail to come to grips with, internal doubt. What about
the attitudes of others? The clinical situation described calls for some
immediate medical intervention. This could include the participation
of a pediatrician with neonatal experience, a neurologist or neuro-
surgeon, and, possibly, an array of other professional specialists.
What will their values be? This question will be impossible to answer, but the physician who calls upon them should be certain that
they are aware that the desired outcome is a living infant with as
much functional ability as it is in their power to preserve or augment. Clarity on this issue is fundamental to a concerted treatment
plan and vital to each specialist's communications with the family.

Beyond this, the committed physician should seek opportunities to openly discuss the value basis of medical care with colleagues whenever possible in order to develop awareness of this issue and to foster unanimity of clinical approach. The infant's physician should also be willing to confront others whose attitudes are unacceptable and to risk criticism or censure from those who are cynical of life-committed ideals. How far each person wishes to go in order to advocate for equal treatment within the medical community is an individual decision. Physicians usually have opportunities to influence policy making at the administrative level via the hospital or medical school's committee structure or through local medical societies, and it is also relatively easy for a physician to influence the community at large by becoming involved with school boards, school committees on the handicapped, community task forces, legislative committees, and countless other similar activities. Participation in community deliberations that affect medical care, the development of programs, and other supports for the handicapped is a necessary activity for the physician who wishes to bring about positive change. To forfeit input is to risk that decision-making citizens will enact measures based on values and priorities that are in conflict with the needs of the handicapped. Physicians' responsibility for attitudinal change includes both the critical clinical moment and advocacy activities aimed at bringing about systemic alterations. Perceiving oneself as a change agent is far different from the usual physician self-identity, but it is this very perception that enables one to approach a difficult clinical situation with the confidence that one is doing more than just preserving a life.

Approaching the parents of the severely handicapped child requires an even greater commitment as well as skill, honesty, and understanding. The bond between the physician and these parents may last a lifetime and will profoundly affect each life it touches, including that of the physician. Learning to communicate meaningfully to parents can bring great personal and professional satisfaction. Conversely, those who do not may experience frustration and alienation that can result in their becoming insensitive to parents' needs and strengths and ultimately to hostility when either fails to meet the other's expectations.

What is the nature of the honesty the physician must bring

to the clinical situation we have described? First of all, parents must know the facts of the situation as these facts exist. The physician must present them with clarity and skill and without medical jargon, carefully estimating what the parents can meaningfully absorb in their emotional turmoil. The initial approach to the presentation of these facts is crucial to the parents' understanding and acceptance of the situation. An insensitive presentation (at this or any other time) is not only clinically unsound but is in itself an act of brutality. Secondly, the physician's honesty must include the admission that one cannot usually predict an outcome with any real assurance. Nevertheless, the physician must be prepared, as soon as the parents are ready, to answer their questions regarding the potential for corrective, supportive, and habilitative services and programs. This requires an intimate first-hand knowledge of such services and programs (or the prompt identification of a knowledgeable consultant). Without such information, the physician is unprepared to fill his role as advisor to the parents and, in fact, is unsuited to play any decision-making role in regard to the survival of the infant. Awareness, not only of what is currently available, but of the habilitative potential of one's community, is as essential to the life-sustaining view as is the conviction that all living beings have the potential to develop. Initially, the physician may have no other choice but to coordinate interventions on behalf of the infant.

As the child grows older, however, the focus should shift from medical or medically related needs to educational and "vocational" or habilitative needs. As this shift occurs, the physician should surrender the coordinator task to another appropriate professional, while retaining input regarding medical concerns. It may be that the parents will continue to seek out the physician as a trusted advisor. If so, the physician must be extremely careful not to preempt the roles of other involved professionals or to make unilateral decisions in nonmedical areas. The physician's role at this point should be to interpret to the parents the comprehensive plan devised by the various professional members of the intervention team that comes to be structured around the child. No matter how severely handicapped the child is, a careful, step-by-step, comprehensive developmental plan is required. No child or adult need be consigned to a lifetime bedridden existence. There have been repeated demonstrations of remarkable progress in even the most severely handicapped when interventions are vigorous. Even if progress is minimal, a daily schedule can be devised that ensures that the child will be out of bed and placed in the most optimal situation. No child or adult need be "written off" or considered a "vegetable."

The physician's honesty should also include the willingness to disclose to the parents the nature of her internal convictions regarding the survival of severely impaired infants. The parents have a right to know, and they should be helped to communicate their own feelings on this issue to the physician. Without this mutual understanding, the physician–parent relationship is subject to ongoing mistrust. Neither the physician nor the parents, however, should confuse their right to explore their own internal convictions with the infant's right to survive. That right is inalienable, and it is increasingly likely that it will be legally upheld with potentially grave consequences for those who violate it! Our scenario described a life-committed physician who wishes to advocate for the child and is not sure how this can be done in view of the parents' supposed belief that the child should die. First of all, parents' fear and confusion are very often expressed as their "belief" that the child's death is the best solution simply because no other acceptable course is offered to them, and they cannot begin to imagine how they will deal with the situation. A physician who is unequivocal about the value of the child and is prepared to discuss a supportive course with assurance can do much to allay parental fears and confusion. At such times the input of other parents who have faced similar situations may also be extremely helpful, and many communities have set up parent-information groups with "hot lines" to provide such support immediately. It is also necessary that *all* the professional persons who communicate with the parents adopt a uniformly supportive approach, and it is the managing physician's responsibility to see that this approach is taken. If the parents persist in their wish that the child should die, the physician is not obliged to concur and is not relieved of the responsibility for preserving the child's life. The parents cannot mandate the child's death. They should be informed, however, that they do have the option of surrendering their guardianship of the child and this may prove their only viable option if they are intractable.

The physician also has the option of obtaining a court order that will allow treatment to proceed over the objection of the parents, although this may be time consuming when prompt action is necessary. Collusion between the physician and parents for the purpose of ending the child's life by withholding ordinary means of support or treatment intervention can be interpreted as a criminal act. Of course, this does not apply to situations in which all reasonable efforts have already been made to try to save the child, but it is likely that hospitals and physicians will increasingly be obliged to show documentary evidence of such "reasonable" efforts. Many severely impaired infants do not survive despite all efforts to save them, but, if these efforts have been honest, then the infant's demise need not leave in its wake guilt-scarred physicians and parents. Only the most insensitive persons or those with the staunchest of internal defense systems could participate in the planned demise of an infant and emerge unscathed unless, of course, society encourages such actions and relieves all attendant guilt. If society does so, the triumph of brutality will have been complete and the human value issue, like the children, long dead.

It is frequently stated that it is economically unfeasible for society to provide for the severely handicapped or that resources used on their behalf are necessarily denied to other needy children with more potential. Why must we accept as inevitable that human services needs should compete with one another in this way? Why must we give priority endlessly to fulfilling our materialistic desires when so many of us have so much already? Why must we squander resources on pursuits that do not benefit humans at all, or even threaten to destroy us? Those who believe that society should not continue to move in these directions have no choice but to confront their own complacency and to advocate actively for the kind of society they want. Is there any other way for this process to start than for it to be generated out of the most deeply held convictions of each individual?

The Declaration on Human Rights and Responsibilities concludes with this statement: "Recognizing that we, in our society, too often compromise our human values by treating people unjustly, and recognizing my responsibility to myself and others, I pledge dedication in my daily life to working for the support and realization of these goals and values." There is no measure of professional expertise that can replace this dedication in the service of values. There is no more important alliance than that of parents, professionals, clients, and other citizens as they work toward mutual life-supporting goals. There is no greater responsibility than the responsibility to oneself to keep alive the courage to search for solutions to human problems that do not dehumanize any of us. The severely handicapped call forth that courage.

Except as noted in the body of this chapter, the author has elected not to list references. Readers are asked to respond to the content of the chapter by examining their own convictions concerning the issues discussed, and not by accepting any of the material on an authoritarian basis.

Are any human beings expendable? The author explores this question as it relates to the survival of severely handicapped infants, viewing them as prototypical of those whom society devalues. Do we go far enough in committing resources and technology in the service of human values or do we consciously or unconsciously dehumanize others and, in the process, brutalize ourselves? This chapter describes an alternate course of humanistic activism, with particular focus on the dilemma of the physician caught up in conflicting parental, societal, and personal values at a critical moment of decision.

Case Presentation for Problem Solving

John Mahun was born after a normal full-term pregnancy. The mother was twenty-eight and the father twenty-nine years old at the time of his birth. There were three other siblings, aged two, five, and seven. The child had some cardiac–respiratory difficulties at the time of birth. His weight was six pounds, and he was noted to have multiple congenital anomalies, such as a cleft palate and equinovarus deformities of the lower extremities. He remained in the hospital during the newborn period for approximately two weeks, during which time casts were placed on the lower extremities after consultation with an orthopedist. He was fed via dropper and syringe because of the cleft palate, and the parents were taught these techniques. He was eventually released to their care at home. At the age of about two months, he became listless and unresponsive and was admitted again to the hospital, and found to be in congestive heart failure. A consultation by a pediatric cardiologist and a complete cardiac workup revealed a large interventricular septo defect, with pulmonary hypertension. John was placed on a digitalis preparation in order to control the heart failure. It was determined that at a later date cardiac surgery might be in order so that the heart defect could be repaired, but it was felt that this should be delayed until the child was more stable and had grown to a larger size.

At about the age of four months, John began to have seizures and was referred to a pediatric neurologist. At this time phenobarbital was prescribed, which appeared to control the seizures considerably. Developmental evaluation at six months of age showed that John was functioning at only a two- to three-month level. Physical growth was noted to be below the third percentile for his age.

At this point, the parents, together with the physicians who have been involved with John, have considered possible courses. It has been noted that placement out of the home in an institutional setting might be an alternative. The parents and physicians also have discussed the possibility of a fatal outcome if cardiac medication were discontinued. All of the discussants were equivocal about taking this action, and the parents were advised to consider carefully how they felt about it.

Some questions that could be asked in this case presentation are: (1) What approach to the parents would you have suggested in the immediate newborn period? (2) What kinds of supports do you think would have benefitted the parents when they initially brought the child home from the hospital after the newborn period? (3) Who else besides the physician and the parents might participate in the present discussion of possible outcomes? (4) Assuming that the withholding of cardiac medication could prove fatal to John, what implications are there in making such a decision? (5)

Were the child to die, despite efforts to preserve his life, how do you think the parents would react? How should they be counseled? (6) If the child died as a result of withholding treatment, how do you think the parents would react? How should they be counseled? (7) If you became aware of a situation in which passive or active termination of an infant's life were being considered, what would you do? (8) If the present child were to live, what kind of comprehensive habilitation program would you envision? (9) Could you describe a community-based system of services that could encompass such a program? How should the cost of such a system of services be borne? (10) What are the current financial implications for parents who seek services in the community? (11) What do you think might be the effect of a severely handicapped child on other normal siblings if the child continued to live at home? (12) What do you think might be the effect on the family members if the child were placed in an institution? (13) How many alternative residential options can you conceive? (14) What do you think is the most viable of the alternative solutions in a situation such as the present one? (15) What is the nature of this dilemma? Is it moral, political, economic, cultural, religious, or technical?

Chapter **12**

Perspectives of Parents
of Disabled Children

Richard M. Switzer

For many parents, a dependence upon professionals begins with the statement: "There is a problem with your child." Fear, anxiety, and often depression follow as the physician either bluntly or gently announces a serious disability. The medical terminology, of which the parent is totally ignorant, helps not at all, but deep within each parent's heart is the feeling and the hope that maybe something can be done.

To add to the strain, parents of children whose disabilities are diagnosed sometime after birth frequently receive the horrifying news in a sterile, unfamiliar setting, such as an impersonal medical center. So often the local hospital does not have the technology, the expertise, or the supportive personnel to make the required assessments.

The specialists who must be called in for consultation more often than not do not know the parents and may even be unfamiliar with the family physician. Although a specialist may have good intentions and may try to be consoling, understanding, and empathetic, he rarely has the time to deal with both parents holistically and to help them face the shocking news they must bear. How ideal it would be if other personnel could assume the burden, other personnel who by training and personality could temper the onslaught of sadness the parents must face. Yet, rarely are such professionals available, and, even if they are, parents may still seek out the specialist they really want to talk to—the doctor herself. The situation is a difficult one for which there is seldom adequate preparation.

To most laypersons, the world of the disabled is new and unfamiliar. Such terms as *muscular dystrophy, multiple sclerosis, spina bifida, dysautonomia,* and *paraplegia* are but complex words that denote a disease state. From the terms themselves, parents do not even know which part of the body is affected. Even the parent with experience with one disability will react as a novice to another. It becomes just a new word to add to the vocabulary. And then the questioning begins. "Will the child live?" "Can she play and learn and talk?" "Will she walk?" "Can she go to school?" "Will she need surgery?"

As the process of facing disability in the new child continues, parents realize that a joyful pregnancy, upon which so many hopes were placed, may end in a kind of tragedy. The outcome is far different from any of their expectations. The translation of these never-to-be-realized hopes into revised aspirations for the newly born handicapped child is rarely the concern of any professional, and so they remain unresolved and a source of sadness to the parents.

The family—grandparents, cousins, and nephews—has to be told, and the explanations have to be made repeatedly. "Yes, she will be able to function." "*No,* she may not be able to walk without crutches." "*Yes,* she can go to school." These are just some of the wearing interactions with which professionals seldom deal. Finally, feelings of guilt have to be faced. Did one of the parents carry the genes? Was it an accident during pregnancy? Was it smoking or alcohol? Why has God done this to me?

The problems that parents of disabled children face always appear to be new, urgent, and unique. Will the child need special postnatal care? Will reparative surgery be prescribed? Are there particular requirements for feeding or sleeping? How soon will a prosthetic device be helpful? Will special drugs have to be administered? The excitement and the swiftness of those early postnatal days almost seem important in themselves and to themselves. Families rally together, siblings show sympathy, and concerned relatives and friends offer help. But as months go by, the disabled child becomes less and less the focus of popular attention and more the object of pity, regret, frustration, and hopelessness. Everyone seems to have concluded that coping is the parents' responsibility, but most parents do not know how to handle these new and changeable attitudes.

Almost without exception, parents look for two miracles. The first is a cure: the treatment, the procedure, the drug that will make the child whole. The second is related to the first: Who will lead the child to normalcy? The first is rarely gained except in those congenital disorders that can be totally corrected by surgery, such as a patent ductus arteriosis. The second involves the most terrible never-ending search that parents will ever experience; for there is not the single expert but instead a series of professionals, each of whom will have a role to play and each of whom likely will begin to play that role from a narrow perspective. The great strength in this system is that unique individual expertise representing diverse disciplines, views, and concepts can be brought to bear on the problem. The great weakness is that only in the most unusual situation will the professionals act like a team, viewing the disabled child and her family holistically. Sadly, in some disease states, such as Duchenne dystrophy, the best of expertise and the most integrated of services cannot change the prognosis of death.

Early in childhood the disabled infant will need a detailed physical and medical evaluation inventory by a physician—one who specializes in rehabilitative medicine. The child may be treated within the hospital confines or receive evaluation and treatment as an outpatient with the careful cooperation of the family pediatrician. If the child suffers from a neuromuscular insufficiency, physical therapy will undoubtedly be prescribed. Another specialist enters the scene. The parents must learn the exercises that the child will have to perform at home under their constant direction, and, as the child progresses into her early years, the problem of mobility—crutches, litter, or wheelchair—has to be faced. More pain, more exercises, more trying.

A third specialist—the occupational therapist—can help significantly in encouraging the use of the affected muscles by carefully using crafts and games, even at the preschool level. The disabled child who picks up a wooden spoon and stirs it in an empty bowl is playing just a normal game as a normal child does, but the disabled child is also preparing for life and the activities of independent daily living.

Other experts come onto the scene, some early, some later, but since speech and hearing are affected by many disabilities, the evaluation of these modalities and the prescription of training and aids should be done very early. Speech and language programs require close and constant cooperation of the family, for daily attention and practice are essential.

The normal child grows and matures because the senses of touch, smell, sight, sound, and kinesthetics are all constantly feeding her mind with information. The child who has a physical restriction generally has incomplete sensory stimulation that will be reflected in her knowledge of the environment and her response to it. Early in the child's life, the fifth specialist, the psychologist, will test the child. He will also view the family relationships and counsel all concerned. The father's role must be emphasized. Although most of the father's time is usually occupied with holding down a job, the father–child relationship is especially important to the disabled offspring whose physical restrictions limit her in the activities in which fathers and children normally participate together. The sibling's role is one of great significance and of great concern. If the disabled child is regarded as special—as a brother or sister who must always get first choice—or is the child in the family to whom no one says no, sibling rivalry and resentment are almost certain to follow. Needless to say, more than one disabled child in a family increases the potential complications.

On the other hand, some siblings are unusually helpful and kind, and the whole family may even come to feel that having a disabled child is a privilege. Yet, even if sibling rivalry is not demonstrated, professionals and parents must not ignore overall effects on the healthy siblings, for their life styles and perceptions of the world are significantly affected. Their existence would be very different if the brother or sister were not disabled, and at one point, perhaps in their adolescence, they may raise difficult questions about their family dynamics. Professionals also should not overlook the feelings parents have about the attention and time they devote to the different children. Much guilt can be aroused, or they alternately may feel resentful that the healthy children make demands upon them when they are already tired from caring for the handicapped child. Even when parents do look at their situation objectively, they still must face a major dilemma: There is only so much time in a day, and the nondisabled children can do more for themselves. But less interaction with the parents may then produce feelings of neglect on both sides. Opportunities for healthy children can be limited by their staying home and helping to care for the disabled child, as well as by financial resources being devoted to this child's needs. There are no easy or right answers to such conflicts, but professionals must be very sensitive to parents having to cope with yet another dimension of the disability on a day-to-day as well as a long-term basis.

As childhood progresses, the family of the normal child thinks of school beginning with first grade or kindergarten and now, more frequently, preschool. The parents of the disabled child must consider preschool as an essential maturing experience in the goal for independence and self-sufficiency. Yet, in our nation, preschool programs for severely disabled children are still very scarce in spite of the fact that experimental programs, such as the one conducted at Human Resources School, have demonstrated that the experience is of great importance in the physical, intellectual, emotional, and psychological development of such children.

Disability also costs money, and our society has evolved so that medical care, once an end in itself, is now just the beginning of the total rehabilitative process that will follow the child throughout her life. The economic burden that families must face presents another threat and source of feelings of defeat. Rarely can priorities or life styles be changed so dramatically as to make new finances available for the disabled child. The most that can be hoped for is sufficient public assistance to prevent other essential family functions from becoming too abnormally curtailed. Dilemmas that often arise from lack of financial support may result in a diminution of emotional support and essential family ties to the child. This is most apparent when a child has to be institutionalized. The acceptance of any kind of public support often results in the loss of privacy, a required sharing of personal finances and plans to strangers, and negative feelings about the entire process, which can be subconsciously reflected back on the disabled child.

Another dimension capable of generating anxiety and despair is a guarded long-term prognosis. Professionals and parents must remember that professional pessimism, although an attempt to be realistic, can be exaggerated. Sometimes the data base upon which to make a firm prognosis just does not exist. Yet, the early years are developmentally the most important for prognoses to be considered carefully. Of course, there is nothing to keep parents from going ahead with stimulation and educational programs even if medical personnel (often the only ones consulted during the early years) do not believe they will be beneficial. However, without encouragement, many parents do this with anxiety and even fear that they may harm the child. It is important that specialists in education and rehabilitation are consulted early and that the parents have every opportunity to contribute to the development of their child. It is equally important that prognoses be considered carefully, since they can easily determine the quality and quantity of environmental experiences provided. In my experience in directing a school for severely disabled children for fifteen years, I have seen professionals from all disciplines be incorrect in their prognosis of a child, not only in terms of life span, but in terms of educational and career potential.

Jimmy is a key example. Born with osteogenesis imperfecta, this young man was confined to minimal home-bound education until he was fourteen years old. Bound in a rigid body cast with diminutive legs and arms, which would seem never to be able to support muscular action, Jimmy revolved his whole life around his amateur radio set and television. With only two to three hours of homebound instruction per week, often offered by inferior, untrained teachers, Jimmy was both learning disabled and educationally deprived. He lacked skills in reading; he lacked abilities in mathematics; and he had literally no experience in peer relationships.

Then Jimmy was referred to Human Resources School. His pediatrician objected strenuously, for Jimmy suffered some ten to twenty fractures a year while confined to bed. What would happen to him in a litter, within the confines of a school, where other teenagers would come in physical contact with him? How could he survive the temptations of competitive sports, of trying too hard physically, and how could he ever make up for the educational insufficiencies that resulted from his home-bound teaching?

Jimmy came to our school, and he learned well. Though litter-bound, he engaged in competitive sports, from touch basketball to bocci to pitch-and-putt golf. Jimmy grew in wisdom, psychomotor skills, and hope. It took many months for his parents to become accustomed to his new-found freedom, but they did come to accept it. Adjusting his total body cast so that he could sit sideways on the front seat of a car, Jimmy successfully completed our adapted driver education program and was licensed to operate a motor vehicle in New York. To be sure, one driver education instructor resigned rather than try to teach a cast-bound boy to drive, but drive Jimmy did. He graduated as valedictorian of his class and then entered a major eastern university, where he chose a program in prelaw.

At the university, Jimmy was elected president of the student council. Then he entered law school, from which he has also graduated. Now a practicing lawyer who often must wheel his litter through cellars and back alleys to get into court rooms located in unadapted buildings, Jimmy has proven that both parents and professionals may not envision what motivation and sheer bravery can attain. Certainly, Jimmy continued to suffer fractures, for that is the nature of osteogenesis. Certainly, Jimmy suffered, and will always suffer, frustration from his lack of mobility, but he is now a professional, a man of attainment, from whom professionals and parents can learn much.

As an individual who was born with cerebral palsy, I found that having a disability greatly affected the direction of my life. This was not so much the result of physical restriction, although reduced arm and leg function is obvious, but the fact that so many people had already made up their minds about what I could and could not do. It began in my early school years and continued when I was an undergraduate in college. At first, I was not allowed to become an education major because a "limping teacher" just could not be a good teacher; I would be too traumatic for the children in the classroom. The grades I was given conveniently went down, along with my hopes and aspirations. Needless to say, the situation did change; a college official intervened and recommended that I be given a chance to prove myself.

In our nation, the physically disabled child has traditionally been relegated to homebound education. In most school districts this area of education has been grossly neglected; the children have received minimal instruction, often taught by teachers with little or no training in this specialized area. As the result of both federal and state legislation, the activities of advocacy groups, and experimental pilot schools, the attitudinal and architectural barriers that once prevented regular education for the disabled child are rapidly being removed. Indeed, present federal law requires formal affirmative action programs, and a recent court decision (North Carolina, 1977) has gone so far as to require a college to pay for a sign language interpreter for a deaf student enrolled in a summer program.

Mainstreaming, a word that will soon be commonplace in our language, is now the official goal in our nation (Public Law 94-142). Whenever possible, disabled children must be offered educational opportunities in the neighborhood school in the least restrictive environment. Although the concept is noble, the practical application presents a severe problem in the relationships between the professional teacher, the child, and other rehabilitation professionals. In fact, teachers in both our public and private schools have had little or no experience in educating seriously disabled children. It will be so easy to excuse them from gym, exempt them from drama and music, and eliminate them from class activities because they cannot function well. Indeed, to be completely practical, there will be thousands upon thousands of disabled children for whom the neighborhood school is not the best answer at this point in time. The special school meeting special needs must remain. Otherwise, if the disability is severe, the student will be the "freak," the social outcast, the one who is the butt of jokes in a school with nondisabled peers.

This is not to say that these attitudes should not and will not pass. Young children in an integrated setting, in fact, seem to be showing the way. A peer–peer program experimentally introduced at our school in cooperation with a neighboring public school clearly indicates that, with careful guidance by teachers and administrators, prejudice against the disabled can be eliminated. But we are far from establishing such programs nationally. Mainstreaming has been the hope of many educators for years. However, we must all recognize that if it is introduced universally without adequate preparation, the disabled child who presently is in a well-organized, goal-identified program could be transferred to a chaotic, disorganized situation to meet the letter of the law and the spirit of the times. A real dilemma emerges for parents and professionals. Do we allow such children to be trail blazers, to pioneer the effort for those who are to come later? Shall we force our disabled children to participate in those plans that meet the legal specifications here and now but that, in reality, are inadequate for them? Will parents and children have their hopes raised by terms like *individualized education program,* and *least restrictive environment,* and then have these same hopes frustrated or shattered because of inadequate school finances? Yet, the parents are told they have the right to demand such programs and related services.

The lack of adequate training of the professionals within the school systems could be a major problem in implementing the new regulations. The president of one of our nation's largest teachers' unions recently commented that although federal law now calls for an individualized education program to be developed for each disabled child, the attainment of such programs will be hardly possible with cuts in school budgets. For example, a hydrocephalic child may require a reshunting of the tube that drains the brain case, but many schools do not even have a school nurse experienced in this procedure. Parents also have the right to help develop the educational goals for their children. They have the right to review the proposed programs that will meet these goals and to help in the development of short-term measurable objectives. Furthermore, they have the right to demand specific educational services without regard to availability. The whole process is to be the result of a team action: the parents, teacher, guidance counselor, administrators, school psychologist, school physician, remediation specialist, and "other individuals" at the discretion of the parents and school authorities.

At the present time, many parents may not feel prepared to play a role in their child's educational programming in the manner in which schools have carried out this process. On the other hand, some school personnel are threatened by parents' participation or else appear condescending. Parents can experience a real dilemma when representing other parents on a committee for the handicapped but when outnumbered by the professionals by at least six to one. Parents of each child who must approve of, and should also participate in, their own child's plan may need special support from the professionals until they feel comfortable. Both parties most likely will grow with experience in understanding each other's contributions as will the meaningfulness of the contributions themselves. The intent of the regulations and procedures is sound and, as has been true of many other areas of social change, implementation becomes more efficient and comfortable with experience.

Throughout the disabled child's total rehabilitative and educational process, parents are told that "professionals know best." After all, their life's work has been devoted to these fields. "Be a nice parent, and cooperate, we know what to do" is the repeated litany. Indeed, the professionals often do know best, but they also often do not. Moreover, professionals should remember that in the case of most disabled conditions it has been parents' efforts which have brought about the programs and adaptations we take for granted today. Parents must frequently state their case and views from a lack of specific training, from a "gut reaction" about what they think is best for their child. The professional, whether a physician or a teacher, can too often dismiss the parents' concepts: "an emotionally involved parent."

However, lack of emotional involvement often keeps the professional from seeing the real, dynamic picture of the developing child. Professionals who deal with disabled children only during working hours and in an office setting often do not understand or even acknowledge the exhausting and mentally challenging nature of rearing a seriously handicapped child. They can be too quick to label parents incapable or neurotic. Moreover, there is no standard family with standard problems. Each family group is an entity unto itself with its own dynamics. Each must have its problems identified and solved individually, and, indeed, each will have different problems of varying degrees of complexity. To be effective, the professional must experience the individual family's functioning first-hand. An office "translocation" is just not the same; yet, in practice, many professionals operate from their offices and cannot even find time to visit the home.

The concept that good parenting of any child requires a great deal of knowledge and all kinds of preparation is gaining increasing acceptance by both professionals and parents. Witness the unique growth of parent education courses and experiences at all age levels in our nation. If such experiences are considered valuable for parenting normal offspring, they are much more essential for the parenting of a disabled child. Professionals can make their own task easier by participating in this thrust, by offering workshops and conferences, and by supporting all kinds of opportunities for parents of disabled children to help one another. Such parents are very often effective counselors and have a wealth of practical knowledge of which professionals are not even aware.

But the concern on the part of parents that professionals lack first-hand experience with the daily living problems and the emotional complications of disabled children is a real one. All the facets of a handicap, objective and subjective, may otherwise be difficult to grasp. Parents may very well communicate inadequacy in the particular area in which a professional is interested, but she cannot fully appreciate the overall strain they are under and the resulting tension in the child. There have been too many conclusions that the child's adjustment would be normal "if only the parents would behave differently."

The parents may also communicate depression and even paranoia about their situation. Over a period of time that a professional in one time and place seldom recognizes, the parents may have had enough experiences objectively to give them good reason to be depressed and paranoid. Services for their children take long to locate, names do not always match the actual services, health insurance is difficult and expensive to come by, a particular program finds an official reason to exclude their child or children; the list could be extended indefinitely. One mother recently voiced her anxiety about where she and her husband were going to continue to obtain enough money to meet all medical and related needs of their young daughter, who had cerebral palsy with a number of handicaps. They had already become involved with a number of different agencies and clinics, each for a different purpose. When asked what one program in particular, which seemed a logical source of major support, was providing, the mother responded, "They will pay for three pairs of shoes."

Professionals who themselves have had disabled children may be able to empathize quickly with other parents. However, they must realize that by virtue of the very fact that they are professionals they may have had fewer obstacles. Status as well as knowledge can make a significant difference in such circumstances. In any event, the present professional who is bemoaning the parents' liabilities may be the tenth one they have seen, and a number of the past nine interactions may have been negative.

Parents must be aware that helping professionals usually attempt to look at each child as an individual and then be realistic about the accomplishments that the child can attain. Parents must also be aware that each professional, because he is a specialist, views the child with a jaded eye. Rare indeed is the professional with the skills, the background, and the emotional traits that allow her to view the child as a whole person. Specialists must be aware of the limits of their knowledge, all of which may have been gained from their education and their clinical experience. For example, I have seen the pediatrician shocked at the osteogenesis child playing in a competitive sport, because the physician's experience with osteogenesis is concerned with skeletal fractures. I have often seen children reach attainments and achievements that other professional educators would find to be impossible. Parents, teachers, physicians, social workers, rehabilitation specialists must always be learners, and frequently the child is the best teacher.

I do not believe that a professional must be disabled in order to truly understand and be effective. But certainly a professional must be able to identify and to have had a first-hand experience, an intimate relationship with handicaps in order to cope with the total gestalt. The real professional has sought out these experiences by working with and for those who have handicaps. She must have role-played; she must have, even in a vicarious way, experienced at some level of the continuum the lot of the disabled. As we identify the increased abilities of disabled individuals, more and more of them are entering the helping and healing professions. Their very presence will serve as a meaningful force that will influence other professionals with whom they train and work.

There do exist emotionally involved parents who either have their sights set too high or too low for their disabled children. At Human Resources School, the faculty and staff fight two generalizations. The first is "My child can never attain your goals" and the second is "There are no goals my child cannot attain." Both are expressed only as the result of what parents honestly believe and hope, but sometimes they are too close to the situation to maintain perspective. If parents are at a point where they can be of little help to their children psychologically or physically, for whatever the reason—perhaps they are not even requesting all the services their children need—the individual professional has to ask herself about her obligation to intervene and improve the quality of life for the child's sake. The child cannot help herself, neither will she be able to do so later on, and she has no other advocate. A situation could arise in which parents cease to cope with the child's difficulties and essentially ignore his special needs. This can present a real dilemma for the professional, if the parents do not respond to counseling and other supportive services. Home and family interactions, whatever their nature, may be the absolute center of the disabled child's existence, so removal is difficult to contemplate.

One way in which professionals can broaden their understanding of, and feeling for, children suffering very severe or fatal conditions is to make home visits to a number of them, not just the few children for whom they might have particular responsibility. Children can also be encouraged by parents and professionals they trust to communicate their own perceptions of the disability. These frequently provide insight to professionals as well as parents about the ongoing emotional dilemmas. We may not often actually encourage these children to express their feelings about themselves, possibly because we are uncertain of our own responses, especially if a child has a terminal illness. Taping or writing may be less anxiety-producing to both the child and the adult. The following is a short story, "The Brain Machine," written by a wheelchair-bound boy suffering from muscular dystrophy. His awareness of the progression of the disease is apparent. But he communicates much more.

> Dr. vonFlight had finished his prize computer brain machine, which took ten years of research and study. Day by day the machine was helping the doctor to brush his teeth, comb his hair, and put on his shoes. The machine was Dr. vonFlight's pride and joy. He couldn't live without it. The months go by, and the doctor is getting more dependent on the machine. Each morning he sits up and turns it on. The machine helps him get out of bed. The machine helps the doctor brush his teeth. Late in the afternoon an electrophysicist calls up the doctor. The machine answers the telephone. The doctor talks on the phone and the electrophysicist asks the doctor if he knows the answer to a problem. Dr. vonFlight must ask the machine.
> Ten years have gone by. The doctor now must have the constant dependency of the machine. It happened so suddenly. The machine broke down in the morning when the doctor went to have his teeth brushed. The doctor went mad. He had to sit down all the time and couldn't do anything. A day later one of the doctor's friends came to see how he was doing. He saw the doctor sitting there. The doctor explained to his friend what had happened. The doctor's friend thought for sure he was mad. He called up a psychiatrist. The psychiatrist came over and the doctor told him what had happened. The leading psychiatrists of the country met and talked about what they would do with the doctor. They finally decided to put him in a little room where a nurse has to take care of him. That is how machine can take over man.

> *Thomas Roy*

I submit that what we know about the potential of a disabled child or even a teen-ager is but a fraction of what can be known. Thus, both the professional and the child should experiment with limitless parameters and goals. The educational process must have

several simultaneous objectives. We must teach the child to think
before responding, to identify a problem, and to set upon a course
by which the problem can be solved. We must inculcate in each
child an appreciation of what is good and beautiful, an understanding of esthetics. We must never grovel but always help the child
reach heights of appreciation even greater than our own. Coupled
to these goals must also be the practical task of preparing the disabled child for independence, the ability to become financially self-
sufficient through productive work.

Although much in our society is funded by state, federal,
and private grants, no child in his adult years should be relegated to
the status of ward. The dignity of holding a job, earning a living,
paying taxes, and being part of a growing economy of our nation is
an American goal. Self-reliance is far more than living independently, being able to toilet one's self or arrange for transportation. It
includes much more than special grants and unique educational opportunities. Self-reliance stresses responsibility so that each handicapped person can reach the fullness of her capabilities. This is why
all education of the handicapped, in my view, must have as an underlying theme career education, the recognition and enhancement
of those traits, skills, and personality characteristics that one day
will help the disabled child become an employed adult. In our culture, one's "vocational self" is part of identity. The goal is equally
important for adolescents and young adults with a limited life span.
We have too long hastened the end of their lives psychologically, if
not physically, by exclusion from programs because they are not a
"good investment." Professionals must examine the morality of such
practices, even if they are not their own. They are capable of influencing attitudes much more than they have in the past. In this
area where skill analysis, job requirements, and task simplification
must be coupled with hope and motivation, we all have much to
learn.

When we cast off the protective cloak of professional pedan-
ticism, when we can look to each other for guidance, when parent
and specialist can penetrate each other's emotional barriers, the disabled child and, indeed, all children, will be better served. Sometimes we as parents, teachers, physicians, administrators, and re-

habilitation specialists create our own barriers, carefully locked to protect the empire of knowledge and concern that we feel is ours. When we unlock those guarded doors, the same keys will open the vistas of independence for our children. A young girl severely afflicted with muscular dystrophy wrote a poem pleading for better communication:

Empathy goes a lot farther than sympathy.
Sympathy is wanting to help someone in need,
While empathy is actually offering him a helping hand.
Sympathy is wanting to cry when you cry,
While empathy is actually shedding some tears.
Sympathy is wanting to help an old lady across
The street, while empathy is actually letting her
Take your arm.
Sympathy is wanting to console a mourning widow,
While empathy is actually feeding her fatherless
Children.
Sympathy is wanting to comfort a broken heart,
While empathy is actually mending it.
While sympathy just grazes the soul, empathy
Actually penetrates it.
So empathize, don't sympathize, and you'll
Be happier if you do.

Denise Hawkins

Case Presentation for Problem Solving

Billy entered a private, state-operated day school at the age of one. Based on medical and psychological testing, he was diagnosed as a spina bifida child who was incontinent of bowel and bladder, having a shunt procedure done six months after birth. He was able to walk with the aid of crutches and bracing. Psychological testing was difficult at this early stage. He followed an early childhood program in this school, with specially trained teachers, until he was five. During this period, he received annual evaluations, both medical and psychological. At five-and-a-half, his Verbal IQ was 52 and his Performance IQ was 34. The special school staff recommended that Billy continue through the first grade and go right through a special education program at the elementary level.

During the five years Billy attended the school, his parents received psychological counseling concerning his prognosis and potential. His mother and father both wanted to know when Billy would be able to attend regular school. The father was a lawyer and they were an upper-middle-class family. The two other children were aged ten and two. During Billy's kindergarten year, both parents read about Public Law 94-142 and felt that the law mandated that Billy be mainstreamed into a public school. They immediately met with the school authorities, who agreed that they were mandated under 94-142 to try to admit Billy into a regular first grade class. The problem was reviewed by the local district's committee on the handicapped. The committee recommended that Billy continue in the private school at least through the second grade to determine whether or not he would be able to read as a normal child. The parents disagreed with the committee and went to the school board to demand that Billy be admitted to a regular first grade program in the fall of the year.

Some questions that could be asked in the case presentation are: (1) Were the procedures followed by the public school correct? (2) If you were the parents, what questions would you initially have asked of the public school concerning both acceptance and program? (3) If you were the principal of the private school, what recommendations would you make to the parents now if there was difficulty with the school board? (4) As principal of the private school, what recommendations would you make to the public school if the school board contacted you?

Chapter 13

Professionals in the Public Schools

Edward R. Lisbe

I have seen idealism easily transformed into disenchantment in many interns or other students I have supervised. Apprentices in social work, psychology, administration, counseling, and teaching all want to make their unique impact on the slow-moving monolith of the public school. "The man who sinks his pickaxe into the ground wants that stroke to mean something," is Saint-Exupéry's (1939, p. 292) description of this energy. Too soon, however, the fire dies. Too soon, when the pressures become greater, the question "How many mountains *should* be moved?" becomes "How many *can* be?" Eventually, if all energy is drained, the question may become, "How can *I* survive?"

Young professionals need not suffer this spiritual annihilation. It is the responsibility of all of their instructors and field supervisors to help break this cycle. Nothing is more critical. Many of us come to a career choice out of a deep, personal conviction that we have found a route to the mountain top. We follow "the path with heart" as Carlos Castaneda (1968, p. 106) learned from his teacher, a Yaqui Indian "man of knowledge." In addition to acquiring specialized knowledge and skills, individuals who have chosen a professional path need two critical supports. They need help in keeping their dreams alive and in building an awareness of the pressures to be faced in doing that. The pressures must become as real to emerging professionals as their dreams.

I was always a dreamer. The difference now is that I carry the dreams in my pocket instead of on my face. The shift occurred somewhere between my first and third year of struggle as a voice for children with teachers, principals, parents, and social agencies. I never fully understood why we were not on the same side; I only knew that I tended to see with a vision different from those around me. While my colleagues were honing their diagnostic skills for an attack on the latest categories of "learning disabilities," I quietly read books by Jonathan Kozol (1967, 1972), a perilous journey for a young graduate student and novice professional in the public schools. My earliest dilemma was in deciding whether or not to continue searching for a truth, the finding of which I knew would be like cutting the oxygen supply from a candle. For, if as I believed, children were failing to read not only because they were dyslexic or minimally brain damaged or slow learners or disadvantaged but because schools as institutions were not designed to help students become persons first, then what could I do? Thus, the nature of my task began to take shape: to change the entire face of public schooling in the United States. My dream was to achieve for the disenfranchised and disinherited children of the world in education what Jonas Salk had accomplished in medicine. For a graduate student, few goals are unattainable!

My days and nights were filled with the dreams from which glowing auras of self-importance are fashioned. I would be the successful change agent. With my knowledge and desire I would, like Atlas, carry all the weight of the world on my shoulders. The nights were particularly inspirational, the stillness and stars combining to nourish ever-growing portraits of the knight on a white horse. Whether or not I could achieve a universal impact with my work was never a question; the only issue was to find the surest way. I laugh easily at myself now. How thankful I am for the quiet smiles that keep me from looking backward with present knowledge to evaluate earlier innocence and the seriousness with which I took my beginnings. The smiles help me to appreciate my first stepping stones across the river, however misguided they might have been. With a light heart, I can appreciate the worth of the whole process; without the lightness I would have wishes for swifter "knowledge." All of my dreams are now tarnished; many are broken. But the laughter helps me to see how lifeless a graduate student would be without them. Unrestricted vision may be a gift present only once in a professional's life. Each of us has inside ourselves a piece of good news. To share that with others is why we enter the helping professions. What we need to learn is how to keep the news alive through the times when no one is reading the paper.

Looking to reach the lives of more children, I left school psychology after several years to concentrate on teacher training. Reflections on wins and losses within the school experience are cloudy because numerous perspectives take shape: How many mountains were there? How high? Which ones were climbed? How fast? Who helped? What climate surrounded the mountain range? Did I use dynamite? How scarred is the mountainside from my climb? Schools are too large, the issues too far-reaching for an individual to make a finite evaluation of impact. The effects of battles fought along the way may be measurable, but the results can never be tallied. I affected some lives and missed out on others. I did not change the world. *Winning,* then, was not the standard against which I saw my accomplishments. Rather, it was *going the distance with my dreams.* To keep them, I learned to hide them better, to make them less vulnerable to attack. The rainbow colors within me are not as brilliant as they once were; my life raft has been often punctured and deflated. Yet, the colors look deeper and richer, the raft stronger with its patches. I went the distance and I still have my piece of good news.

Immense personal energy is necessarily expended for that kind of success over the course of a career. Responsiveness under constant pressure with thoughts, feelings and behaviors that are congruent with a personal values system can drain inner resources to depletion. The realities of "people work" require a presence unlike other fields where processes are replicable. Carpenters follow blueprints, automobile manufacturers use molds, accountants work from forms, and pilots read instrument panels. There are no such guidelines when one human being faces another, where the uniqueness of each encounter requires uncompromising intensity. Thoughts of the effects of such cumulative stress of a great many such interactions over the course of time are unsettling. The breadth of human dynamic complexities in the helping professions—medicine, psychology, counseling, social work, education—was brought home to me one afternoon early in my career. In the space of an hour, after concluding a traumatic parent conference that had been interrupted by phone calls from two principals, I was visited in rapid succession by three high school students, a teacher, and a probation officer. The conference involved relating to some parents a decision made by the committee on the handicapped that their child needed special educational services. No matter what sentiments or educational philosophies surround that announcement, it is never easy for parents to learn that school authorities consider their child to be *different*. One principal was having trouble with a third grader throwing a tantrum, and the other was requesting help with an irate parent. The students, suspended for a fighting incident, wanted me to speak with the principal on their behalf. I listened to the teacher who had personal problems at home, and I gave my information to the probation officer who was wavering on a decision to place a student in foster care.

Reflecting on this experience at the end of the day, I realized with alarm the commitment I had made in becoming a member of the helping professions. In schools, particularly, the opportunity for intervention in the lives of others is unique. Professional skills to be exercised with the magnitude of this responsibility must be outstanding. A devotion to effort and excellence far beyond anything I had previously given in my life was required. I needed razor sharp mental agility, an ability to shift directions as quickly and easily as a porpoise, and, like a cheetah, the ability to reach top speed again in seconds. Quiet with these and other thoughts, I sat for several hours, searching for an answer. I found that I wanted to live each moment of my life to the extent of its possibilities, and the vastness of the school psychologist's role would allow me to do this. My resolution that same night to never intentionally abuse the position was a value I held throughout my years of service and is the one of which I have always been most proud.

Such values, though, do not make one a professional. Neither does the possession of a degree grant this status: doctors, psychologists, lawyers, teachers, and other certified helping professionals who treat their degree as a license to *practice* will remain forever distant from their patients, clients, and students. Those who see it as a license to *learn* will touch lives. There is a capturable moment when one becomes a professional. For each of us, there is a turning point, a special time or place where we cross a line. Kopp (1972, p. 4) describes the journey of the seeker, a passage that cannot be anticipated or hastened: "The cool water of the running stream may be scooped up with open, overflowing palms. It cannot be 'grasped' up to the mouth with clenched fists, no matter what thirst motivates our desperate grab." One becomes a professional by reacting with natural responsiveness to a flow of events. Out of this process comes a moment of special significance, a piece of eternity never to be repeated anywhere.

Such a turning point came for me in the winter of my first year in the schools. My superintendent had called to "ground" me for several days. He asked that I stay out of the schools and remain in my office while he tried to work out the complications arising from a decision I had made and acted upon the day before. It took no more than a second after the close of the telephone conversation to return the receiver to its cradle but, in that instant, I became a professional. A picture flashed through my mind of a delicately balanced scale weighted with *safety* on one end and *risk* on the other, and I realized that maintaining that vital balance was what professionalism was all about. I became aware in that moment of the gulf between my personal needs and the role for which I had been hired. I knew that if I had a future, it would be filled with choices for which finding answers would not be easy. The constant dilemma would be to act in accordance with my beliefs without jeopardizing a position that enabled me to be an advocate for children in the schools.

The incident that precipitated the call involved my action the day before in helping a fifteen-year-old girl, whom I shall call Tracy, to run away from home by crossing state boundaries. Although I had made the decision after a careful consideration of alternatives, I had not foreseen all of the consequences. Tracy's guardians, relatives who had reared her since she was four, were now threatening to sue me and the school. I had picked her up at school in the morning, driven her to the airport and bought her a ticket to fly to another state to live with her sister and brother-in-law. This is drastic action for a school professional to take. Beyond the specific issues, I had acted out of a growing uneasiness about the charade of "help" we profess to offer children. We talk, make phone calls, contact agencies, hold meetings, and write reports, but we may send the child back to an environment that we who have choice would not select unless a gun were to our head. A counselor had spoken to me that week of her frustration at having to send a certain child home to a probable beating each day. I was beginning to question my own sincerity with the children I faced. I no longer knew whether I was playing a game or was there to help. I am sure this mounting frustration about my motives was a factor in my decision in this situation. Tracy had been hospitalized the previous year after taking an overdose of pills. If she succeeded in killing herself the next time, I would not be satisfied with the legal protection my school position gave me. I could envision a final school or medical report stating, "She had been seeing the school psychologist regularly." I felt strongly that something more than talk was necessary. No one can ever say with certainty which of the two goals, a cry for attention or an attempt at self-destruction, is intended by a person who swallows an excess of pills. And, even if it is the former, the latter may be the result.

Here was a girl becoming, over the course of two months, more and more hysterical about her treatment at home. Never physically abused, she claimed that her relatives only wanted her social security check each month and that they did not show her love or affection or other emotional support. She said she was yelled at rather than talked to, frequently locked in a room, allowed none of the personal freedoms normally accorded a high school adolescent, not allowed to use the hot water in taking a shower, and generally degraded about her looks, personality, and intellect. In all ways, she was not being affirmed as a worthwhile human being. The issues as I saw them were as follows: (1) Emotional abuse cases are rarely defensible in court. I was, therefore, involved with (2) a potentially suicidal, (3) underaged girl, unable to legally extricate herself from her predicament. The effect on her (4) appeared to be worsening, and I (5) could not contact her guardians because I had agreed to the girl's request for confidentiality.

The sister in another state, a neighbor, and several friends who had been to her house verified much of Tracy's story. I contacted the department of social services and was told they could not help because the complaint did not fall under their definition of abuse or neglect. A family court judge told me that a good defense attorney would be able to tear apart a case like this, and a lawyer from whom I sought advice said he would not involve himself with this kind of problem. With legal recourse to removing the girl from her home apparently not possible, I thought of three alternatives: (1) continue to speak with her in the hopes that counseling would be enough, (2) speak to her relatives without her consent to try to reconcile the issue through problem solving, or (3) help her to leave home if that was her desire. I rejected the first option because her distress seemed to be increasing rapidly, and she had once before brought harm to herself. I did not wish to see that happen again. To pursue the second alternative would have been too great a compromise of my values. I hold trust inviolate. I also believe that a child knows his parents better than I. To think otherwise would be presumptuous, and to act without this girl's consent would be an abuse of my position, although according to traditional ethical guidelines I might have done so. The third option became very attractive when Tracy's older, married sister called with an invitation for her to come to stay with her. Through several phone conversations, I perceived the sister to be mature, reliable, and sincere in her offer. She described in great detail the home life, schooling, and extracurricular activities that would be available. Relocation seemed to be the ideal solution when Tracy announced one day that she was leaving home and requested my help to get to her sister's. I arranged for her flight, called her sister, and, in the morning, helped her to leave.

I have had frequent letter and phone contact with Tracy since her departure years ago. The change in environment seemed to open her up to a new world. She is a happy, healthy young lady, bursting with enthusiasm about her life, full of a laughter that I never saw during our time together. Children are entitled to this kind of happiness. Emotional scars are long lasting; yet, as a culture, we do little to help children whose bruises cannot be seen. I supported Tracy because there was no socially acceptable way for her to improve her situation. Freedom of movement should not be strictly an adult prerogative.

However, the risks were considerable, both legal and professional. For aiding and abetting a runaway minor across state lines I was subject to arrest. Had anything gone wrong with Tracy's trip, I probably would have gone to jail and been sued for damages. She might have been hurt, her sister might not have been there to meet her, or she might have changed her mind and disembarked at a connecting airport. Many things could have happened over which I had no control. I did not think of these issues in acting as I did. After talking with my superintendent, the district attorney was able to convince Tracy's relatives that my intent was not criminal, and they did not press charges. Later, I learned from a lawyer that a court might be sympathetic to a psychologist's ethical judgment in responding to a dilemma for which there are no meaningful guidelines.

The professional risk was not only to my then-current job but also, perhaps, to any other school position I would try to find in the future. I created a difficult dilemma for my superintendent who was faced with a furious school board, an angry high school principal, and an apparently naive school psychologist who had without doubt exceeded the duties for which he was hired. A superintendent has no procedures to follow here. Beyond the guidelines, like any professional, he can reach only as far as his own human experience will take him. In allowing me to continue within the school system, he demonstrated a supreme act of faith that I would, in the future, operate from the school's frame of reference as well as my own. His faith was warranted because I had learned through this experience that my responsibility was as much to the school as it was to the children. My superintendent also knew of the congruence between my actions and my own life process. He did not fault me for responding to a dilemma out of my deep moral convictions, even though the result was not in the best interests of the school. Through his response to me, I learned more of what it means to be a professional. I believe he made his decision out of an awareness, above all else, of the genuineness and sincerity with which I approached my work. This taught me that there are no more important qualities than these for a professional to model in earning the respect of his peers.

With hindsight, I see that my eagerness, not my values, created the risks. Faced with the same situation again, I would continue to be emotionally supportive of a student who needed to make a change, but I would not take part in the implementation procedures unless it was absolutely necessary. Tracy could have waited for her sister to wire the money to her neighbor, made her own flight arrangements, and located another ride to the airport. My overprotectiveness during the final hours was unnecessary. In all other respects, my position would be the same. Children have few alternatives for airing personal or family problems. Because of this, I consider it my *ethical responsibility* as a school professional not only to provide services, such as support and safety, but also to encourage students to use them. Where else but to the school can a child look for help? Schools and their potential for providing a caring person occupy a unique space in the lives of most children.

In one particularly tragic incident of noncaring, I felt silent rage for the faculty of an entire building. I had been away from the high school for some time and returned to find in my mailbox a note dated three weeks previously from a student urgently requesting to meet with me. I called for her and within minutes saw a shell of a human being walking down the hall toward my office. I saw in her lowered head, hunched shoulders, averted eyes, and slow shuffle a despairing soul. As she came closer, I added to the composite picture a wan complexion, nervousness and fright—not at seeing me but at being alive. She was totally without spiritual energy. I took her hand and reflected softly to her what I was seeing in her body language, "You look as if you have lost all reason for living. I am glad that we will have a chance to talk." After several quiet moments, I saw a tear form in one eye, followed soon by a flood as she became racked with sobs. We spoke then for several hours. I discovered to my sadness that she had been with these feelings since she wrote the note and that in all that time not one person in the building stopped to be with her as I had. For three weeks, she attended school with her insides raw, and no one noticed. What a tragedy for her to be in the midst of so many people and to receive no help. The question is not one of caring. Most educators care for children, or they would not be in the profession. The issue is rather, one of awareness. Teachers must begin to see more than lesson plans, administrators more than procedures. The idea that only a psychologist can reach out a hand to an unknown student in pain must be dispelled. And for the psychologist to perpetuate the myth would be an unfortunate misuse of the assets a school has available for children.

I am suggesting a need for expanded awareness as a way to most effectively use a school's human resources. The professional's dilemma is twofold: to see with more than ordinary vision and to make responsible choices with that sight. We have to look continually beyond the behaviors and between the words of our students and peers. In explaining a method of "stopping the world" to his apprentice (Castaneda, 1968), Don Juan spoke of a *seeing* that happens only when one sneaks between the worlds, the world of ordinary people and the world of sorcerers. Professionals must develop and sharpen such powers, for it is only when we are fully aware of our worlds that we can be truly effective change agents. The inherent difficulty with such an approach is that insightful vision leads to a realization of an ever-increasing multiplicity of issues. Professional wisdom would seem to be in knowing where to stop the process, if that is possible, in order to formulate the major issues clearly. The following two examples are reconstructed conversations, overheard in elementary school offices.

A school secretary speaking to a fourth-grade teacher: "My niece is three-and-a-half years old and is already reading. A brilliant child! She'll surely be a problem to her teacher, though, when she gets to kindergarten. I know she'll be bored, and then she'll become a behavioral problem. By the time she reaches your grade you will really have your hands full." The teacher's response: "It's really getting tough. Parents press their kids too early, there's all the early television like 'Sesame Street' and 'Mr. Rogers,' and the kids are just learning too much, too fast."

The professional who overhears a simple conversation such as this is faced with many choices. One option would be to have not "heard" it and to continue on with the day's work. An alternative is to ask some questions and raise some issues: (1) need for curriculum revision, (2) education of kindergarten teachers on the current needs of children, (3) an inservice course on motivation of children, (4) parent-community education regarding preschool learning (to counter misinformation handed out by the school "experts").

What about all the questions this situation raises at the present moment? Do I share my thoughts with these two individuals about how the learning process may be stifled, how children are often fitted to school instead of school to children? Or, do I say nothing in order to avoid the risk of alienating two people with whom I need to work in the future—especially the secretary who supplies me with valuable information about children and their families? Should I not inquire about this gifted child? Or, perhaps, follow up with a call to the parents to offer my assistance in planning for the future? Should I at least alert the parents to their rights in future years to ensure that their child receives an education commensurate with her needs? If I pursue this last course of action, what about the potential future problems I am creating for school officials who will be required to provide the special services? I may have helped this child, but what if I am consequently turned down by the same officials on a request for a program that might affect 300 children? Whom have I helped and whom have I hurt? The question is how fast or slow should I go? How much or how little should I do?

If I sought them, I would have enough issues with that one conversation to fill a month's schedule. The importance of these questions is in the asking, not the answering. Is there a sensitivity to the layers of meaning beneath overheard dialogue? An undercurrent of thought and feeling exists in the schools, an attitude about teaching and learning beyond any individual classroom experience, which severely affects the quality of education received by the children. Professional awareness means *seeing* this undercurrent in the scores of conversations that take place daily in the halls, offices, and teachers' rooms of any building at any given time. If the school psychologist or other professional is to make change in the overall current of children's lives, it is these issues that must be brought to the surface with as great an urgency as responsiveness to direct referrals.

The school situations I speak of occur with such regularity that possibilities for intervention are often overlooked. Each morning hundreds of children disembark from school buses with feelings of anger, hurt, depression, and loneliness. This emotional energy is brought into a teacher already overburdened with the tasks of teaching. A bus driver is more than a transporter of bodies. When drivers are interviewed, perhaps a psychologist or counselor present as a child advocate might get a feeling for whether or not an applicant understands the needs of children. Perhaps, a course in communication skills for all drivers could be required so that a sad child boarding an early morning bus might hear, "Hi, Carol, you look a little down in the dumps, hope things get brighter for you," and be more able to face the day. These are the issues toward which a professional's antennae must be tuned. This is where his eyes must be trained to see.

A familiar scenario in schools involves the midyear entrant. Laden with meaning not apparently obvious is this one act play I observed on one such occasion:

A mother walked into the building with her nine- or ten-year-old son in tow. One glance at a tough, hard face with piercing cold eyes, attached to a swagger of self-importance, told me that this was a child who would not easily fit into a fourth or fifth grade classroom of obedient youngsters. The mother's first words, "I just moved here from Pittsburgh and want to register my son, Jerry, for fourth grade," were to the principal, who happened to be standing near the reception desk.

As I ideally would have it, the principal would have responded warmly with words to this effect:

"I'm happy to meet you and I welcome you to our town and

school. I have a few minutes and I would really like the three of us
to sit in my office for awhile, so that I could tell you a little about
me and about the school. I'd also like to know from you, Jerry,
what you like to do, what your interests are, and how we can best
work together to make you really enjoy your being here. Then we
could meet your teacher, who'll be breaking for lunch shortly, and
she could explain a little bit about her program. Maybe you could
decide with her the best way and time to meet the class and you
could start sometime tomorrow, if that's comfortable for you."

That is what I would have *liked* to have heard. This child
was new, and the principal had time. Besides being genuinely humane, it could have been a significant preventive action. This child
looked to be potentially troublesome, and, if so, he would create
hours of work for teachers, psychologists, counselors, and administrators in the future. All of these professionals have a common investment in the proper handling of such an encounter. The import
of this simple registration procedure is magnified by the ramifications it holds for these and other people in the system.

Here is the dialogue that actually took place:

Principal: "Has he had his shots yet?"

Mother: "Yes."

Principal: (without ever looking at the boy) "Is there anything we should be aware of about his school-
work or behavior? Do you have any questions
yourself?"

Mother: "No."

Principal: (smiling, without emotion) "Well, you can fill
out these forms with the secretary and then
she'll bring Jerry down to room 104. He'll be
on bus 36 to go home at the end of the day."

As the mother thanked him and the principal turned away,
he added, "Please feel free to ask me about anything you have
problems with. My door is always open."

The principal here is in the position of moving a mountain.

With common sense and a minimum of courtesy, he could help this child feel important, and thus create an opportunity for a successful school experience while he also opens the door for his own productive future contact. Instead, he has effectively shut his door forever to this parent and child. It is this principal who becomes most upset when the community voters turn down a budget after months of careful public relations efforts by the school board. "How can they do this?" he asks, thinking of the exposure to education he has generated through such vehicles as the Thanksgiving play, the Christmas choir, and the bimonthly school newsletter. Parents, however, see this for what it really is, glitter without substance, when their basic need for respect, understanding, and involvement are not met on a daily basis throughout the year.

The issue, then, is not so much this child's feelings as it is the broader implications for every professional in a school district. We often tend to operate in a vacuum, invariably to each other's detriment. This principal's callousness, multiplied by similar indifferences throughout the day, will directly affect his own professional life, the lives of the other children in the boy's class, his teacher, his family, the school psychologist and/or the counselor, and perhaps several social agencies. Administrative guidelines list certain procedures for admitting students. It is beyond the guidelines that we need professionalism. Anyone can ask a parent to fill out forms, but a professional must be aware of, and skillful at, implementing more than a basic set of instructions. This is his moral and ethical responsibility to the child as well as to his colleagues. Eradicating role definition within the ranks of school professionals would make this process substantially more effective. A teacher in the building, a nurse, or, perhaps, a secretary might have better skills for this admissions experience than the administrator. There is a wealth of talent in the schools, but we must seriously begin to look at personal qualifications and strengths rather than at certification or professional standing. Knowledge of one's own limits, together with sufficient ego strength to unhesitatingly ask for help—whenever and wherever it is available—should be professional prerequisites.

Too many lives are connected for there to be many insignificant human interactions within a school system. There is a causality that extends far beyond the bounds of a conversation or an activity. A friendly remark to a seventh-grader standing near the courts where the junior high school tennis club was practicing one afternoon led to a successful counseling experience when his girlfriend's brother was referred to me one year later by the principal. Awareness of this interconnectedness, this spider's web of lives in a school both adult and child, is the key for bringing together that special society known as *school*.

Once we see them, we can answer the questions, although the answering will raise additional queries. Here is a sample of my inner dialogue in observing the principal's registration procedure:

1. Do I intercede on the spot to make the child's entrance into a new and probably frightening situation less traumatic?
2. Do I offer to take the child down to the room and try to ease him in as much as possible?
3. Do I speak to the principal later?
4. Do I forget this child and begin designing a model program for future midyear admissions?
5. Do I set up a conference with the teacher? If so, when?
6. What is my reputation so far in this school?
7. What is my relationship on a personal level with the principal?
8. Do I know this teacher or parent?
9. What is my professional history (success/failure) with the principal or teacher?
10. What are the principal's educational philosophies?
11. How does the principal react to advice from subordinates?
12. Should I offer assistance to the teacher and, with my group work ability, structure some activities to help the class more readily accept this child?
13. Do I call the mother at home and offer to visit as a way of introducing the family more positively to the school system?

In addition to choosing from these and other options, I would need to ask even more questions: When would I start? With whom? Who else is involved? Do I need permission or more information? Who can help me? Whose toes am I stepping on? What am I giving up to devote my energies here? To answer these questions I need to have a clear perspective of my goals: Are they long or short term? Do I want to have a wide-ranging impact on the school system, or will I be content to help a few individuals? Young professionals have to ask insightful questions in order to select wisely from alternatives. Their enthusiasm must be tempered by an awareness of tangential issues to ensure the greatest likelihood of success. Well-founded hesitancy and caution are often confused with compromise by graduate students anxious to put out forest fires before putting on their asbestos suits.

Awareness is a vigilance, a habit of attending to a variety of realities wherever they arise. This, itself, is a mission of Herculean proportions. However, the task is even greater. Most beginning professionals see the mountain and many discover a route to the top. But few know how to climb and so hardly any reach the peak. One must have more than ideas. The stereotype of the philosopher is "someone who, when pushed, has nothing more to offer about life than an honest shrug of the shoulders" (Branch, 1977). Dreamers in public schools, when pushed, give up by either surviving or leaving. The pushing occurs in the climb, where we meet others who do not appear to share our dreams. It is here where the pressures build and the dreams die.

A professional's effectiveness in schools is greatly dependent on how well he works with others. If he is to keep his piece of good news, his interpersonal skills must be exceptional. A counselor must be able to persuade teachers to try different approaches with children. A teacher must know how to encourage and support parents. A principal needs the support of his faculty. A psychologist must convince principals that emotional disturbance in children does not lend itself to quick solutions. The results sought in interactions like these are usually difficult to achieve. All of us are creatures of habit, and we prefer to stay with behaviors that are comfortable for us. A professional must learn how to identify and satisfy the safety needs of the people with whom he works in such a way as to accomplish his own goals.

Unfortunately, most graduate training programs do not speak to this issue. The "people skills" taught in counseling courses focus on the characteristics of the helping relationship. They are not directed toward the conflict situations that the students will face in the field. Carl Rogers (1961, p. 397) eloquently defines the helper as one who is "(1) genuine, integrated, transparently real in the relationship, (2) acceptant of the client as a separate, different person, and acceptant of each fluctuating aspect of the client as it comes to expression, and (3) sensitively empathic in his understanding, seeing the world through the client's eyes." This supportive, gentle, respectful, unshakeable presence is a powerful longing in the heart of every human being. I try to live my own life according to this precept. But these words and feelings alone will not help a counselor to make an impression on a principal who believes that children should be seen and not heard. The counselor (psychologist, teacher) needs influencing skills.

Competence must be achieved in *salesmanship*. How can I have my ideas, opinions, or suggestions accepted by another person? How can I sell myself? Proficiency in selling is rarely developed at the graduate level, yet this deficiency is ultimately responsible for more dashed hopes and broken dreams than any other. With steady precision, our convictions are chipped away: "You can't do that." "It won't work." "This isn't the right time, maybe next semester." "Can you prove that it will work?" "You're getting too close to the kids." "The trick is not to smile until December." "I want you to do it this way." "You have to cover the curriculum." "Too many things might go wrong." "If I let you do it, I'll have to let everyone else do it." "You'll understand how things are done once you've been here awhile." Day after day, week after week, hour after hour, we are put off, postponed, deferred, delayed, and shelved. It does not take long for this sort of pressure to start a young professional thinking "tomorrow" instead of "today" and soon, "Well, it probably wasn't very important anyway." To reverse the trend, we must become skillful in selling ourselves and our ideas, in making others receptive to what we have to offer.

If forced to choose one variable which, above all others, accounted for my faring well in a typically conservative school district, I would select flexibility and versatility in my relationships with others. A successful dreamer knows with whom to share dreams and with whom to talk about reading scores. I believe the two keys to acceptance by others are an awareness that people vary in their interpersonal needs and an ability to respond effectively to those differences. My interpersonal priorities were different in each situation, depending upon the priorities of the professionals with whom I worked. This was not a compromise of my values; rather, it was a purposeful accommodation to meet another person's needs.

Early in my career, I tried to start a peer counseling program in my high school. The principal resisted, I pushed, and, although he finally agreed, the program was not as successful as I would have liked because it never received his support. I never reached him because I tried to convince him with explanations from my own perspective rather than his. What he needed was a list of long- and short-term goals, a specific breakdown of tasks involved, outlines, expectations and objectives, detailed time frames, and measurable results. What I gave him was a global plan for helping children, no facts and figures about the probability of success or effectiveness of options, a nonsequentially planned presentation, and no support material. I had dreams about creating better relationships among the students and building their self-esteem. I expected the principal to support me because my goal was so socially acceptable, and I became angry when he fought so hard. But, I was operating strictly out of my own needs and perspective. I believe he would have accepted my proposal much more readily if I had prepared myself according to his orientation rather than mine. The question novice professionals must ask when trying to meet children's needs in the event the other adult is not initially sympathetic is, "What can I do to make it easier for this individual to relate to me as a person?"

The role of interpersonal versatility in the success or failure of any school professional, and particularly one who operates against the mainstream, cannot be overstated. This type of knowledge should help one to anticipate, rather than to be surprised by, the actions of others and thereby stay one step ahead of the pressures. As long as that process can continue, the survival of dreams is possible. In a school where there are so many people with whom to relate, *skill in the development of productive relationships is a professional necessity.*

I am seeing an exodus of competent people from the schools. They do not feel positive regard for their efforts to help children or appreciation of their talents. Friends, whom I know to be lovers of children, are choosing to spend their lives in out-of-school professions for similar reasons. These careers will *never* bring them the joy reflected *just once* in the eyes of a child who has found someone who understands. The loss for both is immeasurable. I believe the real reward for being a professional in the public schools is so subtle that it needs the unearthing intended by this chapter. I have shown the struggle because it is there with a presence equal in power to the dream. And I have become tired remembering what it was like. The outpouring of energy required the stamina of a long-distance runner. But when energy is expended for enhancing and enriching the lives of others, the self is the ultimate beneficiary. In giving to others, we empower ourselves. Personal growth is the result. I have been recounting a fight, not with the school, but within each individual, to always be stretching beyond our capabilities in support of other human beings. Tiredness is just the price of the dream. If all dreams have their price, the return on this investment is blue chip.

Schools are "people places." Maintaining this human perspective is difficult in the crush of teaching, learning, and accountability pressures. Too often the strength of dreams gives way to strategies for survival. This chapter is about the struggle to keep the focus on the people, the life force of any school system. The task is formidable, yet not as hopeless as many would have it be. No one individual needs to be a superman for children. In recognizing that all school professionals—administrators, nurses, bus drivers, teachers, counselors, psychologists, secretaries, and custodians—have the capacity to be helpers, a professional can expand his impact by replicating himself in others. Mountains cannot be climbed alone. Self-awareness, including the pressures to be faced in realizing one's dreams, and the consciousness of the invisible issues and undercurrents present in any large organization are as necessary as learned skills and techniques. There *are* skills that are important, however, particularly one that seems often neglected in training programs. Professionals must be successful influences. They must know *how* to get children's needs met as well as how to listen and be supportive. Recognition of, and the ability to be flexible in response to, the wide-ranging interactive styles of colleagues is a key for influence in schools. Beyond these ingredients, one element stands alone. It is so essential and important that without it, no matter what else is present, little can be accomplished professionally. A commitment to personal excellence is the standard by which all else is measured. Success requires the individual embodiment of superb interpersonal skills with children and colleagues at all times. There can be no rest periods. This presence with other people is an ideal goal that, of course, can never be totally *achieved*. But I have tried to show that the *striving* need never stop.

Case Presentation for Problem Solving

You have been working for one month in your first job as a school psychologist, hired after completing your internship in the same school district. It is a rural school with a student population of 4,500 for which you are the only psychologist. The university where you received your professional training is nearby, so you have access to support from the supervisor of your graduate program. The school district has six elementary schools, one junior high school, and one high school. Your relationships with the superintendent and with six of the eight building administrators are strong. The two with whom you have less rapport, the high school principal and one of the elementary principals, have the most political power in the school and in the community. You perceive them to favor the *good* children and to be less supportive of those with whom they have problems. The superintendent is a man of uncompromising integrity. A man of few words, he is straightforward and fair in his dealings with people and purposeful and clear in his handling of issues. You believe he hired you for your enthusiasm and personal commitment to bettering the lives of children more than he did for any specific professional expertise you had demonstrated in the internship.

Your path crossed occasionally with another psychologist who worked in your district performing specialized functions related to a federally funded reading program. On one occasion, he showed you a report on which he was basing a school exclusion. You saw the following:

1. The assessment was performed by a clinical psychologist in a distant city.

2. It would take at least three hours to reach her office by car.
3. The child was a six-year-old boy.
4. "Retarded mental development" was the diagnosis.
5. The diagnosis was based on an IQ of 74.
6. A forceful recommendation stated that the child was not a candidate for public school kindergarten and should be placed in another kind of education facility for children with special needs (unavailable).
7. The report was typed on less than one page.
8. The report was written in a detached manner that evoked no feelings of personal connection between the psychologist and the child.

You felt uncomfortable reading the report, sensing that something was wrong. The ramifications of such a diagnosis and recommendation on a child's life could be catastrophic, yet there was no sense of sadness evident. The writing was cold and calculated, as if a worker on an assembly line had inspected a product, stamped it, and passed it on. You also felt that an IQ of 74 is not particularly low and that perhaps the boy had been frightened. Many things did not seem to fit together as easily as the report stated. It seemed one-sided in light of the seriousness of its conclusion. The fact that no other possibilities or alternatives were raised seemed unfair.

Your colleague, however, was relying on that paper as grounds for exclusion. Although he was influential in the district, you knew him to usually favor expediency over quality in the work he did with children. There would be no investigation into the validity of the diagnosis or the merits of the recommendations. The child would be exposed to a failure experience that could leave him with permanent emotional scars.

When you handed back the report, you felt as if you were taking part in an execution so, without saying anything to the other psychologist, you decided to make a home visit. This is what you discovered:

1. The parents were feeling extremely alienated from the school and all of its representatives. They felt guilty about the difficulty their son was having and angry about never receiving support. They were very appreciative of your visit and encouraged by the fact that you

were interested in their situation. They promised their full cooperation with anything you wanted from them.

2. George had had two failure experiences with school. The parents
were not judgmental or blaming when they suggested that perhaps
the principal, the one with whom you did not get along, had not
done all that was possible to help. Their opinion was that even
though George was not the easiest child to manage, he responded to
friendliness and warmth, neither of which he received at the school.
He entered kindergarten the previous year before he was ready. He
was only four years and nine months old and was removed after
three weeks due to his evident immaturity. The present year he
began again and did not adjust well to the experience of the first few
days. George claimed one day that he had been treated roughly by
the principal, and he refused to return to school. The school was
convinced that he did not belong there because of his difficulty in
adjusting and because of the psychological report.

3. The IQ of 74 appeared to be invalid: George had been sedated
the morning of the assessment, he had just been in a car for four
hours, he was tested immediately upon entering the psychologist's
office; he did not respond to questions his parents knew he could
answer, and, the parents contended, the psychologist did little to
help him feel comfortable and at ease in the unfamiliar surround-
ings. Nevertheless the test was administered and scored. Given the
conditions, it seemed remarkable to you that the score was as high
as it was.

4. George's behavior did not seem to you to be that of a retarded
child during the time of your visit. His calculated nonresponsiveness
spoke to you as eloquently as if he were conversing with you. De-
fiantly gazing out the window, he glanced backward often enough
to ascertain your continued interest. He seemed to be wanting to
keep a distance between the two of you, a justifiable behavior in
view of his unhappy experiences with other school personnel. As
you were leaving, you tousled his hair and almost saw a smile. He
watched you from the window and you could almost see a glimmer
of hope in his cautious eyes.

The dilemma within which you find yourself here is many-
sided: The case is not yours to handle. Based on your observations,

you believe George to possess at least normal intelligence. If you do nothing he will be excluded from school. His home is zoned for the one school that has a principal with whom you have trouble and who is the least likely of all the elementary school administrators to give George the kind of support and understanding he needs. With your intuition you are challenging the test results of an experienced clinical psychologist. You have just begun your professional career and do not have the history of success necessary to get quick support if you intercede. You are not absolutely certain that George could succeed in school, so the risk to your credibility as a diagnostician would be considerable if you were able to get his readmission and he did not succeed.

Some questions that could be asked in this case presentation are (1) Would you intercede with the psychologist currently handling this case? If so, how would you do it? (2) Do you believe you have an ethical responsibility to become involved, knowing the probable outcome if you did not? (3) If you took over the case, what would be your first steps with the school? With the boy? With his parents? (4) What kind of evidence would you pursue to counter the results of the psychological report? (5) Would there be any benefit to be gained by contacting the psychologist who wrote the report and presenting your findings? (6) Are there other professionals in the school or community who might support and substantiate your position? (7) If the child were readmitted to the school, what steps would you take to ensure the greatest likelihood of his success? How would you plan his first day? What preparatory work would you have to do? What contingencies would you have to plan for? (8) Which school should he attend? Would another school be better, or should he try his home school first? (9) Should you involve the superintendent in these proceedings? If so, when? In what ways might he be able to help? (10) What do you see as long-term effects of your intervention decision?

Chapter **14**

Dilemmas in Child Abuse and Neglect

Alma S. Friedman, Maureen F. Cardiff,
Alan P. Sandler, David B. Friedman

Child abuse has been defined as any interaction or lack of interaction between a caregiver and a child resulting in nonaccidental harm to the child's physical or developmental state (Fontana, 1971; National Center on Child Abuse and Neglect, 1975). Abuse usually means the infliction of physical harm to the body of a child by other than accidental means. Neglect usually means the failure to provide necessary food, care, clothing, shelter, or medical attention. Sexual misuse (including incest) and the exploitation of children for sexual or financial purposes are detrimental to the physical and mental health of children and must also be considered as child abuse

(Walters, 1975). However, these issues have their own dilemmas and will not be considered specifically in this chapter.

The extent of the problem varies according to the figures cited, but conservative estimates (De Francis, 1977) indicate approximately 300,000 child abuse and neglect cases in the United States each year, with about 30,000 serious sequelae and 1,000 to 2,000 deaths. Compare these figures with the 57,879 cases of poliomyelitis (21,264 paralytic) at the height of the epidemic in 1952, and consider that many child abuse and neglect cases probably go unreported or pass for "accidents" (Mindlin, 1976; Newberger and Daniel, 1976).

The current philosophy of child abuse and neglect (Pollack and Steele, 1972; Martin, 1976) embodies the idea that 85 percent to 90 percent of parents who abuse children are *not* cruel, inhuman, and deranged. The other 10 percent to 15 percent appears to include the psychotic and severely emotionally disturbed and the difficult-to-reach alcoholics, narcotic addicts, and other substance abusers. Thus, about 90 percent of abuse and neglect situations are symptomatic of family dysfunction and, hence, amenable to treatment.

There are laws against child abuse and neglect in all fifty states (Education Commission of the States Child Abuse and Neglect Project, 1976, 1977) that require certain professionals working with children to report suspected abuse to specific agencies, usually law enforcement and social services, and grant the reporter immunity from civil suit. For the most part, the philosophy that there are three victims of child abuse and neglect—the child, the parents, and the community—governs the legal outcome, and efforts are directed not at punishing the abuser, but at protecting the child and treating the family.

This philosophy is based on current research, which characterizes the usual abusive parents as social isolates with low self-image, often abused and neglected in their own childhood, and looking to their children for the love and attention denied to them by their own parents. The child is usually characterized as being special or wanted, but often seen as "different." The reason for this difference may be real, as in the developmentally slow child, or imaginary, as in the scapegoat child. The actual abuse often occurs at a time of overwhelming crisis, when a child causes special inconvenience or fails to live up to parental expectations. A corollary to this philosophy is that all of us (not excepting any class, race, or group) have the potential to become abusers given the proper conditions, and that stress increases the possibility that we lose our self-control. Recent work on maternal–infant bonding (Kennell, Voos, and Klaus, 1976) appears to indicate that the seeds of abuse may be sown when mother and infant, for any reason, fail to bond in earliest infancy.

The identification of child abuse differs in different settings—the hospital or doctor's office, the child care facility or school, the neighborhood or community. The principles are the same, however: (1) unexplained or inadequately explained injuries; (2) changing explanations of injuries; (3) injuries explained by the parents resulting from child behavior impossible for that stage of child development; (4) repeated injuries, typical lesions, marks (strap marks, cigarette burns); (5) inexplicable changes in a child's physical condition or behavior; and (6) changes in adult behavior toward a child. These clues are all common ones and raise suspicion. It is considered sound practice to hospitalize an infant or young child for protection and to allow time for exploration. Careful examination of the child and exploration with the family enable law enforcement, protective services, other involved professionals, and the courts to reach some conclusion about the possibility or probability of abuse and the child's need to be protected. The courts make the ultimate decisions.

Therapeutic modalities include temporary or permanent separation of the child from the abusing adult by day care, crisis care, care by relatives, or foster care and attempts to treat or rehabilitate the offending adult through various combinations of self-help groups, special forms of counseling and support services, and conventional psychotherapy. Early reuniting of children with their natural family is the prime goal. The courts and community protective services oversee this process.

It would appear that society has the problem well under control. Nothing could be further from the truth. The standards for decision making in the field of child abuse and neglect are ill-defined; the decisions made are often arbitrary and based on expediency. Therapeutic services flexible enough to meet the multiple needs of the families involved are not available. Preventive modalities, such as education for parenting and family–child community support systems, are highly inadequate. The individual professional may feel helpless to influence the system in relation to an individual child or family. However, professionals working in the field can examine the strong and weak features of the system, the existing rules and guidelines, and the dilemmas. The individual professional can and should be a change agent and an advocate for children and their families in a complex and changing field if the professional will face up to the dilemmas that go beyond the existing guidelines. The following are eight of the major dilemmas confronting professionals who work in the field of child abuse and neglect.

Dilemma 1: Gray Areas in the Identification Process. Professionals working in the area of human services are constantly faced with the necessity of making important decisions based on inadequate, incomplete, and inconclusive data (Schmitt, Grosz, and Carroll, 1976). Nowhere does one find a better illustration of this than the identification of child abuse and neglect (National Center on Child Abuse and Neglect, 1977b). True, the law only requires suspicion and does not require precise diagnosis, but the required reporting action sets in motion a process that often profoundly affects the lives of many individuals and families. The professional cannot simply report an incident and bow out as a layperson might. A professional is required to document the reasons for suspecting abuse, supply data to those entrusted with decision-making power, and possibly stand behind these observations, statements, and conclusions in a court of law. In addition, the professional must deal with the response of the family, the lay community, and the professional community to the action initiated.

If the diagnosis is firm, as in the case of a battered child with typical lesions and injuries, such as belt marks, cigarette burns, and evidence of repeated assault, there is little problem and no dilemma in the reporting (Helfer, 1974). Most abused children, however, do not present with such clear-cut evidence and conclusive data. Ordinarily, there is an injury with a history that does not quite fit the injury or an injury not usual in a particular age group. There may be a record of frequent "accidents," or too many or changing explanations for certain injuries or lesions.

The professional then begins to look for clues in the child's and parents' behavior—lack of interaction between parent and child, a withdrawn or an overly friendly child, a parent apparently withholding or falsifying all or parts of the history. However, these indicators are often vague, inconclusive, and may be misleading. Family secrets or hidden agendas not directly connected with child abuse may prompt parents and other family members to cover up or hold back factual material and omit important and relevant data.

Even if one or both parents fit the described pattern of the social isolate with a deprived or abusive childhood and a poor self-image, this does not necessarily indicate child abuse. This "World of Abnormal Rearing" (WAR) described by Helfer (1975a, pp. 26–44) with its role reversals, inappropriate expectations, and use of the child as an extension of self does not always result in abuse. It can only be used as one piece of evidence in the diagnostic process.

The professional must then explore and solve problems in a limited period of time (the law usually sets the limits) and normally under less than optimal conditions (in a crowded emergency room or busy principal's office). The exigencies of the situation often produce pressures from others for and against reporting. For example, a teacher may feel that a particular child is coming to class with too many bruises which the school nurse or school social worker should report, whereas their school administrator may disagree. One member of a medical staff, perhaps a trainee, may support a social worker's opinion that the reporting of an injury as possible abuse is indicated, whereas another member of the staff, perhaps a member of the attending staff, may strongly disagree.

A three-year-old girl was brought to a pediatric emergency center by her mother at the request of the director of the child's nursery school. The director had alerted the emergency room physician, a first-year resident, that she suspected abuse because the child came to school each day with new bruises. The mother stated that both she and the child bruised easily and showed several of her own bruises to prove it.

A medical workup was initiated and the social worker from the SCAN *Team* interviewed the mother. The medical workup revealed only a child with multiple bruises of varying ages and with no identifiable imprints. There were no other injuries, and laboratory studies showed no reason for easy bruising. The mother told the physician that her husband, the girl's stepfather, was strict but never hit the child. She told the social worker that he occasionally lost his temper and spanked this youngster, but never touched their younger boy. The senior emergency room physician objected to the recommendation of the resident physician and the social worker that the situation be reported as possible abuse. He felt that the bruises were not unusual for a three-year-old, active youngster. A consultation with the* SCAN *Team pediatrician to resolve the differences of opinion resulted in a reporting through appropriate channels. A protective services follow-up verified the suspicion that this youngster was a scapegoat in this family.*

Dilemma 2: Relationship Between the Professional and the Patient or Client. Many professionals, accustomed to confidential and trusting relationships with their patients, clients, students, or parents, find the field of child abuse and neglect to be new and difficult. They cannot assure their patients or clients that an encounter will be confidential. In fact, the professional who wishes to maintain some semblance of credibility must (or should) make it clear that the interchange may well be shared with such agencies as protective services, law enforcement, and the courts.

The sensitive professional is aware of the fact that there is a class difference in the identification and reporting of child abuse (Steele, 1975). Of necessity, the poor, minority and ethnic groups, and noncitizens have many more contacts with public agencies, public clinics, and law enforcement. Hence, they are more likely to be reported than are middle- or upper-class citizens whose money, education, and status isolate them from agency intervention. Private health and mental health practitioners and school administrators in

---

* A Suspected Child Abuse and Neglect (SCAN) Team is a multidisciplinary group organized to cope with the problems inherent in the identification and reporting of child abuse and neglect. In a hospital setting, the team might include a physician, a nurse, and a social worker. In a school, it might include the school social worker or pupil services counselor, the school nurse, and the principal.

middle- and upper-class neighborhoods often hesitate to report suspected child abuse because reporting might anger the family and the community.

To further complicate this aspect of the dilemma, professionals who frequently come from middle-class, caucasian backgrounds find it difficult to relate to diverse, racial, ethnic, cultural, and alternate life style differences. They often misunderstand or misinterpret family interaction and dynamics. Poverty, with its concomitant ignorance, apathy, and exhaustion, provides its own dilemmas. It makes many professionals feel guilty and uncomfortable.

Professionals in every field are well aware of the important role of their own background and life experiences in the doctor–patient, counselor–client, or teacher–student relationship. How the professional views his own childhood may affect the entire child abuse and neglect decision-making and problem-solving process, but especially the decision to report or not to report. In this area, the individual professional may find himself at odds with, or in conflict with, the profession as a whole—a profession that has been required to report even the suspicion of abuse.

A young mother brought her three-month-old infant to a pediatric clinic because he was "spitting up" after every feeding. In the course of the visit, the mother handled the baby very roughly and at one point spanked the baby forcibly on the buttocks leaving a hand imprint, which faded very slowly. The physician did not react to the mother's behavior, but the clinic nurse asked if he minded if a social worker talked to the mother. He agreed that this should be done.

In the course of her interview, the social worker turned up several disturbing pieces of information relating to the mother's own abusive childhood, her isolation, and her unrealistic expectations of her baby and herself. Both the social worker and the clinic nurse felt that the situation called for reporting as potential abuse, but the doctor strongly disagreed. He felt that this would destroy any possibility for a good doctor–patient relationship and any possibility of helping this young mother. He stated that his own mother had spanked him with a paddle when he was very young and that he and his wife had shaken and spanked their young infant. He finally reluctantly acceded to reporting to protective services when the social worker agreed to handle the referral. The physician listened with interest, but obvious disap-

proval, while the social worker told the mother about having to report and discussed the possible outcomes. The actual outcome was a protective services follow-up. The mother chose a local well-baby clinic for the infant's medical care, but requested counseling in parenting from the very social worker who reported her.

Dilemma 3: Professional Traditions—"To Do No Harm." Professionals in every field are taught that, beyond all else, they should do no harm. Yet, the law requires activities that sometimes appear to violate that dictum. For example, many x rays that are not medically indicated are being ordered by physicians to avoid missing old fractures or a symptom-free skull fracture that might be important in court. This is not to minimize the importance of finding a battered child when the external symptoms might not be obvious. But radiation can also be dangerous, and often clinical judgment indicates that the risk of overradiation is greater. Physicians also worry that if a rumor circulates in the community that child abuse is going to be suspected in almost every injury, some parents will not seek medical care for accidentally and nonaccidentally injured children. By reporting, school personnel may lose the trust of the student who may have asked that his parents not be told for fear of further beating or other abuse at home. By reporting, mental health professionals who uncover child abuse activities on the part of their adult patients in the course of therapy may lose the trusting relationship so necessary for successful therapy. By reporting, community social workers may cause families to lose welfare status. Reporting may lead to short- or long-term foster home placement or perhaps a series of placements for the child and separation from family and friends. In these and other situations, workers may feel that by their actions they have done more harm than good for both the child and the family in question.

The idea of a child abuse and neglect central registry (Fraser, 1974) creates anxieties in many professionals. Registries are usually set up by law enforcement or social service agencies to collect important data and to allow those charged with identifying child abuse the luxury of a resource for checking on recidivism. Through a registry, the effects of inaccurate or incomplete histories, "hospital-jumping," and moving around of many abusive families in the identification and reporting process will be minimized. Nevertheless, registries have great potential for misuse. The poor and minorities are often overrepresented in registries because of their need to use public agencies. Once a family or an individual gets into such a registry by an allegation of suspected child abuse, the record may never be erased even if the charges are not true. The confidentiality of most registries is also very questionable. Often little discretion is used in releasing information. Sensitive professionals may justifiably wonder if they are "doing harm" by reporting when reporting will result in an entry on a permanent ledger that may follow their patients or clients for the rest of their lives.

Professionals often feel that the agencies required to receive child abuse and neglect reports react inappropriately, unresponsively, or unpredictably. This, plus the individual professional's illusions of omnipotence and the realistic knowledge that without legal intervention they may be able to use the helping relationship to effect positive change, may lead some professionals to the conclusion that they can do it better. Such a conclusion gives them a feeling of moral justification for bending or breaking the law. Professionals must ask themselves if this course of action is worth the risk of severe injury to the child, not to speak of civil suit and malpractice action, if therapy does not work out as expected.

In the present social and legal climate, the professional has no choice but to report suspected abuse (Curran, 1977). The parallel in medicine is the hospitalization of the young child who has a life-threatening illness. The hospital is a difficult environment for children, and separation of a child from parents may be psychologically damaging, but hospitalization may be a life-saving measure. Hence, the physician has no choice but to hospitalize.

Reporting suspected child abuse may cause temporary separation of child from parent (there is trauma in separation even in negative parent–child interactions), expense to the family (parents pay x ray, laboratory, and medical–hospital costs), stressful confrontations with law enforcement, social agency and legal personnel for the parents, and, in the extreme situation, criminal prosecution of the parents. However, as with hospitalization, reporting may also be a life-saving measure for the child. The use of a hospital bed to protect an abused child and allow time for professionals to explore may become an issue, especially if there is disagreement among the staff about reporting.

Just as hospital personnel attempt to modify the stressful hospital milieu for children and their parents, child abuse professionals can modify the impact as well as the eventual outcome of reporting by investing time and effort into the reporting process. The professional can and should be open, honest, empathetic and nonaccusatory: "I am required by law to report, but I know how difficult this is for you and I would like to help." It has been pointed out that the law enforcement–legal process itself may be therapeutic in some child abuse cases. It is also true that the process may be very traumatic and destructive for individuals and families, especially if they already have a rather poor self-image and lack appropriate support systems.

Professionals should be able to protect the child and still be supportive of the parents. The professional can help by being a good listener, informing the family about what to expect, suggesting ways that family members can cope with and modify their responses to difficult confrontations, and by offering to counsel and support individual family members as they proceed through the process. Thus, a supportive professional can help minimize the negative effects of the reporting process. In addition, a well-organized, well-documented report and a sound, trusting relationship between the reporting professional and the agency receiving the report may also smooth out the rough spots in the process, assuring that the professional "does no harm" by reporting child abuse and neglect as required.

Dilemma 4: The Professional's Training. In 1975, Helfer outlined eight reasons "why most physicians don't get involved in child abuse" (Helfer, 1975b, pp. 29–31). (1) Medical school training in child abuse was insufficient. (2) Physicians are not trained in interpersonal skills. (3) Doctors have great difficulty working with members of other disciplines as peers. (4) The drain on time, finances, and emotions for the physician in private practice is extensive. (5) Physicians have a fear of testifying in court. (6) There is minimal personal reward, and the rewards that do exist are hard to identify. (7) When one does get involved, he or she is often confronted with a community service system which is less than helpful.

(8) Physicians have rarely been trained to see themselves as agents for change.

These reasons also apply to other professionals to a greater or lesser degree. There are additional explanations that can be advanced for the unwillingness of professionals to get involved, most of which are treated in the discussion of the other dilemmas. However, training is the key issue in almost all of Helfer's "reasons" and in most of the other explanations advanced.

Professional schools do not prepare their graduates to cope with the realities of working in the field of child abuse and neglect. Most of them provide little or no curriculum time for the subject. Few schools offer training and experience that would provide the student with the necessary coping skills and attitudes. In addition, most professional schools do not train or orient their graduates to understand and work effectively with professionals from other disciplines.

Professionals trained in the fields of law and law enforcement tend to emphasize control tempered by compassion when working in child abuse and neglect. Professionals trained in health, mental health, and social services tend to emphasize prevention and compassion tempered by control. In a recent article, Rosenfeld and Newberger (1977, pp. 2086–2088) addressed the clinical issue of "compassion versus control" in working with abusive families as a dilemma of all the helping professions. They pose the need for a standard that would guide the choice of the intervention model and propose six measurements in the form of dualisms to inform professional decisions.

> 1. Acute versus chronic injury: If the injury is an isolated experience that occurs during situational stress, a more compassionate model might be applicable, whereas recurrent severe injuries might call for intervention more weighted on the side of control.
>
> 2. The abusive incident acceptable or unacceptable: A parent who continues to manifest guilt and concern after an isolated episode may be more likely to respond to a more compassionate intervention model, whereas the parent who shows lack of concern about the injury may well require control. Prolonged observa-

tion may be necessary to accurately assess a parent's reaction. We warn against casual impressions.

3. Social versus dissocial: This measurement addresses the parent's pattern of behavior in reference to the norms of the culture or subculture. In suggesting it, we acknowledge the inability and reluctance of professionals to make such judgments. The greater the degree of social deviance (isolation, alcoholism, drug abuse, criminality), the more likely the need for control.

4. Love versus hate for the child: Of the various symbolic meanings of a child to a parent, the most pertinent to this discussion is valence, or the subjective parental attitude toward the child. If the child is seen as good, a compassionate approach may be more likely to succeed, whereas a child seen as intrinsically bad may need to be protected by a model that emphasizes control of the parent.

5. The child seen as separate from or fused to the parent: This measurement addresses the parent's ability to conceive of the child as a separate entity with needs of its own. A capacity for empathy and appropriate parental behavior is supported by this ability, and a more compassionate model may be applied in a case of abuse. A fused perception of parent and child may support a control intervention.

6. Integrated or disintegrated parental ego: A person with demonstrated (or potential) personality strength sufficient to inhibit destructive impulses may more likely respond to a compassionate approach. The desire to quiet a crying child is universal. The impulse to harm the child if necessary to quiet him is prevalent, if not universal. The lack of sufficient ego strength to deflect that impulse into a channel other than abuse may reflect either transient disturbance or serious ego pathology. If it means the latter, at least one aspect of intervention will have to be control.

Obviously there is a great deal of overlap in these measurements, and none provides the answer when or how to employ compassion and control. Child abuse, like other clinical problems, calls for sound clinical judgment. The identification of assumptions

implicit in present child protective work and the establishment of a rational basis for future thinking about
child abuse will promote the development of a more
effective and humane practice (p. 2088).

Attention to issues such as "control versus compassion" by
the various schools training professionals to work in their individual
disciplines would enhance effective interdisciplinary activities in the
field of child abuse. Training at this level would also make it easier
for many more professionals to become involved, as they would be
better equipped to cope with the issues and the dilemmas.

There are also specific skills, not taught in most professional
schools, that would enhance the ability of the professional to cope
with the issues and dilemmas of child abuse and neglect. Training
and experience in the area of working with law enforcement and
the legal profession and in testifying in court would be invaluable
to health, mental health, and social services professionals (Morris,
1974; Urban Rural Systems Associates, 1976). Without these skills
most professionals are afraid to testify; fail to present testimony and
answer questions clearly, succinctly, and firmly when they do testify;
and, in general, fail to perform, at least in this area, in a professional
manner.

Training professionals to be expert witnesses will help overcome the reticence of many of them to become involved in child
abuse and neglect. The skill and the ability to work with law enforcement and legal professionals will help other professionals cope
with the court procedure and avoid the anger, embarrassment, and
frustration caused by lack of knowledge of the legal system (volun-
teering information not requested), lack of ability to cope with
lawyers in court (not listening carefully to the questions or showing
anger when challenged by a lawyer), and lack of ability to convey
to the legal profession what certain professional disciplines are able
or unable to contribute to a particular case.

The problems in testifying relate, in part, to the encroach-
ment on professional time, with long waits, delays, and postpone-
ments upsetting busy appointment schedules. However, most courts
make concessions to health and mental health professionals and put
them "on call," thus avoiding the long waits outside the courtroom

that other witnesses must endure. The problems relating to differences of orientation and point of view (compassion versus control)
and status contests between the so-called helping professionals and
the law enforcement–legal professionals can be minimized if each is
trained to work with the other. Ideally, these two groups of professionals should work together in training programs and be encouraged to continue mutual interaction in the practice of their
professions (Hansen, 1977).

Dilemma 5: The Fine Line Between Punishment and Abuse.
Professionals are often called upon to counsel parents about child
rearing (Friedman and Swinger, 1977). In the course of this
counseling, they may be required to decide whether a given parental action is discipline, punishment, or abuse. Some of the themes
professionals hear expressed, which serve as clues to the possibility
of abuse, are: (1) "I want to show my child I really care for him."
(2) "A good spanking clears the air." ("It's better than nagging,
lecturing, complaining or giving them the silent treatment.") (3)
"How is that kid going to know who's boss?" (4) "I'm not half as
hard on my child as my parents were on me." (5) "I spank (beat)
my kid because I don't want her to grow up to be bad." (6) "My
old man beat me and I'm glad he did. It really made a 'man' out
of me." (7) Variations of "It hurts me more than it does you." (8)
Indications that the spankings exorcise evil inherent in the child.

The problem is how to differentiate between discipline and
punishment and punishment and abuse (Friedman and Friedman,
1977). Discipline and punishment are not synonymous. Discipline
may be defined as systematic training in orderliness to assure the
safety and physical and emotional well-being of children. The ultimate goal of discipline is to develop inner self-control in the child.
Adults resort to punishment when discipline fails. Harsh discipline
and overpunishment soon become abuse.

With this in mind, the professional working with children
must look carefully at the common themes expressed by parents and
evaluate and interpret their meaning: (1) Are they appropriate to
the time and place? (2) Do they reflect the norms of the culture
and are they the typical verbal expressions of the area and socio-
economic class of the parent expressing them? (3) What is acceptable discipline and punishment in this parent's culture or socioeco-

nomic group, and what is acceptable to the professional? (4) Is there a basic underlying concern for the child? (5) Is the parent's discipline or punishment producing the desired effect on the child? (6) Would the parent be willing to consider alternatives?

There is an additional problem in evaluating the interaction between parent and child. Children have different temperaments and respond differently to controls. However, parents interact differently with different children. One must weigh carefully the parent–child interaction: Is it appropriate or has it become an abusive one? Are the disciplinary measures or punishments humiliating, demeaning, or physically injurious? Are they ones to be normally expected in a difficult parent–child interaction?

Inherent in the dilemma of "Is it punishment or abuse?" is the realization that it is not feasible to report every adult who paddles, demeans, or humiliates a child. Realistically, we can only identify and report the more extreme examples. Many situations fall into a gray area and are not clearly abusive. Society, in general, and health and mental health professionals, in particular, still have the responsibility for helping parents rear their children. In a society that condones corporal punishment, it is often difficult to select those situations that are clearly abusive and, therefore, come under the mandatory reporting laws. Often the professional is forced to decide in which cases harsh discipline or punishment has become abuse, and there are few guidelines. Some physicians use tissue damage as their corporal punishment guideline, but some children bruise more easily than others, so even this is not the definitive answer. The professional must look for the social and family milieu in which discipline has become harsh and cruel and punishment has become unreasonable and abusive.

This dilemma becomes a dilemma within a dilemma to the professional who opposes corporal punishment on professional, ethical, and moral grounds. The U.S. Supreme Court condones corporal punishment in the schools despite the overwhelming evidence that corporal punishment slows developmental and learning processes and that violence against children breeds violent adults. Corporal punishment is condoned despite the fact that children who have been harshly and severely punished are overrepresented in the violent delinquent population and despite the fact that abusing parents are often found to have been abused and harshly punished themselves as children. Corporal punishment is condoned despite the demonstrated fact that there are viable alternatives for parents and teachers that provide a climate that fosters healthy discipline without the physical and psychological damage inherent in corporal punishment. What is the responsibility of the professional who decries this regressive return to "spare the rod and spoil the child"? All professionals, even if not in the field of child abuse and neglect, have the opportunity and a responsibility as they interact with families and schools to teach the difference between discipline and punishment and to help develop the alternatives to harsh discipline and corporal punishment.

Dilemma 6: The Rights of Parents and Children. The Joint Commission on the Mental Health of Children has proposed a "Bill of Rights for Children" (Report of the Joint Commission, 1969; Clemmens and Kenny, 1977), which includes the following:

1. The right to be born wanted.
2. The right to be born healthy.
3. The right to live in a healthy environment.
4. The right to satisfaction of basic needs.
5. The right to continuous loving care.
6. The right to acquire the intellectual and emotional skills necessary to achieve individual aspirations and to cope effectively in our society.
7. The right to acquire care and treatment through facilities that are appropriate to their needs and that keep them as closely as possible within their normal social settings.

However, many children in the United States find their rights abrogated by a society that gives lip service to the value of children but treats them as relatively unimportant and expendable. Society has a great deal of knowledge and expertise in the area of child rearing and education, but our institutions—home (parents), school, community, and court—often fail to apply this knowledge and expertise in the best interests of children (Goldstein, Freud, and Solnit, 1973; Hobbs, 1975b). When laws are passed, the rights of children are often overlooked because children have no vote.

The recent child abuse laws would appear to be an exception, but there are feelings and attitudes about the rights of parents and other adults that interfere. Corporal punishment, banned for adults in prisons, is allowed, even encouraged, for children at home and in school. Society places the rights of parents over the rights of the child to be protected from violence—"parents must be allowed to discipline and punish their own children"—and then we add hastily, "but not abuse them." We have already pointed out the fine line between punishment and abuse. And even if the community and the law do step in, the child is often without a knowledgeable advocate when a case goes beyond protective services and reaches the court. The recent trend toward the assigning of a *guardian ad litem* helps in this regard, but unless the abuse is gross, the rights of adults, if not the rights of parents, predominate (Fraser and Martin, 1976; Fraser, 1976–1977).

In 1975, Kempe and, more recently, the Feshbachs (Feshbach and Feshbach, 1976) have caused great concern in some segments of society by suggesting opening the family to the community and to society to enhance the health of children. Kempe proposed the use of "health visitors" similar to those used in Scotland. "Visits from a health visitor do not significantly infringe on the parent's right to privacy but demonstrate that society has the obligation to assure access to the child during the first years of his life rather than waiting until he first enters school at the age of five or six. . . . Effective utilization of health visitors in providing preventive pediatric services to all children would avoid some children being lost to the health care system and not receiving the care (and protection) they need" (p. 694).

Feshbach and Feshbach (1976, p. 164) state: "A major barrier in the education and communication to parents of effective and psychologically sound socialization practices is the secrecy that surrounds this area of interaction. . . . We believe that how a parent rears a child should be an open matter, available for discussion, help, and inquiry. . . . We would like to emphasize that we believe that the most effective route to the 'invasion of parent privacy' is through education and the provision of concrete support mechanisms for the assistance of individuals in their critical social role as parents. Thus, reciprocity is a critical element in our proposal to remove the nonconstructive shield of privacy currently surrounding parent socialization practices—parent rites. Parents have a right to expect help and receive assistance from their community in regard to information, guidance and child care resources. Children's rights will then be served in two fundamental ways. The community will function as a resource to the parents, which is *their* right, and as a protector and advocate for children, which is *their* right."

Professionals working in the field of child abuse and neglect cope with this dilemma in their everyday problem solving and decision making. The individual professional represents society and the community and must consider the conflicting rights of parents and children in every case of suspected or proven child abuse and neglect.

A ten-year-old boy was hospitalized for a hairline fracture of the skull, a large, swollen bruised area of his forehead, and numerous linear marks across his back and buttocks. In presenting the history to the admitting physician the father, a prominent insurance executive, stated the youngster had fallen while running and hit his head on the floor. He later admitted that he had pushed his son's head against the floor in anger after the youngster had done a poor job on a homework assignment. He freely admitted to strapping the youngster frequently "to be sure he doesn't become one of those hippies."

The youngster's mother appeared to be in complete agreement with her husband. She commented that they wanted their child to be a success and, therefore, set high standards. On one occasion when his parents came to the hospital to visit, the youngster ran up to his mother with a partially completed woven pot holder in his hand. "Look what I'm making for you, Mom," he blurted out, "and I think I'll be able to finish it before I come home!" To which his mother responded sharply, "What do you mean you think you'll finish it? You'll finish it and it better be carefully done!"

In juvenile court their lawyer argued that these were parents with very high standards. "Perhaps in this instance father lost his head and went a bit too far, but that only showed a parent's love for his child. After all, parents have the God-given right to discipline their own children and keep them from going astray. Big brother, in the form of government agencies, should not interfere and break down parental discipline."

The court decided that the youngster should live with his

grandparents for six months after which there would be a review hearing. Parent counseling by a therapist acceptable to the parents and the court was arranged. Court supervision for the plan was provided by the protective services division of the department of social services.

Dilemma 7: What Is Neglect? Child abuse reporting laws have been broadened to include child neglect or the failure to provide reasonable care and proper attention to, and protection for, children. This neglect includes, among others, the following areas: (1) willful failure to furnish necessary food, clothing, shelter, medical assistance, or other remedial care; (2) willful infliction of unjustifiable mental suffering; and (3) willful endangering of the health of a child. These guidelines seem quite clear. However, the wide spectrum of what constitutes neglect makes the identification and reporting process very difficult and creates a very real dilemma.

To *neglect* is to ignore or disregard, to fail to care for, or to fail to attend properly or sufficiently. The failure may result from carelessness or by intention. What constitutes "proper or sufficient attention"? How can the professional prove willfulness or carelessness? There is no agreement among professionals on the necessary ingredients of adequate child care. By reporting the suspicion of neglect as the law requires, the professional may victimize the marginal family whose failure to provide "adequate care" is due to social, psychological, or cultural factors beyond their control and not due to lack of concern for the child's well-being.

What are the qualities of adequate parenting that may serve as a standard? It is generally believed that they include the following: (1) love and the opportunity for bonding; (2) adequate and appropriate stimulation; (3) protection from harm (physical and emotional); (4) provision of models of appropriate behavior; and (5) provision of adequate food, clothing, and shelter. Varying degrees of each of these qualities may be present in any individual parenting process. They must each be considered in an appropriate sociocultural context.

The assessment of the degree of deficiency of each of these qualities that would constitute neglect by parents and the assessment of pathology and psychopathology in the child due to these deficiencies is very difficult (Fraser, 1976). There are usually no improbable stories, belt marks, or typical fractures to use as clues. Even the definitely undernourished infant may present problems. The designation "failure to thrive" (FTT) is used to identify infants whose growth is well below (usually less than the third percentile) appropriate standards for chronological age (Leonard, Rhymes, and Solnit, 1966; Barbero and Shaheen, 1967; Smith and Berenberg, 1970; Evans, Reinhart, and Succop, 1972; Rutter, 1972; and Whitten, 1976). Failure to thrive may be an important manifestation of parental neglect (Powell, Brasel, and Blizzard, 1967), but organic problems such as heart disease, kidney disease, malabsorption, and neurologic or endocrine dysfunction must be ruled out before settling on a psychosocial diagnosis. A trial of adequate care and feeding can confirm this diagnosis, but whether FTT is due to "willful neglect" is usually still at issue. The "parental deficit" may be due to a variety of sociocultural, economic, and psychological factors and remediable by the provision of appropriate educational and supportive services.

The parent who refuses to obtain needed medical care for a child is guilty of what has been termed "medical endangering." In some of these situations, the court assumes temporary custody of the child and assures necessary medical care. This decision is relatively clear if the failure to obtain medical care is life threatening, but what about the situation in which a parent refuses so-called preventive care such as immunizations? Where does the professional caring for children draw the line? There are many practical, ethical, moral, and religious considerations that cloud the issue.

How does the individual professional evaluate the qualities of adequate parenting when faced with a specific family situation? When does the individual professional decide that a specific problem situation constitutes neglect and should be reported? We know that affectionless parenting and lack of models of appropriate parenting may cripple a child emotionally and be passed on from generation to generation. But how does one measure affection and lack of a model? We know that children thrive with appropriate parental and environmental stimulation and wither physically, emotionally, and intellectually if deprived of it. But how does one evaluate appropriate stimulation? We know that children should be protected from harm and provided with adequate food, clothing, and shelter, but who sets the standards? Is failure to use an automobile child protection device considered neglect, or should the use of such devices be a parental prerogative? When do repeated "accidents" become "failure to protect"?

Careful physical and psychological evaluation of a child may give clues to the answers to some of these questions. Physical and behavioral abnormalities may or may not be due to parenting deficits. In fact, the parenting deficit may, at least in part, be a result rather than a cause. However, in either case intervention is indicated, and failure on the part of parents to accept help in these situations may be the best indicator of neglect. This concept is especially important in considering family situations in which there is a severely emotionally disturbed or mentally ill adult or severely disruptive intrafamily relationships.

The professional's dilemma in the area of neglect does not end with identification and reporting. Most professionals have no problem with the use of foster home care for children exposed to physical abuse, although even in abusive situations, many children prefer their own home to the best of foster homes. The separation from the abusive parent or parents may be life-saving. The issue is not as clear in neglect situations. The comparative outcomes of remediation in foster home versus natural home have not been adequately studied. The professional is often called on to decide whether remediation is possible without at least temporary foster home placement. This separation may be therapeutic for both parent and child, or it may lead to further deterioration of the parent–child relationship. A therapeutic trial of working with the parents while the child either remains at home or in temporary foster care may be the ultimate evaluative tool and is the one most often employed in clinical practice.

Dilemma 8: The Trauma of Working in Child Abuse and Neglect. Professionals working with abused children and their families must cope with many personally traumatic and anxiety-producing experiences that often cause mental and physical exhaustion (Ebeling, 1975). Typical of these are the initial encounters with the child and his parents, which cause many professionals intense feelings of anger, outrage, sorrow, pity, and revulsion. If workers have not yet clearly separated their feelings about their own childhood, these serve to intensify the emotional impact of the encounter. The usual response to the abused child and his plight is one of sorrow and pity, although an element of anger may enter in if the worker tends to identify with the parent and sees the child as a provocateur. On the other hand, the parents may arouse feelings of anger, outrage, and revulsion by their perverse actions, and the professional may find it difficult to understand how anyone could treat a child this way. Considering what life experiences of the parents may have brought them to this confrontation, the worker may feel pity. These ambivalences make it difficult for the professional to keep in mind that there are two victims in every child abuse situation—the child and the parents—and that there is a need to *protect the child* and *rehabilitate the parent.* Neither can be sacrificed at the expense of the other. Even experienced workers will find that they have wide swings of feelings and inclinations, sometimes in the direction of protecting the child and sometimes in the direction of protecting the parent. These may be based on the worker's own feelings or frame of mind at a particular time as much as on the data he has gathered.

The professional's initial encounter with a suspected abusive family may provoke strong feelings of anger, resentment, and fear in both the parent and the child. They are likely to turn these feelings against the worker as he is the most accessible agent of the establishment and the initiator of steps that may well lead to both separation of the family and possible punitive action against the parents.

Further anxiety and anger may be produced in the workers by awareness of problems in dealing with their colleagues. They have probably already experienced reticence to become involved in suspected, potential, or actual abuse and neglect situations on the part of some of them. This reticence often results in hasty, inadequate, and inappropriate referrals. These colleagues' pejorative remarks about the issue of child abuse often reflect their own inability to handle the situation and their feelings. Their insistence that the worker assure them that the final outcome will be a salutary one and their refusal to look at the realities of the situation increase the difficulties of reporting. Although one professional has no legal responsibility for the actions or lack of action of another, many professional workers in the field of child abuse and neglect try to use these encounters to train and reorient their fellow professional colleagues.

Professional workers may also be burdened by their own feelings about the unpredictable responses of the system to which they must report and the realization that they have little or no control over the evolving situation. Experience will have taught them that long delays and unforeseen outcomes lie ahead. Although additional data may be accumulated as the family progresses through the overburdened and understaffed legal and social service system, this data may be no more reliable than that originally accumulated by the original reporting professional. These data also may be used to arrive at unexpected conclusions.

Another trauma comes from the professional's fear of the ultimate consequences of identifying and reporting a particular family, especially the fear that such suspicions may be in error. These consequences have impact on both the child and the family. The role of the worker in initiating the process and of the inadequate community treatment resources awaiting the family influences the professional. But the possible consequences of not reporting cannot be ignored.

These traumas culminate in severe pressure on workers who lack an adequate support system for themselves and who may not have developed a community network to ease the pressure. Sometimes they may even begin to doubt their own judgment. Peers may distance themselves, and coworkers may be in as much need as the child abuse specialists. If the specialists are to survive, it is essential to develop supportive resources of their own and to force society to accept their need for supplemental professional support. If this is not done, the consequences may well be deterioration in their work, debilitation in their personal lives, and an early flight from the job. Every trained worker who departs must be replaced. The replacement may well be untrained, inexperienced, and no better able to cope than his predecessor. Replacements may likely follow their predecessors in leaving and continue a never-ending cycle to the detriment of all concerned.

There are models for problem solving. Each traditional professional discipline approaches the issue of problem solving in its own idiosyncratic manner (Lazare, 1973). If we examine these models from the point of view of child abuse problem solving and decision making, we find that individually they all fail to answer the dilemmas; a more holistic model is required.

In the "medical model," the physician begins with problem identification or diagnosis and proceeds to problem solving or treatment through developing a data base. This base includes a social history and personal profile. Decisions are formulated on this data base and that difficult-to-define entity, clinical judgment. This model also includes, ideally, patient and family health education with the health professional assuming an empathic stance and appropriate distancing. The distancing serves to achieve a healthy "doctor–patient relationship."

This model does not meet the needs of the professional working with abused children and their families. The exigencies of the situation seldom allow time for the development of an adequate data base. The law defines the action to be taken and leaves little room for clinical judgment. The lack of confidentiality interferes with the empathic stance and the healthy doctor–patient relationship.

In the "social model," the social worker studies the child in the family, home, and community. The worker observes and evaluates the responses of child and family to the milieu, to the immediate and ongoing family-social situation and to the problems at hand. The social worker uses observational and interviewing skills to develop a data base and, as in the medical model, combines this base with clinical judgment in the decision-making process. This model emphasizes mental health education and, as in the medical model, an empathic stance, appropriate distancing, and a healthy worker-client relationship.

This model also falls short in working with abusive families for reasons similar to those described under the medical model. In both models, treatment begins ideally with the first diagnostic encounter. In child abuse, treatment is frustrated by the need of most families to deny abuse, as well as by the law, which often requires therapy by a new group of professionals in a different setting from the reporting facility.

In the "psychological or behavioral model," the psychologist either determines the behavior to be modified, establishes the conditions under which it occurs, determines the factors responsible for the behaviors (here and now), selects a set of treatment conditions and arranges a schedule of retraining (social-learning theory), or he explores and examines early psychologic determinants, then clarifies events, feelings, and behavior using himself and the relationship of the child and family as a therapeutic tool to enhance growth and maturity (psychodynamic theory).

Both approaches in this model also fall short in working with abusive families. The lack of motivation on the part of key members of abusive families and the overwhelming socioemotional needs of most of the families defeat this approach. Mental health professionals traditionally rely on the motivation of the patient and wait for the patient to come to the professional. To effect any change with abusive families, one must actively and aggressively reach out. Furthermore, the traditional nondirective approach may also be ineffective with parents who themselves need parenting and who may need directive counseling in the area of child rearing to get them started in the right direction.

In the "law enforcement–legal model," employed by officers of the law and members of the legal profession, the emphasis is on identifying abusers and punishing them or changing the behavior by requiring therapy. An attempt is made to determine the best interests of (or least detrimental alternatives for) the child. The court assumes the posture of guardian and deputizes others, such as Department of Public Social Services (DPSS) protective services, foster parents, and a variety of family therapists and parent surrogates, to assist them in this role.

This model falls short for all the reasons stated and implied in the dilemmas discussed in this chapter. Behavioral and socioemotional change cannot be mandated. The reality of most child abuse and neglect situations is that the child eventually returns to the abusing family. The family may well have undergone, at best, minimal change in its basic dynamics despite the voyage through the establishment system.

In the "educational model," the educator determines behavioral objectives, develops a lesson plan for achieving the objectives, and carries out the plan by using the format and setting best suited to the students and the milieu. This model falls short in working with abusive families for similar reasons to those discussed in relation to the other models.

Workers in the field of child abuse and neglect require a holistic model that borrows approaches and techniques from all the described models (Schmitt and Beezley, 1976; National Center on Child Abuse and Neglect, 1977). Abuse and neglect situations have biological, social, psychological, educational, and legal implications, all of which must be considered if problem-solving and management-planning efforts are to be effective.

A four-month-old male infant was brought to the emergency room of a large pediatric facility by his mother. The mother stated that the baby was in good health and doing well until one week prior to the visit when he became irritable, refused to take his bottle, and cried continuously. The day of the visit he stopped moving his left arm and cried whenever it was touched.

Medical workup revealed x-ray evidence of a fresh, spiral fracture of the left humerus (upper arm), a type that can only be caused by a twisting motion, and a week-old linear fracture of the right parietal bone (skull). Physical examination revealed a few scattered bruises of varying ages over the body and extremities and a tender, slightly swollen right arm. The "medical model" thus immediately established that this infant fell into the category of the "battered child syndrome" and the case was reported through appropriate channels.

However, the subsequent problem solving required the use of the social and psychological models by a social worker and a child development nurse specialist. Their exploration uncovered a poor relationship between the mother and her own mother (the infant's mother had been abused as an infant), and the mother and father (the father had a drinking problem and on several occasions physically abused his wife).

At first, the mother pointed the finger at the father as the abuser. As the problem-solving law enforcement–legal procedures progressed, with the social worker and the nurse specialist supporting the mother through the intricate legal process, the mother admitted that she occasionally lost her temper and "shook the baby very hard." She commented, "I don't know how to be a wife or mother."

The court ordered temporary placement in a foster home for the infant and family counseling and a parent education program for both parents. The parents elected to seek counseling at a local mental health facility and to return for parenting education to the social worker and nurse specialist at the reporting facility. Clearly, the problem solving and decision making in this situation required the application of a holistic model. Any single model would have fallen far short.

Are there any guidelines for professionals who must cope with the "beyond-the-guidelines" dilemmas? Perhaps the answer lies in what defines "professional"; that is, knowledge, skills, understanding, and an appropriate use of support systems.

Professionals must develop knowledgeability in all the areas covered by the guidelines. This includes the knowledge prescribed by their own profession and essential to the practice of that profession. It should also include some knowledge normally considered to be in the territory of other professionals if that knowledge enhances coping skills in the area of child abuse and neglect. For example, law enforcement and legal professionals should understand behavioral indicators and family dynamics in abuse and neglect, whereas social workers and teachers should know more about the physical indicators and the tools, such as the x ray, that help to establish those indicators for health professionals. However, the professional must be able to recognize when it becomes necessary to assume the role of another discipline and seek the support of other professionals in the problem-solving and decision-making process.

Professionals working in child abuse and neglect must assure themselves that they have the requisite skills. Skill in interviewing and in evaluating family social situations are basic for working with abused children and their families. Beyond this, professionals should not only develop the skills necessary to function in the model usually employed by their profession, whether medical, social, psychological, educational, or legal, but also develop some borrowed from the other models. For example, the law enforcement officer and the lawyer working in child abuse and neglect must develop skill in exploring the social milieu of families, whereas the social worker and the health professional must learn to cope with the intricacies of the legal system and the courts.

The complex nature of the problem of child abuse as well as the complexity of the interests involved (parent, child, state's interest in protecting the child, the interests of the establishment, and the professionals comprising the establishment) requires that a holistic approach be applied at all levels—identification, reporting, exploration, and treatment. Therefore, professionals in the field must acquire another skill—the skill to work with other professionals, to share expertise, to accept the contributions of others, and to avoid protecting their own area of knowledge and jurisdictional boundaries.

Professionals must understand themselves—their past experiences and their present inner selves, their strengths and their weaknesses, their insightful areas and their blind spots—to be sound professionals in any specialization. In working in child abuse and neglect, each professional must understand people—often people from very different backgrounds and with very different life experiences, including child rearing, life styles and value systems. This includes not only patients or clients but also professionals from other disciplines who approach the problem of child abuse and neglect from different training backgrounds and perspectives. Physicians are concerned with diagnosis and treatment but often are placed in a rather special counseling role by families they treat. Social workers seek to improve conditions within and around their clients by exploring problem areas and providing counseling and supportive services. Law enforcement personnel are concerned about apprehending those who break the law but also serve and protect the community and society. Courts and legal professionals are part of a system that determines guilt or innocence and assures that justice prevails and that individual rights are protected. Other professionals, such as nurses and teachers, have special training and perspective that they bring to the field.

Using all available support systems when working in child abuse and neglect can be especially important to the individual professional. SCAN Teams have been organized across the country in hospitals, schools, agencies, and communities. The composition of the teams varies with the setting, but the principle is the same: an interdisciplinary team of professionals (and sometimes paraprofessionals) pooling their knowledge and skills, and supporting and providing balance for one another. The worker who does not have the luxury of a SCAN Team can and should develop an analogous group using available coworkers in his own setting and individuals from the community. For example, one principal in a rural setting uses a public health nurse and his office secretary on his SCAN Team.

To survive the trauma of working in child abuse and neglect, the professional worker must have adequate support. There are four basic elements to this support system:

1. Other professional staff with whom the professional can share feelings and responsibility. The SCAN Team is an ideal solution for this aspect of the support system.
2. An ongoing inservice training and staff development program that can be shared with fellow professionals, such as training in how to prepare for court appearances when called to testify in a child abuse case. Training and supporting one's colleagues is in itself rewarding and, in addition, makes the day-by-day struggles easier.
3. The professional worker must develop personal consultative resources, people to whom she can turn to discuss difficult aspects of a given situation. This aspect of the support system may include people from a variety of community agencies and individuals with whom the professional feels comfortable and able to share ideas and feelings.
4. The support system involves the development of an escape valve and, hopefully, someone to whom the professional can turn for personal advice and counseling. The escape valve may be just having a hobby; the counselor may be a therapist or someone who is a good listener.

Although the law outlines specific steps to be taken by professionals who suspect child abuse and neglect, there are still many dilemmas facing the individual professional in specific suspected child abuse and neglect situations. The difficulties caused by the dilemmas can be minimized by (1) graduate and postgraduate training in child abuse and neglect for professionals entering the field, (2) the use of multidisciplinary and interdisciplinary problem-solving and decision-making models and teams, and (3) an appropriate support system for the individual professional.

The discussion of the dilemmas highlights the need for changes, not only in our child abuse and neglect problem-solving and decision-making system, but also in our national policy toward children and families, currently a low priority. Perhaps, some changes in the child abuse and neglect system will help; for example, a more flexible system with more treatment options will allow the individual professional to choose between compassion or control, easing some of the identification and reporting problems. More important, however, would be a comprehensive health and mental health care and social services system that would emphasize prevention and that would provide support services, including viable choices and alternatives for child care for *all* families and education in child rearing for *all* parents with the goal of enhancing family functioning.

Case Presentation for Problem Solving

On Friday afternoon, Ms. Nagol received a call from the emergency room that there was a new case for her to evaluate. Ms. Nagol is a social worker on the Child Abuse Team at Children's Medical Center and was on call that day. Dr. Baker of the emergency room staff was concerned about an angry young mother and her five-week-old baby. They had been referred from a local community hospital because of the baby's skull fracture. The mother had taken the baby to the hospital the previous night because of a bump on the head. She had been given a return appointment for today when the x rays would be reviewed. The referral note said the history given by the mother, Laura, was that the injury had occurred while the baby was at a friend's house. The friend's one-and-a-half-year-old child had hit the baby, Karen, with a toy truck. X-ray films placed the fracture in the left occipitoparietal (posterior) area of the skull.

Ms. Nagol introduced herself to the mother and accompanied her to the x ray department for a skeletal survey of Karen, films of the arms, legs, and chest. This was done while they waited for admission papers. The young mother seemed tense and resisted questioning. Ms. Nagol put her at ease by giving her information about the procedure for evaluating injuries to young children. "When young children are found to have injuries that are not completely explained by the history," Ms. Nagol commented, "the hospital has the responsibility under state law for evaluating the family situation to be sure the child is not in danger." After this explanation of the hospital staff's concern for Karen's well-being, Laura's defensiveness lessened, and she became more receptive to sharing information about herself and her family.

Laura described herself as the black sheep of her family and a loner. She left home at sixteen to get married. Her family had not been in favor of this decision. Although there had never been any physical abuse, she did not feel close to her family during her childhood. She did not feel that her mother had given her the emotional support she would have wanted. Laura has been separated from her husband for two years because of his involvement in drugs along with a gradual disintegration of their relationship. He has visited her several times over the last two months. He has been pressing Laura for a reconciliation. Laura is currently living with her older sister, who is twenty-four and employed as a secretary. Laura is twenty and unemployed. Her sister has been trying to help her get a job where she works. Laura presently receives welfare payments and stays home with her daughter, Karen.

Laura said that she had been told that she would not be able to have children. This upset her as she had always wanted them badly. She referred to Karen as her most precious possession, as her friend as well as her daughter.

Laura said that she had not been feeling well on Tuesday and her girl friend, Sharon, had suggested that she let her have the baby overnight. Sharon told her that she was holding Karen on the couch and her son was jealous and threw a toy truck. It hit the baby's head, leaving a swelling over the right eye. Laura doubted that her friend would do anything to Karen as she has a good relationship with her own son, and Sharon and Laura are close friends. Laura was upset about the possibility that someone would need to talk with Sharon. She did not want to get her into trouble.

Ms. Nagol explained the location of the skull fracture to Laura, expressing the concern that perhaps Karen had received that injury at another time. Laura asked if it was possible for it to have occurred two weeks ago. She described an incident in which Karen had been in her arms, and she had turned quickly to answer the door. The baby's head hit one of the wood posts of her sister's old-fashioned bed which Laura had been standing next to. Karen cried at first but seemed all right.

Laura insisted that there had been no other trauma. She said she never gets frustrated and would not hit the baby. She described Karen as easy to care for. There had been no problems during her pregnancy and delivery, but Laura remained in the hospital for a week. She had lost a lot of blood following the delivery. The baby left the hospital at three days and was cared for by Laura's mother. Ms. Nagol's first impression of Laura was one of an anxious, young mother who seemed to see herself as an independent self-sufficient person, but in need of some reassuring.

A follow-up interview was tentatively set for Monday as there were problems with transportation over the weekend.

Dr. Stone, pediatric resident, took the admission history from Laura after she returned from x ray. She repeated the same explanations to him but seemed annoyed at further questioning about the incidents. Dr. Stone focused his attention on the other areas of the examination and Laura settled down again. Karen's birth weight had been five pounds, seven ounces. She was slightly premature (six weeks by dates). Laura had sought medical advice for Karen's colic at six weeks at the community hospital where she delivered. Karen had had a diaper rash for one week prior to this visit.

When Dr. Stone examined Karen, she weighed six pounds, fourteen ounces. She had a bruise over the right eye and a diaper rash. The radiologist found two skull fractures in the left posterior area, one fresh and the other, a large healing depressed fracture. There were several small chip fractures at the ends of the long bones in her legs. These were older than seven days. The chest x ray showed five fractured ribs (three on the right and two on the left). These were less than seven days old.

When Ms. Nagol saw Laura on Monday, she told her of the additional injuries and expressed her concern for Karen's safety. She told her that because of the multiple injuries, it would be necessary for Laura to talk with an investigator from the special child abuse unit of the local child protection agency. Laura seemed more upset over the injuries than the fact that she would have to talk to an investigator. She asked Ms. Nagol if in pressing on Karen's stomach to relieve pain from gas, the ribs could have been broken. She explained that she had placed her hands on both sides of the infant's body and pressed on the stomach with her fingers. Both Laura and her sister had done this but neither had heard anything crack.

Much of the remaining conversation was focused on comforting Laura and reassuring her that she would not lose Karen. She feared her own mother would say negative things about her to try to get custody of the baby. Ms. Nagol explained that her openness and willingness to look at her situation and work on solving the problems would be in her favor. Laura was assured that children remain away from their parents for long periods of time only when help is not accepted by the parents and there is a lack of interest and motivation. The interview ended with Laura's acceptance of the need for the referral to the child protection agency. Ms. Nagol promised that the investigator would talk to her first before contacting any of her family.

Investigator Wilson called Ms. Nagol the following day and told her that his impression of the mother had been similar to hers. Laura was cooperative and had related all of what she had told the hospital staff. In addition, she had given the history of frequent and somewhat severe headaches for the past two months. They were upsetting her. She seemed to have less patience with Karen when she had one of these headaches. She thought that she had not been as careful with the baby when she changed her diaper and on several occasions had jerked her legs.

Laura agreed with the social worker at the hospital and the child protection agency investigator that it would be better if Karen did not come home right away. She needed some time to get a job. Ms. Nagol had suggested a mental health clinic in Laura's neighborhood for counseling. Laura continued to visit Karen regularly in spite of the transportation difficulties. The nurses on the ward observed appropriate mother–child interaction.

Ten days after Karen was admitted, she was discharged to a temporary foster home following a detention hearing in juvenile court.

Some questions that could be asked in this case presentation are: (1) How would you present this case in juvenile court if you were the court social worker? (2) Would you recommend criminal charges against the mother? (3) Do you feel that this mother has the ability and the potential to be an effective parent? (4) What are her strengths, weaknesses, and potential resources? (5) What do you see as the major dilemmas for the individual professionals involved—physician, hospital social worker, child protection agency investigator, law enforcement officer, court social worker, lawyer, judge? (6) How would each problem-solving model contribute to the decision-making process? (7) What type of recommendation would you make to court? (8) What would your recommendations be for a treatment plan?

Chapter 15

Beyond the Guidelines: Opportunity and Responsibility

Judith S. Mearig

The authors in this volume have conveyed the message that becoming a committed professional person is not for the faint-hearted. They have criticized much more than they have praised; in many instances they have expressed their dissatisfaction with the "system"; they have described a variety of frustrating situations, especially for the children and families involved, that are a challenge to a professional's ethical responsibility. DiBuono states it succinctly: "Injustice exists and flourishes, and the professional who is part of it must either see it or blindly perpetuate it." He notes that the professional membership may, in fact, harbor values that contradict the stated purpose of the discipline. Mendelsohn would include as one of these values the need for power. After many years of experience, he relates his disillusionment with his initial conception of professionals and goes so far as to make a distinction between traditional and professional ethics. DiBuono puts it slightly differently when he says that professionalism and humanism are not necessarily synonymous. Mendelsohn believes that a major revamping is needed in professional priorities, one that can be achieved only by a concerted effort of many individuals, at least in medicine. Morse sees the disillusionment of young professionals as a widespread phenomenon. Lisbe describes the shattering of his early dreams but has found a way in which he can retain his basic ideals and goals in his work with children in a public school system.

Hobbs and Rhodes recommend that professionals engage in an ongoing examination of the underlying philosophy of their discipline and its practices. Hobbs observes that "It is easy for a professional person to accept without examination the philosophical foundations of his discipline. After years of training and long association with teachers and colleagues who share a common set of values, it is extraordinarily difficult to step aside and question one's value postulates or even be aware that some questioning of assumptions would be productive." Rhodes asks helping professionals to go through this process in examining the origins of a basic concept assumed in much of their functioning, that of abnormality. He illustrates this concept's cultural relativity as well as its potential to satisfy psychological needs of its proponents.

There seems to be agreement among the authors that values permeate almost every professional act. Morse notes that the burden of being an ethical agent in what is at best a quasi-ethical society is not a simple one to bear. Also, it is easy to ignore what he refers to as "first causes," values related to one's concept of human nature that underlie moment-by-moment decisions but that can fade into the background when professionals are very busy. The ecological context in which professionals work today is complicated, as Knitzer, McGowan, and Smith make clear, with numerous external forces influencing, and sometimes appearing to dictate, a professional's behavior and decisions. It often seems reasonable not to question too much but instead to fit into the ongoing tide of events. One frequently begins to define as right or ethical what is immediately feasible and acceptable to others. But a professional forfeits his special trust and independence if he allows this to happen. Hobbs' statement that the final authority for ethical and moral choice must rest with the individual professional person reflects the position of all the authors.

In the analysis of the problems and dilemmas encountered in meeting such a responsibility to children, consensus concerning some key issues appears to emerge. This chapter will examine the authors' major concerns and conclusions, incorporating additional implications and recommendations for the individual professional person as well as for the profession as a whole.

The power dimension of a professional's functioning has to be brought fully into consciousness and examined. At first glance, it may seem that this aspect is of particular concern to physicians, and Mendelsohn and DiBuono criticize the concentration of power in the medical profession. However, if one examines the many components of professional power, he will realize that all professionals can exert significant control over their clients' lives. Hobbs notes that this occurs regardless of the intervention technique employed. Everything from direct "doctor's" orders and behavior modification procedures to the more subtle methods of counselors following a humanistic philosophy is included. All incorporate definite goals for the recipient, who is interacted with in a manner intended to reach these goals.

Kessler gives a poignant example of the misapplication of behavior modification when a child is placed in a packing crate as a "time out" procedure to stop her crying. Yet, ironically enough, many professionals seem to feel they are extracting themselves from any personal responsibility for power over someone else's life when they engage in, or approve of, behavior modification. It is the technique and the reward that are crucial, they maintain.

Hobbs explains the limitations of behavior modification procedures once basic needs are satisfied: "In the long history of humans, with its many ups and downs, what seem most powerfully to shape the behavior of men and women are the exercise of competence; the commitment of oneself to others; the intimacy and comfort of reciprocated private affections; the delights of discovery in nature, art, and music; the intimations of immortality through gods or good works; the benison of needed aloneness; the belief in the possibility of the future; and the valuing of freedom and dignity. When such complex contingencies as these are to be contrived, by what name shall we call the contriver?"

We also must distinguish between public and private power of the individual professional. Public power can add to or detract from the child's welfare, depending on whether it is used to advocate for him in situations where nonprofessionals are relatively helpless or to circumscribe the development or availability of services. Examples of the latter might include the initial resistance of the medical profession to Medicaid and the present psychiatrist–psychologist debate over who should control diagnosis and therapy under any proposed national health insurance plan.

Mendelsohn's comment about our society's investing of physicians with special power, public and private, because of their involvement with the beginning and the end of life is worth reiterating. Others might believe that the doctor's unique skill in any physiological crisis is equally deserving of power and privilege. I am reminded of a medical friend's relating how a colleague always held a stethoscope out of the window when he realized a policeman was following his speeding car. After a few such incidents with the same officer, he was surprised one day when the police car passed him with handcuffs dangling out of the window!

The kind of omnipotence many people attribute to their physicians should not be taken advantage of, as Mendelsohn stresses. However, we should consider whether there is a qualitative difference between medicine and the other helping professions that comes from dependency. This dependency can be preserved, in part, by the medical profession. Not only are some of the requisite knowledge and skills difficult to perfect, the total repertoire is usually highly restricted to the membership and those related helpers whom medicine carefully controls. Furthermore, although the other professions often resent medicine's power and associated procedures, they seek to imitate them in many instances.

Private power with concomitant isolation from public criticism has caused more problems than it has alleviated. Hobbs and Biklen suggest that it has not contributed to a professional's moral

competence, and illustrations in other chapters would seem to substantiate this view. Of course, there has been some inroad into this
private power by the public. Hobbs points out that involvement of
government and the general public in professional affairs is a good
thing. "Professional traditions of privacy and secrecy often deprive
him [the professional] of a valuable source of instruction. . . . an
informed public with open avenues of criticism can be the professional's best friend." Bersoff (1975, p. 372) noted that a reason
codes of ethics may actually be at variance with the law (especially
recently) and may fail "to provide adequate bases for behavior is
their ethnocentrism. . . . Thus, codes represent the professional
group's point of view and are rarely developed with help from the
consumers who receive the professional services." In discussing
closed titles, Fischer states the assessor's own development is restricted when records are unavailable to consumers and dialogue
cannot occur. Bersoff also suggests making consumers part of professional ethics committees and publishing cases brought before
them, so that students and professionals (and consumers) become
more aware of the practical applications of principles. The process
probably would resemble that used in publishing judicial decisions.

Consumer boards are becoming involved more frequently in
the administration of community health and social services, and
Rhodes mentions the proliferation of self-help groups, some of
which see themselves in competition with professionals. Rhodes has
also written of an ultimate rebellion of the "helpee" population
(1972). Knitzer and Kessler cite the professional's complacency
and misuse of power as major factors in the initiation of the lay
child advocacy movement as well as in the marked upsurge in accountability requirements. With third party payments increasing
steadily, accountability must be faced as an integral phenomenon in
professional life. McGowan notes that this emphasis on product is
more inherent in bureaucracies; professionals traditionally have
stressed process. Smith corroborates such differences in goals. There
are additional ethical problems. The professional could be under
pressure to produce some objectively measurable result by a certain
time, whether or not the change involved is the most important one
for the child, or the process employed uses the professional's best
judgment and skills. Kessler and McGowan warn of the ethical

implications if professionals select clients on the basis of their prognoses for progress in areas easily measurable and important to external reviewers. On an even more pragmatic level, paperwork increases significantly with third party payments, and the bureaucratic
operations McGowan describes come into play.

There was another ethical difficulty, of course, when peer
review was essentially the only kind of accountability mechanism for
professionals. Errors due to inadequate skill or knowledge as well as
to poor ethical judgment were very seldom acknowledged to the
public, even though in certain situations the person affected should
have received some redress. Professionals must reassess how they deal
with their mistakes. Kessler illustrates the underlying dynamics of a
number of these in clinical practice with children, some due to
internal, and some to external, factors. She discusses how the mistakes might be avoided, but she also observes that professionals must
acknowledge their fallibility, to themselves and to parents. Professionals should be able to admit lack of knowledge without feelings of
failure, and parents must realize the emotions experienced by professionals. DiBuono makes a similar point. Kessler notes that although there are some unanswerable questions, there are other
problems to which someone else may have a solution, and a consultation or referral should reassure the client of the professional's
integrity.

Another kind of accountability problem can arise in child
abuse. Friedman and associates point out that the professional often
must make quick judgments in less than ideal assessment circumstances and ones that he can substantiate with formal evidence able
to stand up in court. He may lose the confidence or faith of the
parent or child if he errs, not to mention the risk of possible damage
to the parent–child relationship. Moreover, removing a child from
the home on a neglect petition could conceivably cause additional
harm by separating the child from the parents. X rays to verify suspected physical abuse can be harmful. Parents also may be subjected to large expenses and possible criminal prosecution if the
child is kept in the hospital because of suspected abuse. Nonetheless, the professional must make a judgment, and his greatest accountability is to the child, who may suffer no matter what he decides: physical abuse if he remains with the parent or separation

trauma if he is removed from the home. This is a real but unavoidable dilemma. It may be eased by having a multidisciplinary team to reduce the possibility that something of significance is overlooked or misinterpreted. Friedman and associates describe the procedural steps involved.

Many professionals experience a dilemma in deciding how to react to colleagues' mistakes or unethical behavior. Friedman and associates note that there is no legal accountability for these, but, as Fischer points out, there is ethical responsibility. Dilemmas then can arise in ascertaining how best to proceed. The psychologist in Fischer's case presentation grapples with this question, and Lisbe voices a similar concern. Statements of professional standards indicate the first step is to talk informally to the individual involved, but if unsuccessful in achieving any resolution in this manner, the professional should contact an ethics committee. However, unless they are very directly involved in a situation, many professionals hesitate to take either of these actions. Is this inaction unethical? Even more difficult are the beyond-the-guidelines situations. Yet, if one professional feels strongly that a child's welfare is being compromised by another professional's action—or lack of it—he should not stand by silently. There are additional questions that may be asked. What about honesty with a client concerning another professional? Suppose the client is not yours, at any point, but you are aware of what is happening to him. And do professionals have a responsibility to instruct clients in what constitutes high quality services, according to recognized professional standards?

Consent has become a central concept in both the misuse and the reduction of professional power. Biklen vividly illustrates how it has been employed to veil coercion: The client loses something important to him by withholding it. The granting of consent should not be interpreted to mean that the professional is not responsible to use his own judgment. Parental consent, if not encouragement, to school personnel to physically punish their children and the inoculation of children with hepatitis for research purposes are examples of this abdication of professional judgment. In addition, Biklen observes that many injustices have been committed by professionals because of the absence of at least one of the three required components of consent—capacity, information, and voluntariness. The basic intent of consent is to protect the child (or other client), not the professional, but in practice the emphasis has often become reversed. John's case in Biklen's chapter is a prime example.

To give people full information about a procedure to which they are to be subjected has not been standard procedure. Yet, many clients have assumed there was no potential harm by the very fact that nothing was mentioned, as in the cases of birth control devices and x rays. The doctor ordinarily "orders" x rays and that is the end of the transaction, consent is not often requested; if it is, information about possible harm is not provided, as Biklen points out. A particular dilemma exists for professionals in administration of treatment to children. An example is medication to control "hyperactivity." Should possible side effects or long-term effects, such as reduced physical growth, be explained to children, and should they be asked to give their consent? Can parents ethically give consent for them? Under what conditions should parents have the right to place their children in an institution?

Individual professionals have an obligation to ensure that the children with whom they come in contact actually receive the services they need. Given the state of organization of services presently existing in this country, this could be an almost impossible task to implement at times. However, Knitzer, Kessler, McGowan, Lisbe, and Smith emphasize this responsibility for the very reason that there often is no one else to assume it. Knitzer, Kessler, and Smith make reference to Polier's (1975) designation of "professional abuse of children" for the neglect of a needed advocacy stance. Many new services are beginning, but a number still have "exclusion clauses" or limited inclusion criteria. Moreover, matching the child with the proper service and coordinating all services involved are still haphazardly done in many instances. Knitzer, Switzer, Friedman and associates, Kessler, and Lisbe all provide illustrations. In Switzer's chapter, the mother's relating of the response received from an appropriately labeled program for her multiply handicapped child is a very poignant example: "They will pay for three pairs of shoes." Knitzer's families found out about some programs accidentally or through neighbors, although there still were exclusion policies with which to deal. Nominally, we have so many programs, but where are the children who fit into them exactly? What happens to the ones who do not? The diminution of program and service fragmentation is a professional responsibility according to Polier (1975) as well as these authors.

The individual professional's ensuring that children actually receive needed services could include, among many possibilities, providing services oneself for which there is no reimbursement, finding reliable services if they are not readily available, implicitly criticizing other professionals, and following through on both direct services and referrals to see what actually happened to a child. Friedman and others note the reluctance of professionals in child abuse to refer if they do not trust the referral agency's procedures or competency, and Kessler and Knitzer provide examples of harmful referrals. The enormous amount of time frequently required to ensure that children actually receive needed services must be faced. Anyone who has gone through all the steps, from beginning to end, knows the investment demanded. And seldom are there third party payments to cover many of the activities necessary. Some professionals give this kind of time freely because they have it; others do so even if it creates a hardship. Some want to contribute very little if they are not reimbursed financially. A clear expectation in each profession that members share this kind of responsibility might be helpful. Perhaps individual values must be the ultimate guide, but it does seem that professions should be concerned with the great variation in contributions that presently exists. What are the ethical approaches that can be taken?

Quality of services can generate many dilemmas. One is the question of whether consumers should be made aware of high quality or uncommon services even if these are very unlikely to be available to them. I am sensitive to the great variation in services provided to boys suffering from progressive muscular dystrophy, partly on the basis of geographical location and partly on the basis of value judgments of professionals. For example, it is possible to do surgery and long leg bracing for many of these boys, so that they will walk and remain independent for years longer than if not given this intervention. Psychologically as well as physically (less weight gain and deformity) this seems worthwhile, especially since the increasing dependency of the boys is one of the most depressing aspects of the disease. However, these orthopedic services are performed in relatively few places, because it is not universally believed that the results of surgery and the necessary exercise program are worth the investment, on the part of the professionals or the boys. The latter will eventually have to be in wheelchairs—and die—anyway. But the point is that the worth of the investment is a professional value judgment in most cases. The boys or their parents cannot make the decision if they are not made aware of the possibility of the surgery or if distance and finances are a major barrier. Also related is the basic question that all professionals must address: "Is health care a right or a privilege?" An additional ethical question, particularly of interest to parents, is the proportion of funds that should be designated for basic research relative to that spent for clinical and community services to improve the quality of life for children for whom discovery of a cure or prevention will be too late. Children and their parents see on television a sum as high as twenty-seven million dollars collected in twenty-four hours, and wonder how it benefits them.

Kessler stresses the importance of "following through," not always easy if distance and time are involved. The professional not only makes sure services are actually received and lets children and parents know his interest was not momentary, but also acquires his own information for future planning and decisions. Kessler provides good examples of the "out-of-sight-out-of-mind" phenomenon that professionals too often allow to occur. Smith cites a different kind of "following through" dilemma. A number of adults who had been adopted are now determined to trace their natural families. The professional must deal with the apparently negative outcome of a policy earlier thought sound, with issues of confidentiality sometimes creating dilemmas. "Following through" has an additional implication: that of continuing to provide or locate appropriate services as the child develops and his needs change. Otherwise, even significant progress can be lost if planning is left to an agency or school officially responsible for the child that does not provide the needed individual accommodation. Knitzer (1971) noted that the lay child advocacy movement evolved, in part, because professionals were not monitoring services. She asserts in this book that professionals should help families develop skills to cope with bureaucracies and other ecological barriers often encountered in obtaining services.

Lisbe and Kessler raise the question of where the line should be drawn in professional caring or involvement in children's lives: Does one take the child home, request custody, or provide money? A resolution of such dilemmas may begin with the determination that these are a child's real needs. If they are, the professional is responsible to see that they are met. If someone else can more appropriately or more effectively fill the need, the original professional makes the link. If not, he may have to do it himself. He should consider all the ramifications if he actually moves out of his professional role into a more personal one, although sometimes the two appear to blend easily. I recall a court session in which the family pediatrician and I were witnesses for a family attempting to regain custody of its ten children, who were removed by social services because their home was not physically adequate. The pediatrician had loaned her car on Sundays to the parents so they could visit some of their children who had been placed in a group home eighty miles away. The social services attorney rather sarcastically asked the pediatrician if it was customary for her to loan her car to her patients. Of course, he was attempting to establish that she could not be "objective" about this family. Personal generosity was a component of the pediatrician's action, but, from a professional standpoint, she felt that the maintenance of the relationship between the parents and the children was an important need. And no one else seemed willing to provide transportation.

System, institution, or agency barriers can hinder the individual professional in securing services for children. However, this individual has prerogatives and public power he would not have as a layperson. He is not powerless, although there is a temptation to use these obstacles as a rationalization for inaction. Kessler describes projection of responsibility onto some external factor, whether it be parents or an ecological force, as one of the mistakes professionals make. McGowan stresses that the individual professional can acquire knowledge about the workings of a bureaucracy that will allow him to use it as a tool to help children. She points out that the professional's major allegiance is to the child; an employee's allegiance is to the employer. Therefore, professionals who work within a bureaucracy must strive to keep their independence of thinking. This is not always easy to do, as Smith indicates in the case of a social worker whose judgment, based on a direct interaction, can be overruled by an office supervisor. Yet, "The workers have the right and the duty to make sure that their knowledge and skills are not subverted in violation of their best professional judgment."

McGowan notes that we need bureaucracies to deliver many of the services we believe are needed by children. Moreover, there will likely be more rather than less of them if expansion of services ever occurs. Therefore, it is especially important for the professional to understand how he can function effectively within bureaucracies, as well as to help shape them to better meet children's needs. McGowan analyzes nine major differences between professionals and bureaucracies in goals and manner of functioning. She emphasizes that if a conflict remains between needs of the child and those of the bureaucracy, the individual professional's responsibility is to the child. An alternative to increased bureaucratization might be a plan envisaged by Hobbs at the Center for the Study of Families and Children (1977) whereby as much support as possible would be channeled directly to families.

It should be noted that the individual professional has a general responsibility to work for the primary prevention of the need for her traditional services. A basic ethical question arises whenever helping professionals provide services to "correct" a condition. Researchers naturally concentrate upon underlying causes, but the clinical professional also should have a preventive role in his direct interactions with children and their families. It might be said that the professional's greatest ethical responsibility is to try to put himself out of business. Mendelsohn criticizes what he considers to be spurious preventive medicine, but there is a vast continuum of services, with crisis intervention at one end and primary prevention at the other, and some would argue that many kinds of work with children are preventive (Caplan, 1961). The professional can offer expertise at all points on the continuum in terms of specialized knowledge and skill, but since time is finite, each individual must decide the proportion spent in various emphases. Settings such as schools are especially conducive to primary prevention activities. Involvement of helping professionals in the election or selection of public officials who have significant power in children's lives—such as a family court judge or social service commissioner—could be another primary prevention endeavor.

An individual professional can initiate change in a larger system, but there are certain steps he should follow if he wants to have any hope of success. He must beware of quick solutions in his eagerness to initiate change. Lisbe notes, "Well-founded hesitancy and caution are often confused with compromise by graduate students anxious to put out forest fires before putting on their asbestos suits." The professional must have sufficient knowledge of all aspects of a problem, analyze his own abilities and chance for success (his present status in the organization may make a difference), be able to specify the hoped-for outcome, and choose and plan his strategy carefully. A collaborative strategy is best; a mediatory one may be effective; an adversarial approach should be used only as a last resort but may be necessary at times. The professional also must examine his sanction to intervene. Sometimes professional ethical standards constitute legitimate sanction. McGowan views the client's well-being and desire as a crucial sanction.

If the goal is to change a procedure, the individual professional should be able to present viable alternatives. The danger to be avoided, however, is overgeneralization and application in inappropriate circumstances, as Smith notes. Large organizations are particularly vulnerable to this practice. Fischer observes that sometimes professionals do not make a real effort to initiate changes in a larger system when they actually would be listened to because of their recognized expertise. A recommendation will have even more force, of course, if the individual can gain support of his professional group. But this is not always possible.

Risks must be taken by the professional at times, but it should be remembered that the child or other client is most at risk. Morse says the professional is really at risk only when his position is in jeopardy, which may be the real test of ethics. However, he must be prepared for rejection or at least disapproval by his colleagues. This could include informal economic sanctions if he is in any kind of independent practice. Kessler suggests that colleagues' uneasiness when a professional does something more than usual for a child may, in part, be due to shame. Another aspect of the risk-taking process involves disagreeing with professionals who have previously worked with the child (and whom the parents may have rejected) and going in a new therapeutic direction. Time is an important factor. The wisdom of the risk may not become evident immediately, and, in the meantime, a professional may be looked upon with disapproval by colleagues for stepping out of the mainstream. Of course, there is always the chance that the risk taker will be proven wrong. Or, if over a long period of time his judgment proves to be right, the chances are that no one else will remember the original disagreement. But the individual may rejoice in the child's progress.

A most difficult situation for the individual professional is one in which virtually no other colleagues or agencies share the same beyond-the-guidelines philosophy. Perhaps a seasoned professional with a history of overall success behind him can sustain his independent and risk-taking stance over a long period of time, but it is doubtful that an inexperienced individual can survive long without at least one other person's support. Some of the authors (Friedman and associates, Lisbe, Mendelsohn, Kessler, and Morse) make reference to this need, and the range of possibilities for support is great, from Friedman and associates' formal scan Team to Lisbe's identification of sympathetic colleagues. But the intensive and extensive kind of professional functioning discussed in this book cannot be sustained very long without support.

This pessimistic prognosis extends to actual effectiveness; any professional who has felt the helplessness of seeing something occur or not occur in a child's life in spite of his efforts or protestations knows this frustration of feeling he is right but powerless. Ironically enough, the very independence of thinking that should characterize a professional can be his downfall among his colleagues. In addition, if the system resents any questioning of its practices, it may be able to ban him politically from many activities and settings later on in which he might be more effective. Such a situation can result in a dilemma to which Morse refers. Many professionals never consider accepting positions where they are most needed, but where probability of success is very low. And, at what point, if already in such a position, is it ethical to leave, knowing the system then will probably continue in its usual way?

Morse indicates that the individual professional must estimate how much stress he can withstand prior to becoming involved, but it may be unrealistic to expect young professionals to predict with much accuracy their tolerance before they actually have undergone such experiences. This is another reason why opportunities to deal with dilemmas during the professional program are important. Estimation of stress tolerance is important not only for decisions about accepting or remaining in job situations; it can also be critical for decisions about whether to risk in a particular instance. Withdrawing in the middle of a venture could conceivably be more harmful to a child and his family than if action were not initiated. For this reason, estimation of one's own stress tolerance probably could be added to McGowan's list of steps in the decision-making process about whether or not to intervene. The question has also been raised whether some individuals are too sensitive to enter the helping professions. Most likely the authors in this book would opt for more rather than less sensitivity and view this quality as the energizer to effective advocacy for children. However, an extremely sensitive individual must recognize this trait as a potential vulnerability as well as an asset. Lisbe's presentation of this perception and his actual functioning perhaps speaks most directly to this point.

Hobbs, McGowan, and Knitzer all note the importance of having adequate knowledge before making a decision to depart from customary practices. The analytic and procedural steps McGowan outlines, referred to above, are vital. Lisbe illustrates how these steps are followed in an actual situation. He also gives an example of risk taking with little forethought, eventually successful, but he notes many elements that might have gone awry. He explains the balancing of an individual professional's responsibilities to the child and to the school in a manner that retains the child's best interests as the first priority: "a picture flashed through my mind of a delicately balanced scale weighted with safety on one end and risk on the other, and I realized that maintaining that vital balance was what professionalism was all about. . . . The constant dilemma would be to act in accordance with my beliefs without jeopardizing a position that enabled me to be an advocate for children in the schools."

Knitzer notes that risks are not always as great in reality as professionals make them out to be. Not examining them carefully may allow the individual to rationalize that they would be unrealistic for him to attempt and therefore the family, or anyone else, should not expect him to act. In discussing child advocacy in school psychology in a previous article (1974, p. 125) I wrote "Questionable is the position, or defensive nonaction, sometimes taken by school psychologists that if one child is "sacrificed" now it will mean maintenance or establishment of good relationships among the adults concerned, so that more children will be helped later. Actual empirical support for such a position should be examined closely. On an ethical or moral basis, the obligation to the individual child involved in the present seems difficult to ignore. Actually, there are numerous ways of helping children in the future by *working through* the problem of a child in the present, painful though some of the initial steps may be to the adults. Moreover, the author has found that better relationships often emerge eventually (for future children) when those working from different vantage points honestly state their differences and allow themselves to disagree as early as possible in their interactions." The child of the moment should not need to be sacrificed. A child advocate–school administrator communicated this succinctly one day when, impatient with the pace of accommodating children with special needs in schools, exclaimed, "But Robert is now, Johnny is now!" And sometimes children are no more, as I recall from my early experience:

> Jimmy was almost five and suffered from leukemia with an uncertain prognosis. He usually took his necessary injections stoically and, in his own mind, probably hoped for better days. There was nothing he wanted more than to go to school. But his birthday was something like December fifth and the cut-off date for kindergarten entrance was December first. (There was no preschool program in his community at that time.) The parents requested an exception to the age rule from the school administrators and the board of education. His pediatrician and the school psychologist asked also. The response was that no exceptions could be made to the December first deadline; otherwise, many parents would be making similar requests. This child could wait, like everyone else, until the following September. The request procedure went on over a period of a

month, as I recall, but there was no aggressive challenge.

When the school rejection was definite, Jimmy's pediatrician arranged with a college student to have an hour session twice weekly with Jimmy. At this time they planted seeds, colored, worked with numbers, and read and made up stories together. Jimmy proudly referred to "his school." But, of course, it was nothing like a regular daily kindergarten program with a group of children, and he still looked forward very much to going to the "real school" in September.

Jimmy died the following August. I remember writing a note to his parents, saying something about how he had taught many people many things.

Jimmy never quite made it to school. I will always wonder why. And wonder who remained silent when they might have spoken.

Professionals must be extremely sensitive to the countless ethical and moral aspects of classification, diagnosis, prognosis, and treatment choice. Virtually all the chapters in this book touch upon problems or dilemmas in one or more of these choices. Rhodes emphasizes that professionals must not take traditional definitions and concepts for granted. Otherwise, they may be intervening arbitrarily in other people's lives, having sanctions from society, but assuming absolutes where there is only relativity. As Hobbs suggests, the professional does not have to accept any of the nontraditional conceptualizations, but it is important that they be examined and always in his awareness. He must scrutinize the foundation of his discipline and his value postulates and try to comprehend alternative stances. On a pragmatic level, Kessler illustrates denial of alternative approaches as one of the mistakes professionals make in children's lives. The most unethical position, then, would be to take one's own position for granted or, in Rhodes' terms, one's own concept of normality as "right."

Hobbs reminds professionals that science is a system invented by human beings and that there are other construct systems, each with its own unique validity. "The dilemma for the helping professional is in achieving goodness of fit between the theoretical model followed, the diagnosis or assessment of the problem, and the intervention to be initiated. If forcing seems required, another system or model should be considered. But, even if a goodness of fit is achieved without much difficulty, professionals should never lose sight of the fact that their theoretical constructs, language, classification system, and therapeutic procedures are their own invention; they do not reside in the person helped and, in that sense, have no reality of their own. Different systems for ordering exist within, as well as among, different professions." Rhodes uses the Nazi concept of normality and abnormality to illustrate what can happen when the relative and human nature of these constructs is taken as absolute and intrinsic. Kessler notes that mode of assessment and treatment is often determined by the professional's needs rather than by the child's, although this practice is not always seriously detrimental. She also stresses that professionals have a responsibility to see that diagnosis leads to programming and not to leave the child and his family with recommendations too impractical to implement.

Prognosis can have extremely important ethical implications. DiBuono, Kessler, Fischer, Switzer, Biklen, Friedman and others, Smith, Knitzer, and Lisbe all emphasize this point. The major danger is making predictions about a child's development without sufficient data, and this, in turn, can lead to environmental restriction of opportunities for him to learn. This is a case in which professionals should ethically risk error, giving the child the benefit of the doubt.

Professionals must ensure that any classification system they employ is not harmful to children. Hobbs (1975a and b), Mercer (in Hobbs, 1975b) and Fischer (1974), among others, have written extensively about this topic, and their thinking and conclusions will not be repeated here, except to note that the alternative approaches they suggest seem to be fairer to the child than more traditional ones (Mercer's multidimensional assessment procedure and Hobbs' classification of each child's needs with programmed steps to meet them, as reflected in the Public Law 94-142 legislation). Fischer's flexible and individualized use of psychological assessment instruments and techniques also provides a viable alternative. She emphasizes that the assessor must be involved in the assessment, an idea unacceptable to many professionals who, in the past, felt that this practice destroys "objectivity." Fischer would argue that it preserves reality and, furthermore, that the distinction between testing and assessment must not be forgotten. Finally, Brown's (1975) integrating of parents into the formal assessment process introduces a new concept in the purpose and potential of psychological testing.

Protection of power and territorial boundaries has always been a hindrance in achieving a truly benign method of ordering and communicating children's deviations from the average. Much of the classification tradition is based on the medical model, and it is difficult for many individual professionals to think in different terms. But ethically it seems imperative that this be done if some children are being denied opportunities, are becoming socially isolated, or are having their psychological development negatively affected because of a professional's adherence to a constricted classification system. All professionals should consciously acknowledge any system they have locked themselves into. Too often, as Fischer notes, "We have given location on the bell-shaped curve priority over individualized understanding and helping."

There is an ethical question concerning the justification of the continued use of labels with negative connotations in order to make children eligible for services. Similarly, a computer seems to be dictating policy in state institutions when professionals are required to record an intelligence quotient or numerical medical classification. Fischer comments: "Through our IQ-oriented technology, we have created many cases of retardation. Functioning as mere technicians is not only unethical; it is destructive." In some state institutions, it has been necessary for a child to be given a traditional diagnostic classification and an official patient identification number, both entered in a permanent record, in order to receive any outpatient services. Using sanctions of both professional codes of ethics and the child's well-being, this situation is one in which it seems that professionals as a group should take a firm stand and assert their best judgment. In these cases as well as in newly established or funded programs, they should suggest alternative procedures. Professionals must also respond quickly when discriminatory screening and testing programs are implemented on a large-scale basis. Termination or alteration of such programs in the past was often initiated by community pressure groups, although professionals knew all along of the lack of validity of tests and procedures in particular situations. Fischer and Kessler include cautions about the presently popular preschool screening programs in their discussions.

Friedman and associates express reservations about the use of central registries to record child abuse and neglect cases. The dilemma is that, without them, it may take much longer to confirm a pattern of abuse but, with them, there is the risk that families will be negatively labeled and any positive change in their behavior never recorded. This may make them subject to other external interventions much sooner than if their names were not in the registry. The issue of record keeping is an important one, of course, for all professionals. Kessler, Fischer, Biklen, Knitzer, and Lisbe all describe harm to children related to what was written in records. Professionals must take moral responsibility for the use of records, although it is recognized that they cannot have complete control. However, they do have control over what is put into them. The access parents and sometimes children now have to their own files is a positive development and should reduce the inclusion of potentially harmful and undocumented statements. A question still may be raised about the restrictiveness of psychiatric and often other medical records on children. Is there really an ethical justification for these records to be treated specially? One of Fischer's cases involved this practice. The issue becomes particularly relevant when it is realized that such records can be subpoenaed in court and that physicians traditionally have been encouraged to write down impressions as well as actual clinical findings. As Brant, Garinger, and Brant (1976) suggest, a major revision in medical record keeping may be required. Philosophically as well as pragmatically, the best place to start would seem to be in medical education.

Professionals need a more effective interdisciplinary approach to helping children. This has been said for many years, but these authors frequently refer to the lack of it in their experiences. DiBuono and Friedman and associates comment that physicians have difficulty in working with other professionals as peers, perceiving themselves at the top of a power hierarchy. They are also seldom trained as change agents but assume they should be team leaders, and many other professionals share this expectation. However, the case material in the various chapters attests to the fact that the medical profession is not solely responsible for ineffective interdisciplinary functioning. Moreover, Morse notes that in a decision-making group session, whatever the titles and professions represented, the priorities and needs of the professionals as individual human beings also operate. Great skill is required to contribute one's best expertise and judgment while blending them with different perspectives of other professionals.

Sometimes volunteers can better accomplish a task. I have been repeatedly amazed at the effectiveness of a college service fraternity over a period of at least ten years in meeting many emotional, social, and even some financial needs of three severely handicapped children and their family when no other source of help would fit them into their "category." They also met these needs with more insight, less time, more reliability, and definitely less red tape than any service agency (Kaplan and Mearig, 1977). A local minister, likewise, can respond appropriately to most human needs (except medical) and has a particular interest in handicapped children, having started the community's first preschool for them. He sometimes coordinates his efforts with those of the service fraternity. Helping professionals must learn to work more in partnership and not become trapped in territorial boundaries of their agencies or circumscribed conceptions of their roles. The various self-help groups to which Rhodes refers will also come to be viewed as having a valuable function. Required, of course, is the ability to recognize when each kind of special expertise, professional or nonprofessional, is needed. It is the individual professional's responsibility to support whoever can best help the child.

Use of techniques or data from another profession occurs frequently in the normal course of events. However, adequate familiarity with both underlying theory and practice must be attained; otherwise, a child may be harmed or at least inappropriately helped. Friedman and associates cite the need for physicians to have knowledge about legal and courtroom procedures; they believe law enforcement officials should work closely with all helping professionals in child abuse. As another illustration, the same data may be interpreted differently by psychologists and physicians because of different premises; that is often the case in the intelligence analysis of boys suffering from Duchenne muscular dystrophy, as Fischer notes. Finally, social workers may criticize the format of a physician's family interview. These are but a few examples. Misunderstanding or misuse of another profession's techniques and materials probably can be substantially remedied only through joint training of professionals, but awareness of ongoing developments in one another's specialties is an ethical responsibility of all children's professionals. These developments may have important implications for one's own functioning as well as for more fully understanding the child. There is an equal obligation to make sure that new developments of one's own profession are shared with others.

A shift in professional education from exclusive concentration on the specialty area to one that is more interdisciplinary in orientation seems required. Joint practicum experiences and seminars are one vehicle, but the orientation could also be incorporated in coursework and textbooks without diminishing the focus on the knowledge required in that profession itself. In addition, DiBuono and Friedman and associates emphasize the need in medical education for more attention to children with special needs, especially in areas such as severely impaired children and child abuse and neglect. This includes medical factual knowledge as well as dynamics of the problem as it exists in a child. DiBuono points out that medical education has been more oriented toward curing disorders of "intact" individuals. Psychology and social work, as well as teacher education, have analogous gaps in knowledge of basic information about children with special needs. Switzer expresses concern that many school personnel are not prepared to implement the various facets of Public Law 94-142 and asks to what extent disabled children should be trailblazers while professionals learn. The recent emphasis on these children would seem to demand that all professionals acquire essential knowledge if they are to do an adequate job, legally and ethically.

A particular lack among all helping professionals is a holistic approach to severely handicapped children. This becomes increasingly evident as these children are required to receive additional services. DiBuono and Switzer describe the depressing effect this lack can have on a severely handicapped child and her family, especially if the professional in charge understands only a small part of the total dynamics but thinks he must pretend to be in control of everything. Switzer also refers to the sheer exhaustion, mental and physical, that parents experience when a host of individual professionals have to be consulted. Professionals in this work must extend coordination beyond themselves. Experience in working with community services who should supply many of these children's ongoing needs and with volunteers should begin in the training program.

Professionals have a special responsibility to change society's feelings and attitudes toward severely impaired children. Switzer and DiBuono suggest that the first step is for the individual professional to examine his own values concerning these children. Attitudes and feelings toward them can affect prognoses and services offered. More opportunities to become comfortable with seriously impaired children, including informal relationships with them which many students have not had previously, could be made available in professional programs. If professionals have had no association and also have acquired little factual knowledge about the dynamics of the disability itself, it is hardly realistic, or ethical, for them to play the role of expert to parents. DiBuono cites derogatory terms used in medical training about severely impaired children.

Rhodes believes the age-old wariness of many "normal" individuals toward becoming close to people who are different is a defense against being reminded of their own weaknesses and even impending death. "The abnormal ones are the nonexistent ones—the palpable or material symbol for not being. They represent our death. They are the nearest we can come to knowing and acknowledging our own death. . . . We hold this imperfection at bay by holding 'them' at bay, separating 'them' out of the shared being and activities of community—out of the culture which is our phenomenological reality made manifest" (1977, p. 4). There is also the insight provided by Farson (1974, p. 227): "When a child sees a person without a leg, he will point and ask. We wish he wouldn't. We wish he would learn to look away as we have, and pretend there is nothing wrong." DiBuono's comment is very similar in meaning: "Their [severely impaired infants] parents and those professionals who advocate for them are considered annoyances with unrealistic dedication to a cause that lies outside the mainstream and threatens our own sense of well being." Professionals must examine any such dynamics in themselves before they can deal with those in the larger community.

On the other hand, a number of professionals are overwhelmed by sympathetic depression when they have to work with severely handicapped children, particularly those who are terminally ill and steadily deteriorating. They are often not prepared to deal with situations in which they feel helpless and cannot effect a significant change. Informal contact with such children before the professional must take direct responsibility for them can help. Switzer also notes the importance of having handicapped individuals become professionals and believes that their association with more hesitant colleagues can be a bridge to the latters' successfully working with handicapped children. However, professionals who continue to feel genuinely uncomfortable with the severely handicapped probably should not work with them, although the obligation remains to see that these children receive quality services from someone. Individuals who already have demonstrated an ability to relate to the severely handicapped should be encouraged to enter the helping professions and specialize in these services, even if significant financial support is required.

The decision about providing life supports to severely impaired newborns presents a very basic ethical dilemma, particularly to the physicians initially involved. DiBuono outlines the value issues every professional must confront before he can even begin to adequately serve these children and their parents. He states, "The ultimate question is really 'Is all human life *inherently* valuable?' Or, taking an even more daring human perspective, 'Is not all human life of *equal* value?'" Such basic questions, of course, must also be faced by society as a whole; Hobbs noted that public discussion of an issue such as sanctity of life can only be beneficial. DiBuono makes his own position clear, but stresses that it is not necessarily that of "a materialistic society that measures value in terms of health, beauty, strength, intelligence, and productivity." Yet, he notes society's ambivalence in allowing such infants to die; he does not believe we are a death-oriented society. But the parents may not believe they want the child to live, and then the professional, if he holds to dictates respecting the sanctity

of the infant's life, may have to request that the child be removed
from their custody. DiBuono's case presentation of an older infant,
as well as the Canadian church controversy, should impress upon
the reader the immediacy as well as the profundity of the issues
involved. Some hospitals (Johns Hopkins, for example, where the
Kennedy Foundation film *Who Shall Survive?* was made) have had
a policy of not performing restorative surgery on Downs' syndrome
newborns if the parents do not desire it, as Mendelsohn notes. However, a very important variable, often left out in reporting the parents' decision making, is anxiety about the belief that this child can
have no meaningful life and that society will not support the family
in its upbringing. DiBuono discusses the various possibilities for
community support at some length in his chapter, emphasizing that
values mainly determine how a society decides to allocate funds and
services. These children could be provided with much more support
than is presently available if our society were not placing higher
priority on other values, often materialistic ones. Kessler was concerned after the release of the movie *Who Shall Survive?* that
parents were not aware of developmental, educational, and even vocational possibilities for Downs' syndrome children, as well as alternative living situations. She produced the film *A Question of Values*
(1973), which illustrates some of these options and provides a
longitudinal, developmental perspective. Needless to say, these issues
have implications for the valuing of life all along the age continuum,
with the professional always seeming to be in a pivotal role.

Professionals must define their own positions on right-to-life
issues, and they have a responsibility to make these known to the
larger society. It also should be evident that although physicians
may have to deal with such dilemmas initially, all helping professionals eventually become involved in shaping the development and
lifestyle of severely impaired children. DiBuono believes the professional should not only make his views known but actually become
involved in community groups that debate and deal with these issues,
including services that assist severely impaired children. In addition, teachers, psychologists, and school nurses can incorporate objective knowledge as well as value discussions in high school health,
biology, and parent education courses. Integration of impaired with
nonimpaired children at young age levels is also being arranged

more frequently, partly due to legislation. If successful, it may suggest that Rhodes' concept of an inherent fear of abnormality may be learned.

Finally, the often-noted devaluing of children in general in our society should be acknowledged, as should the continuing notion held by some that children belong to their parents and are, therefore, no one else's responsibility. Smith notes the long period of time natural parents often have to decide whether they want to give up custody of a child for adoption. She also cites the precedent-setting English practice of dealing differently with parentless children according to their economic status. Many professionals want to see the family strengthened and the parents given the capability and support to rear their own children more independently, but this does not imply an ownership of them in the sense that the larger society should not be concerned with what happens to the children. The recent Supreme Court decisions concerning the legitimacy of corporal punishment in schools, referred to by Friedman and associates, reinforce the inferior, owned status of children. It is not permissible to strike adults in prisons without great provocation, but hitting children is considered a "traditional" method of ensuring their proper upbringing by parents and by school personnel. Individual professionals and professional groups may be the only adults independent and committed enough to oppose such reasoning and practices. How many do it? Is this not an ethical responsibility?

The parent–professional relationship is slowly changing. Parents are beginning to play more of a partnership role with professionals. This change has come about, in part, through legislation requiring their access to records, consent for external intervention in their children's lives, and participation in education and treatment program planning, as Biklen notes. But it also has evolved because of the gradual recognition of many professionals that parents have unique insights into dynamics of their children's functioning that they could never acquire, unless over a long period of time. However, parents will need support from professionals if they are uncomfortable in new roles, and many professionals will have to learn how to share power with parents. Hopefully, the time will soon come when the partner relationship can be taken for granted so that third party advocates will not be needed to accompany parents in interactions with professionals. A kind of experience I can recall should be disappearing: I accompanied the very polite and patient parents of a boy with a serious language development lag, due to a brain malignancy and associated surgery, to a conference concerning possible vocational training. The greeting was, "You understand, of course, that this school is for normal children."

Switzer and DiBuono emphasize the value of a relationship of honesty and partnership, feeling that parents' confidence in the professional is enhanced if they understand his anxieties and concern over limitations of expertise—his own and that of his profession. In turn, this understanding can alleviate some of the professional's anxieties. Lisbe notes the importance of going into homes in order to understand values of different families as well as physical conditions and interpersonal dynamics contributing to a child's functioning. In the case of a severely disabled child, Switzer stresses the importance of the professional acquiring some idea of what it is like to live with such a child on a day-to-day basis. In one sense, there seems to be no substitute for this firsthand visiting. Professionals traditionally have come from middle-class backgrounds, are often from nonhandicapped families, and obtain an understanding of other people's values only in the abstract. Yet, their own values can significantly influence perception of the very behavior in the child they are trying to understand. Brown and Fischer's giving parents responsibilities in the psychological assessment process also reflects a partner relationship. Moreover, it is one in which new insights are achieved by both parents and professionals. In addition, this procedure demonstrates the blending of assessment into treatment. Parents' interactions with the child may begin to change in the assessment session itself as they discover new responses from the child when they introduce new stimuli or use a different teaching approach.

Another partnership could grow out of Feshbach's and Feshbach's (1976) recommendation that "how parents rear a child should be an open matter, open for discussion, help, and inquiry." However, these authors were suggesting a home visitor system that is somewhat controversial. Official intervention of one kind or another, which may or may not be necessary, could follow. Child advocates and those working in child abuse, of course, might see substantial benefit in a home-visiting plan. The basic question of who, ultimately, is responsible for a child must be dealt with. Perhaps the more preventive governmental participation Hobbs and his colleagues talk about at the Center for the Study of Families and Children (1977) avoids some of the problems. Developing a program whereby families are given the supports required, financial and otherwise, to do a better job of parenting on their own may make after-the-fact intervention into separate aspects of the child's development less necessary.

More attention must be devoted to ethical and moral issues and dilemmas in professional programs. Specific content areas that could be added or expanded to better prepare professionals to cope with children's problems have been noted earlier. In addition, programs should view ethics and the decision-making process itself as integral parts of their students' education. These can be dealt with explicitly and naturally in most courses, seminars, and practicum experiences. Discussion of issues in the abstract also has its place, but as Morse and Mendelsohn suggest, ethics should permeate the entire curriculum. The "when?" and "what if?" questions are just as important as the "how to" ones in professional education. Mendelsohn gives examples of critical ethical issues in a number of course areas. Examination of such issues has to be an ongoing process, and modeling of experienced professionals is important. Morse and DiBuono note that haphazard learning in ethics is occurring at present, but the student may come away with an interpretation very different from the one intended. Mendelsohn says the learning is detrimental. A danger, as Morse points out, is value indoctrination of any kind. However, it would seem that this can be avoided with faculty and supervisor sensitivity. In the modeling process, the older professional should give explanations for her choices and allow the student to question her rationale.

The student also needs someone to help him deal with conflict. Moreover, he should have experiences in actually coping with dilemmas while in the professional program, when emotional support is available and issues can be worked through systematically in discussions with people who are sympathetic but not directly involved in a situation. It is very important that the ideals with which students usually enter a professional program not be lost. Morse says, "The role of the seasoned professional is to know the odds and yet keep at the task, working with the young professional who supplies both the drive for change and time myopia." And Lisbe summarizes the challenge: "Unrestricted vision may be a gift present only once in a professional's life. Each of us has inside ourselves a piece of good news. To share that with others is why we enter the helping professions. What we need to learn is how to keep the news alive through the times when no one is reading the paper."

An exception to professional or ethical guidelines is just that and needs to be carefully justified, planned, and explained. However, it should not be avoided if it is required to help the child. The individual professional must ultimately make this decision himself. Mendelsohn notes that there would be moral chaos rather than ethical standards if individualization without generalization were the order of the day for professionals. Ethics demands generalizations. Fischer, Hobbs, Kessler, and McGowan all stress the importance of fully recognizing the ethical standards of one's profession; Hobbs and Kessler note that these must be revised periodically to incorporate theoretical developments and the wisdom of experience. This ongoing revision process provides an opportunity for the individual professional who demonstrates the need to go beyond the existing guidelines to contribute to the standards themselves. But the authors in this book seem to agree that there will always be significant exceptions to be made to any guidelines that are formulated.

The challenge, of course, is to know when exceptions are justified. Here is where thorough knowledge of all the variables involved in a situation is essential. If guidelines still do not emerge or are not adequate, the "invincible surmise" to which Hobbs refers must then come into play. This is required "when the well-being of another person is seriously at stake" and "both art and science are insufficient guides to choice." Hobbs also states: "As knowledge and understanding grow, the most astute, sensitive, and responsible professional people must begin making choices in advance of, and at odds with, established ethical standards. New circumstances will require new kinds of ethical and moral decisions. The true professional person must accept private responsibility for the constant reconstruction of what is right." Hobbs notes that this is a profound responsibility, one that differentiates the professional person from the technician or the tradesperson, and one requiring a constantly expanding awareness of the issues involved. These are also the instances in which early and personal values come most to the fore in decision making. And, as Mendelsohn states, "Ethics is not a question of motivation or deliberation. Ethics is judged by behavior."

DiBuono gives no references for his position; he believes the reader ultimately must respond to the content of the chapter by examining his own convictions rather than relying on any "authority." Fischer explains how it is possible for a standardized administration of a test to be unethical. Kessler notes the judgment required in taking a child client home to live, and in not informing parents of a runaway threat. Lisbe relates involvement in actions to help a child bordering on the illegal. All the authors at one point present situations that ask the professional to exercise the "invincible surmise." This individual decision-making process taking one beyond the guidelines is not only the distinguishing characteristic of an ethical professional. It may also represent a singular opportunity to make a significant difference in the direction of a child's life. But, as Hobbs indicates, it is a profound responsibility.

References

ABESON, A. "Movement and Momentum: Government and the Education of Handicapped Children—II." *Exceptional Children,* 1974, *41,* 109–115.

ABESON, A., BOLICK, N., and HASS, J. A. *A Primer on Due Process.* Reston, Va.: Council for Exceptional Children, 1975.

Ad Hoc Committee on Advocacy. "The Social Worker as Advocate: Champion of Social Victims." *Social Work,* 1969, *14,* 16–22.

American Psychological Association. *Ethical Standards of Psychologists.* Washington, D.C.: American Psychological Association, 1953.

American Psychological Association. *"Revised Ethical Standards of Psychologists."* APA Monitor, 1977, *8* (3), 13–14.

American Psychological Association. *Ethical Principles in the Conduct of Research with Human Participants.* Washington, D.C.: American Psychological Association, 1973.

American Psychological Association. *Standards for Providers of Psy-*

chological Services. Washington, D.C.: American Psychological Association, 1975.

AXINN, J., and OTHERS. *The Century of the Child.* Philadelphia: University of Pennsylvania Press, 1973.

BARBERO, G. J., and SHAHEEN, E. "Environmental Failure to Thrive: A Clinical View." *Journal of Pediatrics,* 1967, *71,* 5.

BECKER, E. *The Denial of Death.* New York: Free Press, 1973.

BECKER, H. *Outsiders: Studies in the Sociology of Deviance.* New York: Free Press, 1963.

BEEBE, M. "The Development and Evaluation of a Model of Assessment and Intervention for School Psychologists." Doctoral dissertation in process, University of Michigan.

BENEDICT, R. *Patterns of Culture.* Boston: Houghton Mifflin, 1961.

BERGER, P. *A Rumor of Angels: Modern Society and the Rediscovery of the Supernatural.* Garden City, N.Y.: Doubleday, 1969.

BERGER, P., and LUCKMANN, T. *The Social Construction of Reality: A Treatise on the Sociology of Knowledge.* Garden City, N.Y.: Doubleday, 1967.

BERNSTEIN, B., SNIDER, D. A., and MEEZAN, W. *Foster Care Needs and Alternatives to Placement: A Projection for 1975–1985.* New York: New York State Board of Social Welfare, 1975.

BERNSTEIN, V. *Final Judgement.* New York: Parish Press, 1947.

BERSOFF, D. N. "Silk Purses into Sows' Ears: The Decline of Psychological Testing and a Suggestion for Its Redemption." *American Psychologist,* 1973, *28,* 892–899.

BERSOFF, D. N. "Professional Ethics and Legal Responsibilities: On the Horns of a Dilemma." In B. Cardon and others (Eds.), *Law and the School Psychologist: Challenge and Opportunity.* New York: Human Sciences Press, 1975.

BILLINGSLEY, A. "Bureaucratic and Professional Orientation Patterns in Social Casework." *Social Service Review,* 1964, *38,* 400–407.

BLACK, S. *Holocaust.* New York: Bergen-Belsen Memorial Press, 1965.

BLATT, B. *Souls in Extremis.* Boston: Allyn & Bacon, 1973.

BLATT, B., and KAPLAN, F. *Christmas in Purgatory.* Boston: Allyn & Bacon, 1966.

BLAU, P., and SCOTT, W. *Formal Organizations.* San Francisco: Chandler, 1962.

BOSCH, H. *The Complete Drawings of Hieronymus Bosch.* New York: St. Martin's, 1973.

BOWLES, S., and GINTIS, H. *Schooling in Capitalist America.* New York: Basic Books, 1976.

BRAGER, G. A. "Advocacy and Political Behavior." *Social Work,* 1968, *13,* 5–15.

BRAGER, G. A., and SPECHT, H. *Community Organizing.* New York: Columbia University Press, 1973.

BRAGER, G. A., and HOLLOWAY, S. *Changing Human Service Organizations: Politics and Practice.* New York: Free Press, 1978.

BRANCH, T. "New Frontiers in American Philosophy." *New York Times Magazine,* August 14, 1977, p. 46.

BRANT, J., GARINGER, G., and BRANT, R. "So You Want to See Our Files on You?" In G. Koocher (Ed.), *Children's Rights and the Mental Health Professions.* New York: Wiley, 1976.

BRASSELL, W. "Intervention with Handicapped Infants: Correlates of Progress." *Mental Retardation,* 1977, *15* (4), 18–24.

BRIAR, S. "The Social Worker's Responsibility for the Civil Rights of Clients." *New Perspectives: The Berkeley Journal of Social Welfare,* 1967, *1,* 89–92.

BROWN, L. K. "Family Dialectics in a Clinical Context." *Human Development,* 1975, *18,* 223–238.

BURT, R. A., and MORRIS, N. "A Proposal for the Abolition of the Incompetency Plea." *The University of Chicago Law Review,* 1972, *40* (60), 66–95.

CALDWELL, B. M., and RICCIUTI, H. N. (Eds.). *Child Development and Social Policy, Review of Child Development Research.* Vol. 3. Chicago: University of Chicago Press, 1973.

CAMPS, F. E., and CARPENTER, R. G. *Sudden and Unexpected Death in Infancy.* Bristol, England: Wright, 1972.

CAMUS, A. *The Plague.* New York: Knopf, 1948.

CAPLAN, G. *Prevention of Mental Disorders in Children.* New York: Basic Books, 1961.

CAPLOW, T. *Principles of Organization.* New York: Harcourt Brace Jovanovich, 1964.

CASTANEDA, C. *The Teachings of Don Juan: A Yaqui Way of Knowledge.* New York: Ballantine Books, 1968.

Center for the Study of Families and Children (Program). N. Hobbs, Director. The Vanderbilt Institute of Public Policy Studies, Nashville, Tenn., March 15, 1977.

CHERNISS, C. "Is There a Job Satisfaction Problem in Community Mental Health?" *Community Mental Health Journal*, in press.

CLEMMENS, L., and KENNY, T. J. "Prevention of Emotional Problems in Childhood: A Philosophy of Child Rearing." *Clinical Pediatrics*, 1977, *16*, 122–123.

CLOWARD, R., and EPSTEIN, I. "Private Social Welfare's Disengagement from the Poor: The Case of Family Adjustment Agencies." In M. N. Zald (Ed.), *Social Welfare Institutions*. New York: Wiley, 1965.

COX, F. M., and OTHERS. (Eds.). *Strategies of Community Organizing*. Itasia, Ill.: Peacock, 1970.

CUPOLI, J. M., and NEWBERGER, E. H. "Optimism or Pessimism for the Victim of Child Abuse." *Pediatrics*, 1977, *59*, 311–313.

CURRAN, W. J. "Failure to Diagnose the Battered Child Syndrome." *New England Journal of Medicine*, 1977, *296*, 795–796.

Dale v. *New York*, N.Y. Ct. Cl. (March 30, 1973).

DE FRANCIS, V. "Highlights of National Study for 1975." In *Child Abuse and Neglect Reports*. Washington, D.C.: National Center on Child Abuse and Neglect, 1977.

DES PRES, T. *The Survivor: An Anatomy of Life in Death Camps*. New York: Oxford University Press, 1976.

Donaldson v. *O'Connor*, 422 U.S. 563 (1972).

Durham v. *United States*, 214 F.2d 852 (D.C. Cir. 1954).

EBELING, N. B. "Preventing Strains and Stresses in Protective Services." In N. B. Ebeling and D. A. Hill (Eds.), *Child Abuse: Intervention and Treatment*. Acton, Mass.: Publishing Sciences Group, 1975.

Education Commission of the States Child Abuse and Neglect Project. "Model Legislation for the States." Report no. 71. Washington, D.C.: National Center on Child Abuse and Neglect, 1976.

Education Commission of the States Child Abuse and Neglect Project. "Trends in Reporting Statutes." Report no. 95. Washington, D.C.: National Center on Child Abuse and Neglect, 1977.

ELMER, E. "A Follow-Up Study of Traumatized Children." *Pediatrics,* 1977, *59,* 273–279.

EVANS, S. L., REINHART, J. B., and SUCCOP, R. A. "Failure to Thrive." *Journal of Academy of Child Psychiatry,* 1972, *11,* 440–457.

FANSHEL, D. "Status Changes of Children in Foster Care: Final Results of the Columbia University Longitudinal Study." *Child Welfare,* 1976, *55* (3), 143–172.

FARSON, R. *Birthrights.* New York: Macmillan, 1974.

FELLNER, I., and SOLOMON, C. "Achieving Permanent Solutions for Children in Foster Home Care." *Child Welfare,* 1973, *52* (3), 178–187.

FESHBACH, N. D., and FESHBACH, S. "Punishment: Parent Rites vs. Children's Rights." In G. P. Koocher (Ed.), *Children's Rights and the Mental Health Professions.* New York: Wiley, 1976.

FESTINGER, J. B. "The Impact of the New York Court Review of Children in Foster Care: A Follow-Up Report." *Child Welfare,* 1976, *55* (8), 515–546.

FEYERABEND, P. *Against Method: Outline of an Anarchistic Theory of Knowledge.* London: Humanities Press, 1975.

FISCHER, C. T. "The Testee as Co-Evaluator." *Journal of Counseling Psychology,* 1970, *17,* 70–76.

FISCHER, C. T. "A Theme for the Child-Advocate: Sharable Everyday-Life Events of the Child-in-the-World." *Journal of Clinical Child Psychology,* 1972, *1,* 23–25.

FISCHER, C. T. "Intelligence Contra IQ: A Human-Science Critique and Alternative to the Natural Science Approach to Man." *Human Development,* 1973, *16,* 8–20.

FISCHER, C. T. "Exit IQ: Enter the Child." In G. Williams and S. Gordon (Eds.), *Clinical Child Psychology: Current Practices and Future Perspectives.* New York: Behavioral Publications, 1974.

FISCHER, C. T. "Undercutting the Scientist-Professional Dichotomy: The Reflective Psychologist." *The Clinical Psychologist,* 1976, *29,* 2–7.

FISCHER, C. T. "Collaborative Psychological Assessment." In C. T. Fischer and S. L. Brodsky (Eds.), *Client Participation in Human Services: The Prometheus Principle.* New Brunswick, N.J.: Transaction Press, 1978a.

FISCHER, C. T. "Informed Participation: Why Now?" In C. T. Fischer and S. L. Brodsky (Eds.), *Client Participation in Human Services: The Prometheus Principle.* New Brunswick, N.J.: Transaction Press, 1978b.

FISCHER, C. T. "Personality and Assessment." In R. Valle and M. King (Eds.), *Existential Phenomenological Psychology: An Alternative Approach.* New York: Oxford University Press, in press.

FISCHER, C. T., and RIZZO, A. A. "A Paradigm for Humanizing Special Education." *Journal of Special Education,* 1974, 8, 321–329.

FONTANA, V. J. *The Maltreated Child.* (2nd ed.) Springfield, Ill.: Thomas, 1971.

FOUCAULT, M. *Madness and Civilization.* New York: Vintage Books, 1973.

FOUCAULT, M. *Mental Illness and Psychology.* New York: Colophon Books, 1976.

FRASER, B. G. "Toward a More Practical Central Registry." *Denver Law Journal,* 1974, 51, 509.

FRASER, B. G. "The Child and His Parents: A Delicate Balance of Rights." In R. E. Helfer and C. H. Kempe (Eds.), *Child Abuse and Neglect: The Family and the Community.* Cambridge, Mass.: Ballinger, 1976.

FRASER, B. G. "Independent Representation for the Abused and Neglected Child: Guardian Ad Litem." *California Law Review,* 1976–1977, 13, 16–45.

FRASER, B. G., and MARTIN, H. P. "An Advocate for the Abused Child." In H. P. Martin (Ed.), *The Abused Child.* Cambridge, Mass.: Ballinger, 1976.

FRAZER, J. *The Golden Bough.* New York: Macmillan, 1950.

FREIDSON, E. "Dominant Professions, Bureaucracy, and Client Service." In W. Rosengren and M. Lefton (Eds.), *Organizations and Clients.* Columbus, Ohio: Merrill, 1970.

FREUD, S. *Civilization and Its Discontents.* (J. Riviere, Trans.) London: Hogarth Press, 1949.

FRIEDMAN, A. S., and FRIEDMAN, D. B. "Corporal Punishment, Humiliation, Ridicule and Other Forms of Child Abuse." Paper presented at Child Abuse and Neglect seminar, California State University at Bakersfield, January 22, 1977.

FRIEDMAN, D. B., and SWINGER, H. (Eds.). "Parenting and Child Behavior." *Pediatric Annals,* 1977, *6* (10 and 11), 9–109, 10–111.

Gary, W., and others, and United States v. Stewart and others, No. 74–2412 "C" (E.D.N.C.).

GILBERT, N., and SPECHT, H. "Advocacy and Professional Ethics." *Social Work,* 1976, *21,* 288–293.

GILHOOL, T. "An Inalienable Right." *Exceptional Children,* 1973, *39,* 597–609.

GODDARD, H. *Juvenile Delinquency.* New York: Dodd, Mead, 1921.

GOFFMAN, E. *Asylums.* Garden City, N.Y.: Doubleday, 1961.

GOLDSTEIN, J., FREUD, A., and SOLNIT, A. *Beyond the Best Interests of the Child.* New York: Macmillan, 1973.

GORDON, S. "Are We Seeing the Right Patients? Child Guidance Intake: The Sacred Cow." *American Journal of Orthopsychiatry,* 1965, *35* (1), 131–137.

GOULDNER, A. W. "The Secrets of Organizations." In *Social Welfare Forum.* New York: Columbia University Press, 1963.

GOULDNER, A. W. *The Coming Crisis of Western Sociology.* New York: Basic Books, 1970.

GOVE, W. "Societal Reaction as an Explanation of Mental Illness." *American Sociological Review,* 1970, *35* (5), 873–883.

GREENWOOD, E. "Attributes of a Profession." *Social Work,* 1957, *2,* 45–55.

GRIFFITH, J. *Black Like Me.* Boston: Houghton Mifflin, 1961.

HAMDEN-TURNER, C. *Sane Asylum: The Delancey Street Foundation.* New York: Morrow, 1977.

HANSEN, C. "A Program to Introduce Medical Students to the Problem of Child Abuse and Neglect." *Journal of Medical Education,* 1977, *52,* 522–524.

HARPUR, T. "Kill Severely Retarded at Birth: Anglican Study." *Toronto Star,* July 27, 1977, p. 1.

HELFER, R. E. "The Responsibility and Role of the Physician." In R. E. Helfer and C. H. Kempe (Eds.), *The Battered Child.* (2nd ed.) Chicago: University of Chicago Press, 1974.

HELFER, R. E. "The Diagnostic Process and Treatment Programs." DHEW Publication No. (OHD) 75–69. Washington, D.C.: National Center on Child Abuse and Neglect, 1975a.

HELFER, R. E. "Why Most Physicians Don't Get Involved in Child

Abuse Cases and What to Do About It." *Children Today,* 1975b, *4* (3), 28–32.

HERSCH, C. "The Discontentment Explosion in Mental Health." *American Psychologist,* 1968, *23* (7), 497–506.

HITLER, A. *Mein Kampf.* New York: Stackpole, 1939.

HOBBS, N. "Science and Ethical Behavior." *American Psychologist,* 1959, *14,* 217–225.

HOBBS, N. "Ethics in Clinical Psychology." In B. B. Wolman (Ed.), *Handbook of Clinical Psychology.* New York: McGraw-Hill, 1965.

HOBBS, N. "Ethical Issues in the Social Sciences." In W. H. Kruskal and J. N. Tanner (Eds.), *Encyclopedia of Statistics.* New York: Free Press, in press.

HOBBS, N. *The Futures of Children: Recommendations of the Project on Classification of Exceptional Children.* San Francisco: Jossey-Bass, 1975a.

HOBBS, N. (Ed.). *Issues in the Classification of Children: A Sourcebook on Categories, Labels, and Their Consequences.* Vols. 1 and 2. San Francisco: Jossey-Bass, 1975b.

HOBSON, L. *Gentleman's Agreement.* New York: Simon & Schuster, 1947.

ILLICH, I. *Deschooling Society.* New York: Harper & Row, 1971.

JACKSON, J. "Adjustment of the Family to the Crisis of Alcoholism." In E. Rubington and M. Wienberg (Eds.), *Deviance. The Interaction Perspective.* London: Collier-Macmillan, 1965.

JAMES, W. "The Dilemma of Determinism." In A. Castell (Ed.), *Essays in Pragmatism.* New York: Hafner, 1948.

JENKINS, D. H. "Social Engineering in Educational Change: An Outline Method." *Progressive Education,* 1949, *26,* 193–197.

JONES, J. "Self-Help Activists Talk." *APA Monitor,* 1977, *8* (8).

JONES, M. A., NEUMAN, R., and SHYNE, A. W. *A Second Chance for Families: Evaluation of a Program to Reduce Foster Care.* New York: Child Welfare League of America, 1976.

KAPLAN, A. "Social Ethics and The Sanctity of Life: A Summary." In Shils, E. and others (Eds.), *Life or Death: Ethics and Options.* Seattle: University of Washington Press, 1968.

KAPLAN, D., and MEARIG, J. "A Community Support System for a

Family Coping with Chronic Illness." *Rehabilitation Literature,* 1977, *38* (3), 79–82, 96.

KATZ, S. N. *When Parents Fail: The Law's Response to Family Breakdown.* Boston: Beacon Press, 1971.

KEMPE, C. H. "Family Intervention: The Right of All Children." *Pediatrics,* 1975, *56,* 693–695.

Kennedy Foundation. *Who Shall Survive?* (Film.) Washington, D.C.: Kennedy Foundation, 1971.

KENNELL, J., VOOS, D., and KLAUS, M. "Parent–Infant Bonding." In R. E. Helfer and C. H. Kempe (Eds.), *Child Abuse and Neglect: The Family and the Community.* Cambridge, Mass.: Ballinger, 1976.

KESSLER, J. *A Question of Values* (Film.) Cleveland: Mental Development Center, Case Western Reserve University, 1973.

KIERKEGAARD, S. *The Sickness Unto Death.* Princeton, N.J.: Princeton University Press, 1971.

KIRESUK, T. J., and LUND, S. H. "Process and Outcome Measurement Using Goal Attainment Scaling." In G. U. Glass (Ed.), *Evaluation Studies, Review Annual.* Vol. I. Beverly Hills: Sage Publications, 1976.

KITSUSE, J. "Societal Reaction to Deviant Behavior: Problem of Theory and Method." In H. Becker (Ed.), *The Other Side.* New York: Free Press, Macmillan, 1964.

KLAUS, M. H., and KENNELL, J. H. *Maternal–Infant Bonding.* St. Louis: Mosby, 1976.

KNITZER, J. "Advocacy and the Children's Crisis." *American Journal of Orthopsychiatry,* 1971, *41* (5), 799–806.

KNITZER, J. "Child Advocacy: A Perspective." *American Journal of Orthopsychiatry,* 1976, *46* (2), 200–216.

KOENIGSBERG, R. *Hitler's Ideology: A Study in Psychoanalytic Sociology.* New York: Library of Social Science, 1975.

KOOCHER, G. P. (Ed.). *Children's Rights and the Mental Health Professions.* New York: Wiley, 1976.

KOPP, S. *If You Meet the Buddha on the Road Kill Him.* Palo Alto, Calif.: Science and Behavior Books, 1972.

KOZOL, J. *Death at an Early Age.* Boston: Houghton Mifflin, 1967.

KOZOL, J. *Free Schools.* Boston: Houghton Mifflin, 1972.

Kremens and others v. *Bartley and others*, No. 75–1064 in the Supreme Court of the United States.

LAING, R. *The Divided Self.* London: Tavistock, 1964.

LANDIS, B. Y. (Ed.). "Ethical Standards and Professional Conduct." *The Annals of the American Academy of Political and Social Science*, 1955, *297*, 1–124.

Larry P. v. *Riles*, 343 F. Supp. 1306 (N.D. Calif. 1972).

LAWDER, E. A., ANDREWS, R. G., and PARSONS, J. A. *Five Models of Foster Family Group Homes.* New York: Child Welfare League of America, 1974.

LAZARE, A. "Hidden Conceptual Models in Clinical Psychiatry." *New England Journal of Medicine*, 1973, *288*, 345–351.

LEONARD, M. F., RHYMES, J. P., and SOLNIT, A. J. "Failure to Thrive in Infants: A Family Problem." *American Journal of Diseases of Children*, 1966, *111*, 600–612.

LITWAK, E. "Models of Bureaucracy Which Permit Conflict." *American Journal of Sociology*, 1961, *67*, 177–184.

LITWAK, E., and OTHERS. "Community Participation in Bureaucratic Organizations: Principles and Strategies." *Interchange*, 1970, *4*, 43–60.

LONDON, P. *Behavior Control.* New York: Harper & Row, 1969.

MAAS, H. S., and ENGLER, R. E., JR. *Children in Need of Parents.* New York: Columbia University Press, 1959.

MCGOWAN, B. G. *Case Advocacy: A Study of the Interventive Process in Child Advocacy.* New York: School of Social Work, Columbia University, 1973.

MACKEY, R. A. "Professionalization and the Poor." *Social Work*, 1964, *9*, 108–110, 119.

MANN, L. "Psychometric Phrenology and the New Faculty Psychology: The Case Against Ability Assessment and Training." *Journal of Special Education*, 1971, *5*, 3–14.

MARTIN, H. P. "The Environment of the Abused Child." In H. P. Martin (Ed.), *The Abused Child.* Cambridge, Mass.: Ballinger, 1976.

MATSON, F. W. *The Ideas of Man.* New York: Delacorte Press, 1976.

Matter of Quinlan, 70 N.J. 10, 355 A.2d 647 (1976).

MATZA, D. *Becoming Deviant.* Englewood Cliffs, N.J.: Prentice-Hall, 1969.

MEARIG, J. S. "Ethical and Moral Considerations: Responsibility of the Individual Professional in an Urbanized Society." *American Journal of Orthopsychiatry*, 1970, *14* (2), 47.

MEARIG, J. S. "On Becoming an Advocate in School Psychology." *Journal of School Psychology*, 1974, *12*, 121–129.

MECH, E. V. "Adoption: A Policy Perspective." In B. M. Caldwell and H. N. Ricciuti (Eds.), *Child Development and Social Policy, Review of Child Development Research*. Chicago: University of Chicago Press, 1973.

MERCER, J. R. *Labelling the Mentally Retarded Child*. Berkeley: University of California Press, 1973.

MERCER, J. R. "Psychological Assessment and the Rights of Children." In N. Hobbs (Ed.), *Issues in the Classification of Children: A Sourcebook on Categories, Labels, and Their Consequences*. Vol. 1. San Francisco: Jossey-Bass, 1975.

MERTON, R. "Bureaucratic Structure and Personality." In D. Stein and R. Cloward (Eds.), *Social Perspectives on Behavior*. New York: Free Press, 1958.

MEYER, C. *Social Work Practice*. (2nd ed.) New York: Free Press, 1976.

MILLER, R., and WILLNER, H. S. "Sounding Board: The Two-Part Consent Form." *New England Journal of Medicine*, 1974, *200* (17), 964–966.

MINDLIN, R. L. "Background to the Current Interest in Child Abuse and Neglect." *Pediatric Annals*, 1976, *6*, 10–14.

MOORE, W. E. *The Professions: Roles and Rules*. New York: Russell Sage, 1970.

MORRIS, C. "If You're Called as an Expert Witness." *Resident and Staff Physician*, 1974, pp. 76–81.

National Center on Child Abuse and Neglect. "The Problem and Its Management." DHEW Publication no. (OHD) 75-30073. Washington, D.C.: Office of Child Development, 1975.

National Center on Child Abuse and Neglect. "Planning and Implementing Child Abuse and Neglect Service Programs." DHEW Publication no. (OHD) 77-30093. Washington, D.C.: Office of Child Development, 1977a.

National Center on Child Abuse and Neglect. "Symposium on Child

Abuse Indicators and Case Identification," Houston, April 15–16, 1977. Clearinghouse Project, Contract HEW-105-76-1136. Washington, D.C.: Children's Bureau, Office of Child Development, 1977b.

NEWBERGER, E. H., and DANIEL, J. H. "Knowledge and Epidemiology of Child Abuse." *Pediatric Annals,* 1976, *5,* 16–26.

PALMER, J. O. *The Psychological Assessment of Children.* New York: Wiley, 1970.

PANITCH, A. "Advocacy in Practice." *Social Work,* 1974, *19,* 326–332.

PATTI, R. J., and RESNICK, H. "Changing the Agency from Within." *Social Work,* 1972, *17,* 48–57.

PAUL, J., and DES JARLAIS, D. "Labeling Theory." In W. Rhodes and J. Paul (Eds.), *Emotionally Disturbed and Deviant Children.* Englewood Cliffs, N.J.: Prentice-Hall, 1978.

Pennsylvania Association for Retarded Children v. Commonwealth of Pennsylvania, 343 F. Supp. 279 (E.D. Pa. 1972).

POLANYI, M. *Personal Knowledge: Towards a Post-Critical Philosophy.* Boston: Routledge & Kegan Paul, 1958.

POLIER, J. W. "Professional Abuse of Children: Responsibility for the Delivery of Services." *American Journal of Orthopsychiatry,* 1975, *45* (3), 357–362.

POLIER, J. W. "In Defense of Children." *Child Welfare,* 1976, *55* (2), 75–82.

POLLACK, C., and STEELE, B. "A Therapeutic Approach to the Parents." In C. H. Kempe and R. E. Helfer (Eds.), *Helping the Battered Child and His Family.* Philadelphia: Lippincott, 1972.

POLLAK, O. *Human Behavior and the Helping Professions.* New York: Spectrum, 1976.

POWELL, G. F., BRASEL, J. A., and BLIZZARD, R. M. "Emotional Deprivation and Growth Retardation Simulating Idiopathic Hypopituitarism." *New England Journal of Medicine,* 1967, *276,* 1271–1278.

PRATT, L. *Family Structure and Effective Health Behavior: The Energized Family.* Boston: Houghton Mifflin, 1976.

Psychological Corporation, The. *Test Service Bulletin No. 54.* New York: Psychological Corporation, 1959.

QUINE, W. "Speaking of Objects." In *Ontological Relativity and Other Essays.* New York: Columbia University Press, 1969.

RANK, O. *The Trauma of Birth.* New York: Harcourt Brace Jovanovich, 1929.

RANK, O. *Will Therapy and Truth and Reality.* New York: Knopf, 1945.

REISS, A. "The Social Integration of Peers and Queers." In H. Becker (Ed.), *The Other Side.* New York: Free Press, 1964.

Report of the Joint Commission on Mental Health of Children. *Crisis in Child Mental Health: Challenge for the 1970s.* New York: Harper & Row, 1969.

RHODES, W. "Overview of Interventions." In W. Rhodes and M. Tracy (Eds.), *A Study of Child Variance.* Vol. 2: *Interventions.* Ann Arbor: University of Michigan Publications Distribution Service, 1972.

RHODES, W. "Social Values and the Health of Children." Paper presented at Interdisciplinary Faculty seminar, Ann Arbor, Mich., May 7, 1977.

ROGERS, C. *On Becoming a Person: A Therapist's View of Psychology.* Boston: Houghton Mifflin, 1961.

ROSENBERG, A. *Selected Writings.* (R. Pois, Ed.) London: Cape, 1970.

ROSENFELD, A. A., and NEWBERGER, E. H. "Compassion vs. Control." *Journal of the American Medical Association,* 1977, *237,* 2086–2088.

ROSENHAN, G. "On Being Sane in Insane Places." *Science,* 1973, *179,* 250–259.

ROSENHEIM, M. K. "The Child and the Law." In B. M. Caldwell and H. N. Ricciuti (Eds.), *Child Development and Social Policy: Review of Child Development Research.* Chicago: University of Chicago Press, 1973.

ROSENTHAL, R., and JACOBSON, L. *Pygmalion in the Classroom.* New York: Holt, Rinehart and Winston, 1968.

RUTTER, M. *Maternal Deprivation Reassessed.* New York: Penguin, 1972.

RYAN, W. *Blaming the Victim.* New York: Vintage Books, 1971.

SAINT-EXUPÉRY, A. *Wind, Sand, and Stars.* (L. Galantiere, Trans.) New York: Roynal & Hitchcock, 1939.

SANTAYANA, G. *Poems.* New York: Scribner's, 1923.

SARASON, S. B. *The Creation of Settings and the Future Societies.* San Francisco: Jossey-Bass, 1972.

SATTLER, J. M. *Assessment of Children's Intelligence.* Philadelphia: Saunders, 1974.

SCHAFER, R. *Psychoanalytic Interpretation in Rorschach Testing.* New York: Grune and Stratton, 1954.

SCHATZMAN, M. *Soul Murder: Persecution in the Family.* New York: Random House, 1973.

SCHEFF, T. *Being Mentally Ill.* Chicago: Aldine Press, 1966.

SCHMITT, B. D., GROSZ, C. A., and CARROLL, C. A. "The Child Protection Team." In R. E. Helfer and C. H. Kempe (Eds.), *Child Abuse and Neglect: The Family and the Community.* Cambridge, Mass.: Ballinger, 1976.

SCHMITT, B. D., and BEEZLEY, P. "The Long-Term Management of Child and Family in Child Abuse and Neglect." *Pediatric Annals,* 1976, 5, 59–78.

SCHRAG, P., and DIVOKY, D. *The Myth of the Hyperactive Child.* New York: Pantheon, 1975.

SCHUTZ, A. *Collected Papers.* Vol. 1. The Hague, Netherlands: Nijhoff, 1962.

SCOTT, R. A. "The Selection of Clients by Social Welfare Agencies: The Case of the Blind." *Social Problems,* 1967, 14, 248–257.

SHERMAN, E. A., and OTHERS. *Services to Children in Their Own Homes: Its Nature and Outcome.* New York: Child Welfare League of America, 1973.

SHORE, M. F. "Reviews of the Literature." *American Journal of Orthopsychiatry,* 1977, 47 (2), 359–360.

SKINNER, B. F. *Science and Human Behavior.* New York: Macmillan, 1953.

SKINNER, B. F. *Contingencies and Reinforcement: A Theoretical Analysis.* New York: Appleton-Century-Crofts, 1969.

SKINNER, B. F. *Beyond Freedom and Dignity.* New York: Knopf, 1971.

SMITH, C. A., and BERENBERG, W. "The Concept of Failure to Thrive." *Pediatrics,* 1970, 46, 661.

STARR, J. "The Search for Biological Parents." Paper presented at National Conference of the American Association of Psychiatric Services for Children, San Francisco, November 1976.

STEELE, B. F. "Working with Abusive Parents." DHEW Publication No. (OHD) 75–70. Washington, D.C.: National Center on Child Abuse and Neglect, 1975.

STONE, H. D. (Ed.). *Foster Care in Question.* New York: Child Welfare League of America, 1970.

STRAUSS, P. L., and STRAUSS, J. B. "Book Review: Beyond the Best Interests of the Child." *Columbia Law Review,* 1974, *74,* 996–1015.

STUDT, E. "Organizing Resources for More Effective Practice." In *Trends in Social Work Practice and Knowledge.* National Association of Social Workers, 10th Anniversary Symposium, Atlantic City, N.J., May 21–23, 1965.

SZASZ, T. *The Myth of Mental Illness.* New York: Harper & Row, 1961.

SZASZ, T. *The Manufacture of Madness: A Comparative Study of the Inquisition and the Mental Health Movement.* New York: Harper & Row, 1970.

TURNBULL, R. (Ed.). *Consent Handbook.* Washington, D.C.: American Association on Mental Deficiency, 1977.

UNDERWOOD, B. J. *Psychological Research.* New York: Appleton-Century-Crofts, 1957.

Urban Rural Systems Associates' Resource Materials. "Discussion Guide on Medical Witness." Washington, D.C.: National Center on Child Abuse and Neglect, 1976.

VINTER, R. "The Social Structure of Service." In A. J. Kahn (Ed.), *Issues in American Social Work.* New York: Columbia University Press, 1959.

VINTER, R. "Analysis of Treatment Organizations." *Social Work,* 1963, *8,* 3–15.

WALTERS, D. R. *Physical and Sexual Abuse of Children.* Bloomington: University of Indiana Press, 1975.

Washington Research Project, Inc. *Children Out of School in America.* Washington, D.C.: Children's Defense Fund, 1974.

WEINTRAUB, F. J., and ABELSON, A. "Appropriate Education for All Handicapped Children: A Growing Issue." *Syracuse Law Review,* 1972, *23* (4), 1037–1058.

White House Conference on Children 1970 Report to the President. Washington, D.C.: U.S. Government Printing Office, 1971.

WHITTEN, C. F. "Failure to Thrive: Can Treatment Be Effectively Investigated?" *American Journal of Diseases of Children,* 1976, *130,* 15.

WICKER, T. "Fragmenting Children." *New York Times,* May 8, 1977, p. E19.

WOLFENSBERGER, W. *The Principle of Normalization in Human Services.* Toronto: National Institute of Mental Retardation, 1972.

WOODEN, K. *Weeping in the Playtime of Others.* New York: Mc-Graw-Hill, 1976.

Wyatt v. *Stickney,* 325 F. Supp. 781 (M.D. Alabama 1971).

YABLONSKY, L. *Synanon: The Tunnel Back.* Baltimore, Md.: Penguin Books, 1967.

ZISKIN, J. *Coping with Psychologic and Psychiatric Testimony.* Beverly Hills: Law and Psychology Press, 1976.

ZWEIG, P. *The Heresy of Self-Love: A Study of Subversive Individualism.* New York: Basic Books, 1968.

Index